Great Wartime Escapes and Rescues

David W. Mills and Kayla L. Westra

BLOOMSBURY ACADEMIC
NEW YORK · LONDON · OXFORD · NEW DELHI · SYDNEY

BLOOMSBURY ACADEMIC

Bloomsbury Publishing Inc, 1359 Broadway, 12th Floor, New York, NY 10018, USA
Bloomsbury Publishing Plc, 50 Bedford Square, London, WC1B 3DP, UK
Bloomsbury Publishing Ireland, 29 Earlsfort Terrace, Dublin 2, D02 AY28, Ireland

BLOOMSBURY, BLOOMSBURY ACADEMIC and the Diana logo
are trademarks of Bloomsbury Publishing Plc

First published in the United States of America by ABC-CLIO 2019
Paperback edition published by Bloomsbury Academic 2025

Copyright © Bloomsbury Publishing Inc, 2026

COVER PHOTOS: U.S. soldier and combat helicopter approaching. (zabelin/iStockphoto);
Grunge background. (in-future/ iStockphoto); Grunge metal texture. (AnaMOMarques/iStockphoto)

All rights reserved. No part of this publication may be: i) reproduced or transmitted in
any form, electronic or mechanical, including photocopying, recording or by means of any
information storage or retrieval system without prior permission in writing from the publishers;
or ii) used or reproduced in any way for the training, development or operation of artificial intelligence
(AI) technologies, including generative AI technologies. The rights holders expressly reserve this
publication from the text and data mining exception as per Article 4(3) of the Digital Single
Market Directive (EU) 2019/790.

Bloomsbury Publishing Inc does not have any control over, or responsibility for,
any third-party websites referred to or in this book. All internet addresses given
in this book were correct at the time of going to press. The author and publisher
regret any inconvenience caused if addresses have changed or sites have
ceased to exist, but can accept no responsibility for any such changes.

Library of Congress Cataloging-in-Publication Data
Names: Mills, David W., 1965- author. | Westra, Kayla L., 1966- author.
Title: Great war time escapes and rescues / David W. Mills and Kayla L. Westra.
Description: First edition. | Santa Barbara, CA : ABC- CLIO, LLC, 2019. |
Includes bibliographical references and index.
Identifiers: LCCN 2018055595 (print) | LCCN 2019005451 (ebook) |
ISBN 9781440859168 (ebook) | ISBN 9781440859151 (hardcover : alk. paper)
Subjects: LCSH: Prisoner-of-war escapes— History— Encyclopedias. |
Rescues— Encyclopedias. | History, Military— Encyclopedias.
Classification: LCC D25.5 (ebook) | LCC D25.5. M4975 2019 (print) |
DDC 355.1/29603— dc23
LC record available at https://lccn.loc.gov/2018055595

ISBN: HB: 978-1-4408-5915-1
PB: 979-8-2163-9216-3
ePDF: 978-1-4408-5916-8
eBook: 979-8-2160-9200-1

For product safety related questions contact productsafety@bloomsbury.com.

To find out more about our authors and books visit www.bloomsbury.com
and sign up for our newsletters.

I am forever grateful for the love and support of my wife, Ann, and our three children: Sam, Joey, and Jake. Without their patience and understanding, this life would not be possible. I also appreciate the staff, faculty, and administration at Minnesota West Community and Technical College who have supported me in the past, as well as the faculty and leadership in the Department of Military History at Command and General Staff College who have taught me much about being a historian. Finally, I am thankful for my friend, Kayla Westra, without whom this book would not be possible.
—David. W. Mills

Words cannot express my gratitude for my family—Dayton, Madeline, and Claire—for their unwavering support and encouragement. I love you all beyond measure. I am also thankful for my work at Minnesota West Community and Technical College and the commitment of the leadership team to providing access and opportunity to the students in our region. And thank you, Dave Mills, for asking me to be a partner on this project and for sharing your passion for history and learning.
—Kayla L. Westra

Contents

List of Entries   ix

Introduction   xi

A–Z Entries   1

Bibliography   215

Index   227

List of Entries

Air France Flight 8969
Andersonville
Argo
Ash, William
Benuzzi, Felice
Black Hawk Down
Bonaparte, Napoleon
Brickhill, Paul
Buchanan, Jessica, and Poul Hagen Thisted
Burns, Joe Lee
Cabanatuan Prison Rescue
Cavell, Edith
Charlie Company
Churchill, Winston
Code Name Bright Light
Comet Line
Cornelius, Elias
Cowra, Australia
Dakota War of 1862
Dengler, Dieter
Dramesi, John A.
Dunkirk: Operation Dynamo
East German Escapes
Eichmann, Adolf
Fields, Kenny Wayne
Flight 181: Mogadishu Hijack 1977

Flight 571: Tel Aviv Hijack 1972 (aka Operation Isotope)
Fort Stanton
Garros, Eugene Adrien Roland Georges
Giraud, Henri Honoré
Glazier, Willard W.
Grimson, George
Hambleton, Iceal "Gene"
Hamill, Thomas—Civilian Contractor
Harrer, Heinrich
Holzminden: The First Great Escape
Hoover, Robert
Iran Hostage Rescue Attempt: Operation Eagle Claw
Izac (Isaacs), Edouard
Jensen, Agnes
Joseph, Dilip
Kilpatrick, Ralph
Larive, Etienne Henri "Hans"
Libby Prison Escape
Locher, Roger
Long-Range Reconnaissance Patrols
Los Baños Prison Camp Rescue
Lynch, Jessica
Mary, Queen of Scots
Mayaguez Incident
McBrayer, James

Morgan, John H.
Munich Olympics
Mussolini, Benito
O'Grady, Scott
Operation Barras
Operation Chavín de Huántar
Operation Dragon Rouge
Operation Dustoff
Operation Halyard
Operation Jericho
Operation Jonathan
Operation Nimrod
Operations Berlin, Market Garden, and Pegasus
Pekerney, Sasha, and Toivi Blatt, 300 Others
Phillips, Richard

Pluschow, Gunther
Rowe, James N. (Nick)
Ruffatto, Barney
Son Tay Raid: Operation Ivory Coast/Kingpin
Stalag Luft III: Great Escape
Takur Ghar
Tapscott, Robert, and Wilbert Widdicombe
Task Force Smith: Battle of Osan
Third Platoon, George Company
Villingen Prison
Vrba, Rudolph, and Alfred Wetzler
Wattenberg, Jürgen: Camp Papago Park Escape
Webb, Kate
Werra, Franz von

Introduction

For many who entered military service throughout history, the most terrifying aspect of combat was not death, but the possibility of falling into enemy hands as a prisoner of war. Some men of Custer's 7th Cavalry chose to commit suicide rather than fall into enemy hands, an act repeated throughout the history of warfare, from the Siege of Masada through the present day. In almost all of these instances, the fear of falling into enemy hands—and the torture or mistreatment that went with it—was greater than the fear of death itself. This book chronicles a common thread through the many escapes and rescues examined here, and that was the bravery of the men and women who submitted to capture, launched rescue operations, or those who simply assisted the pursued in their quest to escape.

Many military and civilian people examined in this book were taken into custody against their will, either as members of a hostile military organization during war, or as civilians in the wrong place at the wrong time. Those people were terrified that they would be killed, and the uncertainty of their immediate future was more terrifying. Would they ever see their families again? If so, when? These and a million other questions raced through their minds as they raised their hands above their heads, accepting their capture. Once in prison, the idea of escape was a tempting one, but few people statistically ever attempted to break out. The odds were simply not in their favor. They lacked resources, clothing, and language skills—and geography often worked against them. If they were recaptured, they might be killed or endure physical abuse, or perhaps harder to accept, their fellow prisoners might suffer in their place. The men and women in this book were exceptionally brave, risking all to escape their captors.

One of the greatest breakouts from a prison camp was the escape from Stalag Luft III, when 77 prisoners made it out of the tunnel they had dug and to freedom. Most of the men were eventually caught and 50 were executed, but 3 did make it home. Franz von Werra was a German prisoner of war who almost escaped from England by stealing a fighter plane, but he was sent to America after authorities discovered the plot. Once in North America, he leaped from a train, then made his way from Canada to America. He further escaped to Mexico, then South America, and eventually to Italy and home. Nick Rowe was a Green Beret in Vietnam who spent five years as a prisoner. Eventually, he saw an opportunity to escape when a helicopter flew near his location. Rather than a specific escape plan, chance came to Rowe's rescue that day.

Sometimes, prisoners would receive assistance in escape whether or not they wanted it. In the case of the Son Tay raid, American forces attempted to rescue prisoners from a Vietnamese prison camp, only to discover that the camp was empty. The greatest rescue in history was probably the effort to evacuate the British army from the continent at the start of World War II, when over 300,000 soldiers were taken off the French beaches and brought back to England. In another instance, Allied airmen in Italy orchestrated a rescue of over 500 Allied soldiers and airmen before the Germans in Yugoslavia could take them prisoner. Perhaps the most daring rescue was of Benito Mussolini in World War II. His rescuers landed on a mountaintop, freed him, then took off in a small plane and flew him to safety. Often, the most heroic aspect of a rescue was in the minutes, hours, or days after a pilot was shot down behind enemy lines. It took an incredible amount of determination on the part of the pilot not to give up, especially as hunger and other conditions took their toll. For rescuers, often flying in slow and vulnerable helicopters, the satisfaction of pulling a fellow American out of a hostile environment was immense.

Probably the most overlooked aspect of escape attempts was the assistance from members of the population, at great risk to themselves. William Ash was shot down over France, and he received help from many partisans that passed him from home to home, though the Germans captured him and executed many of his friends. The fliers shot down over Yugoslavia were helped by partisans, often giving up the only food they had to feed Allied fliers. Inmates in the Los Baños prison camp would escape and seek food from the Philippine population, then sneak back into the camp to share the food with those who were physically unable to walk or fend for themselves. In their escape, James McBrayer and three other American marines traveled hundreds of miles, assisted by the generosity of Communist Chinese guerillas, and were delivered to an airfield where American planes operated, flying them to freedom.

Wartime rescues, escapes, kidnappings, and terrorist operations make up the crux of the stories contained here, though each one is a little different from the others. The men and women depicted are true heroes, often disregarding their own freedom in order to save others. We have done our best to accurately retell these stories in a way that brings the people and their tales to life. Any errors or omissions are unintentional. We hope that you enjoy the stories about escapes and rescues contained in this book.

David W. Mills
Kayla L. Westra

Air France Flight 8969

Conflict: Terrorism
Captured: December 24, 1994
Released: December 26, 1994

In the early 1990s, Algeria was in a state of civil war. Pilots knew that the conditions they encountered when flying over the country were dangerous, from missile attacks in the air and on the ground. In late 1994, some airlines had discontinued service into Algiers, but Air France had not done so. However, the executives were aware that the city was dangerous, and the airline had gone to volunteers for the flights in and out of Algiers.

On the morning of December 24, 1994, Captain Bernard Delhemme, with the help of the crew, was preparing his Air France Airbus to return from Algiers to Paris. Preparations went as planned until after the passengers were loaded. At that time, four Algerian presidential police boarded the plane to inspect passenger passports. Though the men wore uniforms with Air Algerie logos, their actions and presence unnerved some of the crew. Specifically, one of the flight attendants saw that the men were very well armed and one carried dynamite, which was noticed as very unusual.

The "inspection" was not an inspection, and the men pretending to be Algerian police were part of the Armed Islamic Group of Algeria (GIA). Unknown to the captain and crew, the terrorists planned to blow up the plane in Paris, over the Eiffel Tower. Because of the delay caused by the GIA, the plane did not leave as scheduled, which alerted the Algerian military on the ground, and they surrounded the aircraft. At that point, the terrorists admitted to captain and crew that they were hijacking the airplane, and that they viewed the French, and by proxy, Air France, as infidels. They took full control of the plane while on the ground in Algeria.

The leader of GIA was well known. Abdul Abdullah Yahia was considered a dangerous man, and the other three members of the group carried assault rifles, machine guns, hand grenades, and dynamite packs. At one point, two of the terrorists changed into the pilot and copilot's uniforms so that any snipers would not know they were terrorists. Additionally, they forced the passengers to follow strict Islamic beliefs, such as men and women sitting separately and the women covering their heads. The hijackers were unpredictable, and throughout the event they switched from calm control to terrorist tactics, keeping their prisoners in a state of unease and excitement.

By noon, the media had also arrived on scene to cover the events. The Algerian military and minister of interior began negotiations, working with Captain Delhemme, who was forced to speak for the hijackers. The demands of the GIA were

At the Marseilles Airport on December 26, 1994, French police storm Air France Flight 8969. The hostages were liberated and all four terrorists killed. (Thierry Orban/Sygma via Getty Images)

typical for hijackers: they primarily bargained for the Algerians to release leaders of the Islamic Salvation Front political party, Abassi Madani and Ali Belhadj. The Algerian prime minister, Mokdad Sifi, responded that before they would discuss releasing political prisoners, children and elderly should be released from the plane.

Within two hours, the hijackers wanted to leave the airport, but they could not because the stairs were still attached to the plane. Additionally, the military had surrounded the plane and the path to the runway was blocked. When the crisis team refused to remove the boarding stairs, the hijackers stated they would blow up the plane and kill everyone on board unless their demand to leave the airport was met. To prove they were serious, the terrorists killed a police officer at the top of the boarding stairs. The Algerian authorities still did not comply, and the men got another man, a Vietnamese diplomat, Bui Giang To, and shot him on the boarding stairs.

The plan to rescue the passengers and crew was unknown to those on the plane, but the French government had gotten involved with the crisis and wanted to send troops. The Algerian government declined. The French then sent special forces to Majorca, Spain, which was as close as they could get their elite military force. Once there, however, the Algerian government reiterated that these French special forces were not needed or welcome within Algeria.

In the middle of the night, Captain Delhemme was allowed to check on passengers and crew, and he found people calm. He had been talking with the hijackers, trying to get them to release the passengers and crew. At this time, Delhemme was unaware of the GIA's plot to fly the plane into the Eiffel Tower. The hijackers released women with young children and those who were ill, but 170 passengers were still on the plane. The hijackers repeated their demands to leave the country, and authorities again denied their request. The hijackers then killed the chef, tossing his body out the door. Authorities in France asked that the plane be allowed to leave Algiers, and the Algerian authorities finally agreed.

The plane's auxiliary power had been running since the hijackers had come on board, so the plane did not have enough jet fuel to reach Paris. It was decided that they would refuel at the airport in Marseille. Captain Delhemme was worried that the hijackers would blow up the plane before they arrived in Marseille, and he asked the GIA leader, Yahia, if he planned to kill them all before they could land. Yahia stated that he wanted to do a press conference in Paris. Delhemme was reassured, but again, he was not aware of the original GIA plan.

The plane took off in the early morning hours of December 26. French special forces, the GIGN, were now in Marseille, having traveled from Majorca, and they planned to board the plane at the Marseille Airport. The plane landed at 3:30 a.m., and the ground crews directed them to a remote part of the airport. Again speaking through the captain, Yahia asked for fuel, but nearly three times what was needed to fly to Paris from Marseille. This tipped off the French that they planned to weaponize the aircraft. At that point, the French leaders determined that they would not let the plane leave Marseille.

The hijackers wanted to leave again that morning, but the negotiators got them to take on food and water and empty the toilets. The GIGN were dressed as airport personnel, and the hijackers did not realize they had GIGN personnel on the aircraft. The GIGN men did a reconnaissance of the aircraft, noting what they were up against and leaving microphones on board so they could hear what was going on. The negotiators convinced the hijackers to do their press conference in Marseille, because the major press outlets were in Marseille as well as Paris. The hijackers agreed, and an area in the front of the plane was cleared for this purpose, or so the French authorities told them. They moved the passengers to the rear of the aircraft to protect the passengers when the GIGN forces stormed the airplane.

The hijackers noticed the delays in the arrival of the press, and they became restless. Delhemme was ordered to move the plane closer to the terminal. The captain understood that if the plane was blown up, that there would be tertiary damage to the terminal and people within. The movement of the plane also caused issues for the GIGN forces, but they adjusted their plan and snipers were moved to the roof to provide cover for the group that would rush the plane. The hijackers had determined to get things moving, and they began the process of choosing another victim to kill. Instead of just killing an additional hostage, they fired throughout the cabin, and then fired their machine guns toward the control tower, where the negotiators were located. The erratic behavior forced the French into action, and the raid was ordered to begin immediately.

The hijackers saw the GIGN forces bringing the stairs forward, and a 20-minute firefight began in the aircraft, with hundreds of bullets being fired. GIGN forces entered from the front and back of the plane, and one of the hijackers was killed immediately. Survivors described the scene as apocalyptic and chaotic, and most of the passengers escaped within the first few minutes. Two of the other hijackers were killed, leaving just the one who was in the cockpit with the pilot and copilot. The last hijacker allowed the crew to leave, and he was killed in a firefight with the GIGN forces, about 20 minutes after the raid began.

One hundred sixty-six people survived the firefight on the airplane. Thirteen of them received minor injuries. Nine of the GIGN forces were injured, but only one seriously. Captain Delhemme had been hit in his right elbow and thigh, but he was not seriously wounded. After healing from his injuries, he flew for Air France for another nine years. French authorities thought that the operation had gone well. The story of Flight 8969 was told in TV shows as well as a documentary on *The Age of Terror* (2008), and in the 2011 film, *L'Assaut*.

Further Reading

"The Killing Machine." *Mayday* (Season 2, Episode 3). Discovery Channel Canada / National Geographic Channel, 2004.

Sancton, Thomas. "Anatomy of a Hijack." *Time,* June 24, 2001.

Sof, Eric. "The Hijacking of Air France Flight 8969." *Special Ops* (magazine), October 25, 2012.

Andersonville

Conflict: American Civil War
Captured: Various
Released: Various, 1864, 1865

The name "Andersonville" is one synonymous with grisly prisoner of war camp conditions. Immortalized in fiction and film, the treatment of those at Andersonville was also catalogued by early photographers, who captured the survivors in stark black and white. When the prisoner exchange system between the North and the South broke down in 1863, primarily over the treatment of black soldiers, Andersonville was built. In February 1864, the first Northern prisoners of war arrived at Andersonville, even though it was not finished. Andersonville, officially known as "Camp Sumter," was built by black workers who put up a 15-foot-high stockade around the original 16 acres of land. These men were often allies of the Northern prisoners of war, but alliances were difficult and the workers had little freedom themselves. The camp was eventually expanded to about 26 acres, about 600 feet by 800 feet. Andersonville was built to hold 10,000 men, but at its peak, held up to 35,000. The prison near Andersonville was only in service for 14 months, yet its history is some of the darkest of the Civil War.

Unlike in modern wars, there were no standing military orders for apprehending prisoners of war to attempt to escape. After Northern soldiers in Andersonville built huts with the limited materials available to them, they then started on escape plans. Many diaries exist of soldiers who were imprisoned at Andersonville. These documents detailed what the prisoners learned about the terrain and surrounding area after their imprisonment, and many used these notes in their escape attempts as well as the attempts of those who came after them. The first group of detainees made their first escape attempt a week into their captivity. Fifteen men made it over the wall using a rope before the guards caught them; all were recaptured and given a 64-pound ball and chain to carry around as punishment. The camp leadership instituted the "deadline" after this, which was a smaller fence 19 feet inside the stockade walls. If inmates crossed this line, the guards would shoot them, no questions asked. Several survivors shared examples of guards shooting at prisoners for the sport of it, even if the prisoners were close to the line but not over it.

Some scholars question the survivors' objectivity in their retelling of the conditions at Andersonville, but many accounts corroborated the stories about the terrible conditions and treatment. Many stories about black prisoners, in particular, were told, including how they were not given any medical treatment, and their wounds often worsened and led to their deaths. Lice were problematic for all, and the lack of rations, which diminished as more and more prisoners were brought to Andersonville, exacerbated the illnesses.

Conditions in Andersonville worsened as the war went on. As many as 35,000 men were on 13 acres of land. Sewage and lack of rations made conditions miserable, and there was little to no shelter. Dysentery, scurvy, and waterborne illnesses weakened the men, and most did not survive without treatment. Typhoid fever, worms, and exposure were also issues. Though there was ample wood surrounding the prison, the prisoners were not allowed to use it for shelter or heat, and most had little serviceable clothing. Men became more and more desperate to escape, even though many lacked the strength to muster an attempt.

Conditions at Andersonville, a Confederate prison in Georgia, were overcrowded and unsanitary. (National Archives)

Trainloads of prisoners arrived every two to three days, carrying 500 to 800 new prisoners. Of the 45,000 men who were at one time imprisoned at Andersonville, only 328 succeeded in escaping. Some scaled walls, others bribed guards to get past the deadline and over the wall, and a few simply walked out the gates to freedom. The Confederate soldiers used hounds to track them, and if the dogs caught the prisoners, the escapees rarely survived very long when back in Andersonville.

Several of the survivors of Andersonville told their stories afterward. John McElroy of the 16th Illinois Cavalry first went to Libby Prison upon his capture, and then he was sent on to Andersonville. McElroy's account of his imprisonment at Andersonville was published in several installments in the *Toledo Blade* shortly after the war. McElroy estimated that 19 prisoners a day died, almost 600 per month. In addition to McElroy's accounts, Robert H. Kellogg, a sergeant major in the 16th Connecticut Infantry Volunteers, described what he saw when he entered the prison camp in May 1864, and he also talked about the squalid conditions and how previously hearty men were now walking skeletons. Another Union prisoner, Dorence Atwater, helped to record the names of the dead at Andersonville. He suspected that the government would never see the true list, and he kept a secret list, which he took with him when he was liberated. That list was published in the *New York Tribune* after the war. Newell Burch, a member of the 154th New York Volunteers, was also a prisoner at Andersonville, and had the distinction of being the longest-held Union prisoner during the Civil War, serving 661 days as a prisoner of war. Prisoners in the Andersonville Prison were liberated in May 1865.

After the end of the Civil War, the commander of Andersonville, Captain Henry Wirz, was tried and executed for war crimes. Wirz had allowed Andersonville to be populated with more than four times its capacity, and he was held accountable for the inadequate conditions, water supply, and food rations, as well as the disease that ravaged the prisoners. In 14 months, approximately 45,000 Union soldiers were held at Andersonville; about 13,000 of those men died, mostly from scurvy, diarrhea, and dysentery. McElroy's accounts of trying to assist fellow prisoners give a firsthand account of the suffering. What little medical care was available was not useful, and 76 percent of the men taken to the hospital died there. Former prisoners testified about the conditions of the camp; those who had survived were photographed. Their conditions could not be understated, and many were walking skeletons. Though Wirz claimed he had tried to get more food and supplies for the prisoners of war at Andersonville, the fact that he had not done so, and the fact that so many had suffered under his command, sealed the case for the prosecution. Wirz was sentenced to be hanged, which occurred on November 10, 1865. He was the only Confederate official to be convicted of war crimes.

The stories of the men imprisoned at Andersonville have been widely written about by those who survived and those who studied the prison and the Civil War. MacKinlay Kantor's fictional novel, *Andersonville,* was written in 1955 and won the Pulitzer Prize for Fiction in 1956. In 1970, PBS created a television adaption of a Broadway play about the trial of Andersonville's commandant, Henry Wirz, and in 1990, Ken Burns also included a section on Andersonville in his miniseries on the Civil War. Movies in 1996 and 2008 depicted the conditions at Andersonville as well as the toll on the prisoners of war.

> **Civil War Prisoners of War**
>
> During the Civil War, the idea of how to run a prisoner of war (POW) camp was not well defined, nor were rules of conduct for prisoner treatment established. The Geneva Convention meetings would not occur for another 30 years. However, in 1863, President Lincoln ordered that a code of conduct be instituted to ensure POWs were treated reasonably well, with food, medical treatment, and shelter. Though not opened until 1864, Andersonville did not provide prisoners with food, shelter, or medical treatment. As a result of the harsh conditions, the prisoners at Andersonville established a primitive society within itself. A hierarchical structure developed, and a prisoner's survival depended upon his rank within that society. Prisoners provided food, clothes, shelter, and protection to each other.
>
> Within these groups of prisoners was a hierarchy as well. The group at the top, known as the Raiders, was notorious and attacked other inmates, stealing food and clothing. To counter the Raiders, another group formed, known as the Regulators. The Regulators caught the members of the Raiders, and the Raiders were tried by a judge and jury within Andersonville. Punishments included a ball and chain, stocks, running a gauntlet, or for six unlucky Raiders, hanging.

Andersonville is now a national historic site. The site includes the prison area, as well as the Andersonville National Cemetery and the National Prisoner of War Museum. Since 1971, the National Park Service has run the Andersonville site.

Further Reading

Jacobs, Timothy M. *The 1864 Diary of Union Civil War Soldier Sergeant Samuel E. Grosvenor: A First-hand Account of the Horrors at Andersonville Prison.* New York: Two If By Sea Publishing, 2011.

McElroy, John. *This was Andersonville: The True Story of Andersonville Military Prison as Told in the Personal Recollections of John McElroy, Sometime Private, Co. L, 16th Illinois Cavalry.* New York: McDowell, Obolensky, 1957.

Ransom, John L. *John Ransom's Andersonville Diary.* London: Douglass Brothers, 1883.

Argo

Conflict: Terrorism
Captured: November 4, 1979
Released: January 20, 1981

The 2012 film, *Argo,* was based on the joint covert operation to rescue six American diplomats who were stranded in Iran after the United States embassy was seized in Tehran. Iranian militants stormed the American embassy in Tehran on November 4, 1979, and took 66 hostages. They accused the Americans of spying and trying to undermine the current Islamic revolution. The terrorists insisted that they were just students who had acted spontaneously. However, the terrorist attack was well coordinated, many of the militants seemed to follow a plan, and they knew exactly where to go within the compound. The militants had the approval of the

Ayatollah Khomeini, the leader of the new government, who used the hostage situation to demand the U.S. government return the former shah of Iran. Many of the hostages remained prisoners for 444 days, until almost the exact moment when the president of the United States, Jimmy Carter, relinquished his role as president, having lost the 1980 election to Ronald Reagan.

Although the larger group of hostages was held for over a year, not everyone in the compound was taken hostage in the opening moments of the situation. The militants overlooked the consulate office in the opening moments of the attack on November 4, and 10 Americans used the door within the office that opened onto the street to make their escape. They were free and tried to blend into the morning crowds on the sidewalk, but they did not have a plan on where to go, because they were now in hostile territory. Their best bet was to make their way to a friendly embassy and avoid being taken as hostages. They were unsure what would happen to them if they were taken prisoner by the militants, but they realized that trial and execution were real possibilities.

The Americans broke up into two groups. The first group to exit the consulate office consisted of two married couples, Mark and Cora Lijek and Joe and Kathy Stafford, who knew each other well and were particularly close. Accompanying them was Bob Anders from the embassy, and an Iranian woman who worked in the office and promised to lead them to the British embassy. Unfortunately, when

American embassy workers are welcomed back after being rescued in Iran by the Canadian embassy, February 2, 1980. From left: Robert Anders, Kathleen and Joseph Stafford, Cora and Mark Lijek, and Henry Lee Schatz. The six were given fake Canadian passports. (Bettmann/Getty Images)

they arrived, the British embassy was also under siege, with huge crowds of demonstrators surrounding the area. The Iranian woman offered to bring the group to her home, but the Americans refused, not wanting to put her in danger. The closest sanctuary was fellow escapee Bob Anders's apartment, which was warm and dry, and he had food. The group headed there. Unknown to the five of them, militants had almost immediately arrested the second group of Americans to leave the consulate.

The small group moved several times in the first few days after the fall of the embassy, staying just ahead of the Iranians, who were arresting any Americans they could find in Tehran and taking them to the embassy. The diplomats had contacted the U.S. State Department and let them know the situation, but it was obvious the five of them would have to move somewhere safe, and then a rescue operation would follow. Bob Anders had a friend in Tehran who worked at the Canadian embassy, John Sheardown, and Anders enlisted his help. Sheardown recruited the assistance of his boss, Canadian ambassador, Ken Taylor. They sent a cable to Ottawa, seeking permission for what needed to be done, and a quick response from the capital approved their actions. Canada would hide the American diplomats. Sheardown sent a car to pick up the Americans, and they found their sanctuary for the next three months. The Staffords stayed in the ambassador's private residence, while the Lijeks and Anders stayed with Sheardown. Before long, another American, Lee Schatz, who had been staying with the Swedish ambassador, joined the group at the Sheardown residence.

As soon as the Central Intelligence Agency (CIA) confirmed that six Americans were free within Tehran, a plan came together. Antonio Mendez had worked a number of exfiltration cases in the past and had his team work on a series of cover stories for the Americans. They needed a plausible reason for six Westerners to be in Iran, and most importantly, for them to leave the country. One idea was that the group was made up of English teachers who were looking for jobs, but finding none, decided to leave. Another idea was that they were agriculturalists, but none of them knew much about agriculture, leaving the group vulnerable to an immigration officer who might ask too many questions. Mendez came up with the idea that the group worked for a Canadian film production company out of Hollywood, and that they were in Iran looking for a location to shoot their film. This was the ultimate cover story the agency used.

Coming up with a cover story took creativity, but to pull it together required extensive hard work. Each American required a new identity with a complete set of new documents, including a Canadian passport, driver's license, and pocket litter—that collection of useless but omnipresent paper such as library cards, movie tickets, or receipts that subtly adds to the credibility of a fake identity. Just in case, the agency also created a phony production company, Studio Six. The fake company was staffed with CIA employees who could verify the employment of the six Americans, and they also created a portfolio and movie posters that depicted their new project.

Mendez and an associate, Julio, flew to Europe on January 22, 1981, to complete final preparations, with the exfiltration set for January 27. Mendez and Julio landed in Tehran on January 25, and they went to meet with the Americans to go over their cover stories and the exfiltration plan. The six Americans were nervous, though they were told that the best chance for success required complete confidence in the operation. Movie producers had notoriously big personalities, and this required them to get into character, memorizing their cover stories until they could recite information flawlessly. Disguises were also created. The anticipation was more taxing than the actual exfiltration. The Americans played their parts, getting through customs and security with no issues. The situation grew tense when their flight was delayed for an hour due to mechanical issues, but they boarded the flight bound for Zurich and were out of Iran with no additional problems.

The film *Argo* (2012), though a fictionalized account, won three Oscars. Previously, in 1981, a television movie, *Escape from Iran: The Canadian Caper,* was also released. Books were also written about this event, including Robert Wright's 2010 book, *Our Man in Tehran,* which was also made into a documentary and released in 2013. Several books were also written about the Iran hostage crisis.

Further Reading
Mendez, Antonio, and Matt Baglio. *ARGO: How the CIA and Hollywood Pulled Off the Most Audacious Rescue in History.* New York: Penguin Books, 2012.
Wright, Robert. *Our Man in Tehran: The True Story behind the Secret Mission to Save Six Americans during the Iran Hostage Crisis & the Foreign Ambassador Who Worked with the CIA to Bring Them Home.* New York: Other Press LLC, 2010.

Ash, William

Conflict: World War II
Captured: March 24, 1942
Escaped: Numerous times, but recaptured

Born November 30, 1917, William Ash was from Dallas, Texas, and worked as a migrant farmworker during the Depression. Ash volunteered for service with the Royal Canadian Air Force in June 1940. He earned his pilot's wings and a commission in March 1941, then went to England where he learned to fly Spitfires, the British single-seat airplane used extensively in World War II. On a sweep over France, he was shot down near the town of Vieille-Eglise, near Calais, where he crash-landed his plane. He ran from the smoldering aircraft and into a town, where a woman gave him some clothes for a disguise. The French Resistance helped him further, moving him to Paris, where he stayed with a young couple until the Gestapo burst into the apartment one morning, arresting everyone inside. The Germans executed the couple who hid him. Ash was told he would be tried as a spy, but the German Luftwaffe came for him before that could happen. He ended up at Stalag Luft III, the site of the famous "Great Escape" of 76 prisoners.

Ash was one of the most heavily punished prisoners in World War II, spending over six months in solitary confinement because of his many attempts to escape from Nazi prison camps. Ash's first stint in solitary confinement ("the cooler") came after a prank against the German guards. The guards were trying to count the prisoners when a number of men, including Ash, began to mill about, forcing the guards to start over from the beginning. The guards did not find the prank funny, and Ash and another prisoner took the brunt of the punishment, each spending two weeks in confinement.

Ash's first escape attempt quickly ended in failure. Each week, the prisoners went to a different section of the camp to shower, where the guard counted everyone in and out. Ash found a place to hide under a manhole cover in the shower room. Ash figured he could hide in the space and have his fellow prisoners create confusion upon leaving the shower. The plan worked well until one of the prisoners got into an argument with a guard. The guards were in no mood for play when it came time to count prisoners, and the absence of Ash was quickly discovered, and he was sent to solitary again for another few weeks.

The number of prisoners quickly expanded beyond anything the Germans had envisioned, and many of the prisoners at Stalag Luft III were sent to a new camp 150 miles to the northeast, in Poland. The German Army, not the German Air Force, ran the camp, and they had no idea how devious the Allied prisoners could be. Additionally, the distance between the buildings and the fence was fairly close, making tunnels a possible avenue for escape. However, Ash's first escape attempt at the new camp did not involve a tunnel. While on a work detail unloading a train and when the guards were not looking, Ash dove under the train car, rolled to the other side, and ran for the woods. The Germans noticed him and rode their motorcycles to a point where they could intersect his route. Ash tried to run through the guards, but they threw him to the ground and beat him. He was sentenced to the cooler again. Somehow, Ash had managed to conceal a small file from the guards, and he used this to cut through one of the bars of his cell. He received two more weeks of isolation for his actions.

The day that Ash was released from the cooler, he tried to escape again. This attempt involved crawling to the edge of the compound with two other prisoners, where one of them produced a homemade pair of wire cutters. The prisoner attached the device to the barbed wire and cut it, which resulted in a loud snap because of the tension in the wire. The guards heard the noise and came running, catching the other two prisoners. Ash managed to avoid capture and made his way back to the barracks.

Tunneling to freedom was a common escape tactic of Allied prisoners, and Germans soon developed countermeasures against those efforts. Ash and others realized that an organized escape committee was the only way to increase their odds for success. Prisoners presented their ideas for escape attempts to the committee, who would approve or deny the plan. If approved, the escapee got the backing of the entire escape committee, including labor and technical skills. If denied, the escapee agreed not to pursue the escape attempt. Because England and other nations needed volunteers with varied backgrounds, there were artists, engineers, lawyers, businessmen, electricians, printers, tailors, and any number of professional people with skills to assist in the escape efforts.

Ash's next escape attempt employed these men and their skills. Ash and several others saw an opportunity to construct a tunnel from the toilet facility, underneath the perimeter fence, and to the woods beyond, which was a distance of about 150 feet. While the digging crew expanded the tunnel, the others set to work creating false identity papers, maps, and civilian clothes out of military uniforms. The plan called for 32 men to make their way under the camp through the tunnel on March 5, 1943, and head for various points. Ash and his traveling partner were headed for Warsaw, but were captured after only a few days, as were the other escapees. Ash spent 10 days in the cooler as a punishment.

As a result of the escape attempt, all of the prisoners were returned to Stalag Luft III, except for the sergeants, who were moved to a new camp, Stalag Luft VI, in Lithuania. Ash doubted he could escape from Stalag Luft III, but he was an officer and not being sent to the new camp. However, Ash traded identities with an enlisted New Zealander named Donald Fair, and soon he had a number of escape possibilities once again at Stalag Luft VI. Ash and the others determined the latrines there also made an excellent point from which to begin a tunnel, and the escape committee was soon busy with preparations. When the time came to leave the camp through the tunnel, Ash was at the front of the line of prisoners waiting to escape. He and seven other inmates made it out of the tunnel and away from the camp before the escape attempt was discovered. Ash was on the run for several weeks, staying with a Polish family and helping the community with the harvest. Once he left that family, he was captured within a few days. He was taken to Berlin, where he was told he would stand trial and possibly be shot for his crimes, but he was eventually sent back to Stalag Luft III, where he spent time in the cooler for his attempted escape and for trading identities. While detained, the famous "Great Escape" took place from the camp. When the men heard that the Germans executed the prisoners who were caught, Ash's escape career came to an end. He was eventually released when the Allies overran his camp.

After the war, Ash lived in Britain and wrote a series of novels. He also worked as a reader for the BBC. Reportedly, Ash's exploits were the basis of Steve McQueen's character in the 1963 film, *The Great Escape*. Ash died on April 26, 2014, at the age of 96.

Further Reading
Ash, William. *Under the Wire.* London: Bantam, 2006.
Bishop, Patrick. *The Cooler King: The True Story of William Ash, the Greatest Escaper of World War II.* New York: Overlook Press, 2015.

B

Benuzzi, Felice

Conflict: World War II
Captured: 1941
Escaped: January 24, 1943

Felice Benuzzi was born November 16, 1910, in Vienna, Austria, to an Italian father and Austrian mother. Growing up in the Alps, he was a natural climber and outdoorsman. He entered Italian Colonial Service in 1938, and was in occupied Ethiopia in the late 1930s. He was captured in 1941 and placed in British POW Camp 354, which was located at the base of Mount Kenya.

Benuzzi had a legal degree, and being in a POW camp was difficult for many reasons, but particularly because of the boredom, which led to thoughts of escape. He escaped several times, but was caught each time. An Italian in Kenya, he found it difficult to blend in, and he was spotted and quickly recaptured on his early attempts. He thought about escape, but realized that actually getting to freedom was not likely. At that point, his ideas turned to climbing the mountain, which gave him a reason to plan and plot, as well as something to deal with the boredom. This escape was different from others, however, because Benuzzi planned to climb the mountain, then return to the camp.

Benuzzi received packages from home, including clothing and cigarettes. He stopped smoking and used the cigarettes to barter with other prisoners and guards. He also worked with two other men, Dr. Giovanni ("Giuàn") Balletto and Vincenzo ("Enzo") Barsotti, to plan their route and gather supplies. Benuzzi stole a key, and the three men walked out at midday. After their escape, they marched to the mountain, dealing with illness and weather. At one point, they were within 20 yards of a herd of elephants, and Benuzzi stated how that experience alone was worth getting out of the camp.

The three men made it to the mountain through the forests, but found that where they actually were was a bit different than where they thought they would be. This was a consequence of not having maps of the area. They set up a base camp and rested before climbing. Although they thought they would be at Lenana Peak, they were actually climbing Batian. With questionable tools, including a rope they didn't trust, Benuzzi and Balletto headed up the mountain. Snow and hail hampered their progress, and they had to stop about 5,000 feet up the face. Ice overhangs also caused them problems, and they came back down to base camp, struggling to find the tent and the ill Barsotti. On their second attempt, they tried ascending Lenana Peak, making it to a flag that Brits had hoisted on early expeditions before turning back.

Too weak to continue, the group decided to head back to the POW camp, following the river on their return. It took them 9 days to return, and their rations ran out. They also saw Africans who were bounty hunters who could get 10 pieces of silver for each of them. The trio managed to elude the men, and after 17 days outside of the POW camp, they snuck back in. They were exhausted and were found just outside the main fence. Their punishment for escaping the camp was 28 days in a cell, but they only served 7 days. Ironically, Benuzzi could still see Mount Kenya from his cell.

Benuzzi was repatriated in 1946, and he served as a diplomat later in his career. A highly fictionalized account of this story was the focus of a 1994 movie, *Ascent*. Benuzzi died in Rome in 1988.

Further Reading

Benuzzi, Felice. *No Picnic on Mount Kenya: A Dangerous Escape, A Perilous Climb.* London: William Kimber, 1952.

Benuzzi, Silvia. *No Picnic on Mount Kenya: Felice Benuzzi's Daughter Reflects on her Father's Adventure.* Waterstones (blog), September 30, 2016, www.waterstones.com/blog/no-picnic-on-mount-kenya-felice-benuzzis-daughter-reflects-on-her-fathers-adventure.

"Mount Kenya: Simon Calder Tackles Africa's Other Summit," *Belfast Telegraph,* October 29, 2007.

Steele, Rory. *The Heart and the Abyss: The Life of Felice Benuzzi.* Brisbane, Queensland: Connor Court Publishing, 2016.

Black Hawk Down

Conflict: Terrorism
Captured: October 3, 1993
Rescued: October 4, 1993

Though the events of this battle in Mogadishu are well known, the actual battle was not a movie or a video game, which is how many people learned more about the events of these two days. The battle on the streets of Mogadishu involved guerilla tactics and attacks on American convoys. The terrorists used women and children in the streets as shields. Although American motives for being in Mogadishu were focused on alleviating starvation in the region, the attempts to replace the government did not go well and resulted in warlords running the city and taking the food supplies intended for humanitarian relief. In these conditions, soldiers protected the food shipments and were involved in firefights on the streets. Anticolonial sentiments were intense in Mogadishu, and with newfound freedom from centralized leadership, the local warlords took advantage of the lack of oversight to wreak destruction in their own country.

During one of the firefights between Americans and the men fighting for the warlord Mohamed Farrah Aidid, a rocket-propelled grenade (RPG) shot down an American Black Hawk helicopter, Super Six One, piloted by Chief Warrant Officer Cliff Wolcott and copilot Chief Warrant Officer Donovan "Bull" Briley. Both pilots were killed in the crash, while Delta Force snipers Sergeant Jim Smith and Staff Sergeant Daniel Busch lived through the crash and began defending the site. Smith and Busch were later rescued, although Busch would die of his injuries. A convoy was immediately deployed to the crash site to extract the soldiers, and the 10th Mountain Division, based across the city, mobilized to assist. These soldiers had trained for crashes and how to protect themselves, if possible, until help could arrive, but getting to the downed crew as quickly as possible was important to their survival.

Fighting against Aidid's men was notoriously difficult, as Admiral Jonathan Howe, the head of the 38,000-person Unified Task Force, knew. Women would shoot at soldiers, even if they held a child in their arms. His Rangers knew that they would have a difficult task getting to the crash site because of the tactics Aidid's guerilla fighters used. In addition to using children and women as shooters, they set fires in the street and set up barricades that slowed down rescue convoys. The fighters in the Unified Task Force convoy had thousands of rounds with them and used most of them in a mission, and they also had to fend off RPGs.

The reaction force was not far into their attempt to reach the pilots when they were ambushed, and half of the 75 men were hit within the first hour of the rescue mission. Drivers navigated crowded streets, around fires and barricades, while gunners and other soldiers did their best to keep the injured alive, providing triage and fighting back at the same time. Although the Somali guerillas were unpredictable in their tactics, the rebel fighters were well armed, and their chaotic attacks were effective. The Rangers on the mission had left early in the day, and by 7 p.m. that night, they were still fighting in a three-square-block area. They needed to resupply ammunition, water, medical supplies, and IV bags. Because they had not anticipated the intensity or length of the mission, they also had not brought night vision goggles with them, which further hampered their efforts.

At about 4:20 p.m., another American Blackhawk helicopter, Super Six Four, piloted by Mike Durant, was also shot down by a rocket-propelled grenade. Most of the assault team had headed to the first crash site, but when they got there, they were unable to leave due to the heavy assault from the Somalian rebels. The team set up in several houses to wait out the night. Two Delta snipers, Gary Gordon and Randy Shughart, on board the Black Hawk Super Six Two, were inserted near the second crash site, trying to keep Durant and the others in the helicopter safe. Both Gordon and Shughart were killed and awarded Medals of Honor posthumously. Durant, who had suffered a broken back and broken femur, was now being held by Aidid. The others in Super Six Four were killed by Somali fighters. Pilot Mike Durant, who had been captured, was asked to make videos about the Americans in Somalia. During this process, he relied on his survival training. The group holding Durant ransomed him to Aidid. President Clinton ordered Aidid to release Durant, and the Red Cross assisted in retrieving Durant 11 days into his captivity.

The crash survivors were unaware of the size of the rescue effort; there were 100 vehicles—tanks, armored carriers, and Humvees—in a two-mile-long convoy, which included Americans as well as Malaysian and Pakistani officers and soldiers. At 3 a.m. the following morning, John Stebbins and Tim Wilkinson, two of the crew members from Super Six One, were rescued. Though the convoy had reached the downed crew, there was not enough space in the vehicles to get everyone out. They knew they would have difficulty getting out of the city, so they flew doctors into the national soccer stadium, which was closer and where there was a Pakistani base. Some of the troops headed back to the hangar where the American troops were based, where they reset and went back out the next morning to get more of the missing soldiers. Some of the soldiers were temporarily deaf from the gunfire and blasts from the RPGs. By the time the operation was over, 18 soldiers had been killed and 73 injured.

The story of the battle in Mogadishu is well documented in book and film. *Black Hawk Down: A Story of Modern War* was written in 1999 by Mark Bowden, who had previously written a series for *The Philadelphia Inquirer*. Bowden's book was adapted into a commercial film, which was directed by Ridley Scott. Rescued pilot Mike Durant published *In the Company of Heroes* in 2003. Several documentaries were also published about the events of the rescue, including *The True Story of Black Hawk Down* on the History Channel (2003) and a National Geographic television episode in *No Man Left Behind,* entitled "The Real Black Hawk Down" (2016).

Further Reading
Bowden, Mark. *Black Hawk Down: A Story of Modern War.* New York: Grove Press, 1999.
Durant, Michael. *In the Company of Heroes.* New York: New American Library, 2003.

Bonaparte, Napoleon

Conflict: French Revolution
Captured: April 6, 1814
Escaped: February 26, 1815

Born on August 15, 1769, on the island of Corsica, Napoleon Bonaparte was one of eight children. His father was a lawyer, and the family was middle class but not wealthy. Bonaparte was educated in France, and he graduated from the military academy in 1785. Bonaparte was married twice, the first time to Josephine de Beauharnais, whom he married in 1796. She had two teenage children from a previous marriage, but they did not have any children together. In 1810, Bonaparte married Marie Louise, who was the daughter of the Austrian emperor. They had one son, who became known as Napoleon II. This son was only 10 when Bonaparte died, and the boy only lived to be 21 years old.

Bonaparte rose to distinction during the French Revolution, moving into increasing positions of power until he proclaimed himself emperor of France on December 2, 1804, famously taking the crown from Pope Pius VII and placing it on his own head. He conquered much of Europe during his reign, though the European powers formed a number of coalitions to try to oppose him. The sixth coalition, comprised of Austria, Great Britain, Portugal, Prussia, Spain, Sweden, and Russia, was finally able to stop his advances and remove him from power. Though Bonaparte won a series of small skirmishes in the beginning, his army faced a force more than twice its size and lost to the coalition at the Battle of Leipzig.

In what is known as the Frankfort Proposals, the allies offered lenient peace terms, with Bonaparte keeping his title of emperor, but the size of his lands were significantly lessened. He lost control of many of the gains he'd won through conquest. Bonaparte did not initially accept the allies' offer; they withdrew the offer and offered even harsher terms, stating that France would return to its original boundaries and Bonaparte would lose all of its territorial gains. Bonaparte rejected this offer and was determined to continue to fight, though his administrators in Paris surrendered to the coalition forces in March 1814. By this point, the allied coalition demanded that the French government remove him. When Bonaparte heard of this demand, he ordered the army to march on Paris, but his generals and marshals refused. Bonaparte then tried to abdicate and put his son in charge of the French government, but the allies rejected this proposal. With little choice in the matter, Bonaparte abdicated his throne and negotiated that he be allowed to exile on the island of Elba, an island off the southern coast of France.

Though Bonaparte was allowed to retain his title of emperor, it was a hollow honor. He was allowed to preside only over Elba, which had just 12,000 residents. Bonaparte convinced the British authorities, who were responsible for supervising his banishment, that he only wanted to live in peace and preside over his small farm. Needing something to occupy his time, he threw himself into governing the island, developing the iron mines there, overseeing the construction of new roads, issuing directives on modernizing agriculture, and revising the island's legal and educational systems. He also built up the island's defenses, which included an army of 2,000 soldiers and an imperial guard of 600. The island's defenses also included a small navy.

After ruling much of Europe, it is not surprising that Bonaparte was not content on Elba, and his efforts were just to pass time until he could return to France and claim the titles and power he felt belonged to him. Though Bonaparte had been promised an annual stipend of 2 million francs per year, the new king had had no intention of paying Bonaparte such a sum. Bonaparte was nearly out of the money he had been allowed to bring with him from France, and he knew he had considerable expenses that he could not support going forward.

Unlike most who are considered imprisoned or exiled, Bonaparte had a constant stream of visitors from Europe and received letters from supporters in his homeland. He learned that France had not forgotten him, and that he still carried the support of a significant percentage of the French people. When he heard that the British intended to remove him from Elba and incarcerate him on the island of St. Helena in the South Atlantic, he began to plan his escape. When his official British overseer, an officer named Neil Campbell, returned to England, Bonaparte initiated his plan to return to France. He organized his small naval fleet, and aboard the brig *Inconstant,* made good his escape with over 1,000 people aboard his ships.

Bonaparte had many supporters when he returned to France, and the king who deposed him was generally not popular. Several of his former officers were ordered out of Paris to arrest him, but ended up joining Bonaparte instead. French citizens were afraid that the newly crowned king, Louis XVIII, would outlaw many of the positive effects of the revolution, while others believed that the return of Bonaparte simply meant more war and excesses. Bonaparte pledged to implement constitutional reforms to attract the allegiance of more detractors, but this rang hollow with those who knew him. Without a fight, Bonaparte returned to power on March 20, 1815, and began the period known as the Hundred Days, but not without rankling the British or the other countries of the coalition. At the Congress of Vienna, representatives from Austria, Great Britain, Prussia, and Russia all promised to

> **POW Treatment—18th Century and Beyond**
>
> By the mid-18th century, small professional armies gave way to large national armies that fought for ideology rather than for money. Thus, it became more common for nations to retain captured soldiers as prisoners of war rather than exchange them, forcing their opponents to recruit, train, and equip more soldiers to keep their forces at the numbers needed. At the same time, legal scholars began to write the first laws and treaties regarding the treatment of prisoners.
>
> The term "prisoner of war" became a legal status only after Tsar Nicholas II of Russia organized the Hague Peace Conference in 1899, which each signatory agreed to follow. The provisions for the treatment of prisoners were extensive, but in sum, they guaranteed humane treatment and specified what work prisoners would perform while in captivity. The agreement also required each prisoner to divulge his true name, rank, date of birth, and service number, if issued one. It also specified the treatment and punishment for prisoners who escaped. The Second Hague Peace Conference in 1907 generally affirmed the agreement toward prisoners laid out at the first conference.
>
> The Geneva Peace Conferences in 1929 and 1949 further refined the treatment of prisoners and placed responsibility for the protection of prisoners on the leadership of the powers that captured them. Torture was specifically outlawed as a means of extracting information, but the Communist forces in Korea and Vietnam notoriously violated this provision. Furthermore, the conference clarified the specifications for prisoner facilities, medical treatment, labor, food, and movement of prisoners, among other points. Again, some countries did not follow the provisions.

provide 150,000 soldiers to remove Bonaparte from power for good. Bonaparte, known for his acumen, fought a brilliant campaign, but the coalition forces defeated him at Waterloo on June 18, 1815. He abdicated his position again, hoping to seek asylum in the United States, but he was captured and removed to the island of St. Helena, where a fleet of naval vessels and a unit of the British army ensured he would not escape again. Bonaparte died on May 5, 1821, from what most scholars believe was stomach cancer. He was buried on St. Helena, but later, in 1840, was exhumed and returned to France and interred at Les Invalides in Paris, where other French military leaders are buried.

Further Reading

Braude, Mark. *The Invisible Emperor: Napoleon on Elba from Exile to Escape.* New York: Penguin Press, 2018.

MacKenzie, Norman. *The Escape from Elba: The Fall and Flight of Napoleon, 1814–1815.* New York: Oxford University Press, 1982.

Brickhill, Paul

Conflict: World War II
Captured: March 17, 1943
Escaped: Assisted but did not attempt to escape

A native Australian, Paul Brickhill was born on December 20, 1916, in Melbourne, but the family moved to Sydney when he was 11. The third of five children,

Brickhill went to work early in 1931, when his father lost his job and the family needed additional income. A friend, Peter Finch, helped him get a job at a paper in 1932, and by 1940, he was working as a junior editor. The events of the rescue at Dunkirk caught Brickhill's attention, and in early January 1941, he enlisted with the Royal Australian Air Force. He did his training in Australia and Canada, as well as in the United Kingdom.

Brickhill was eventually deployed to North Africa, where he flew a Spitfire as part of the Desert Air Force. Two years and two months later, while flying a mission in Tunisia in March 1943, he was shot down and captured after he landed the plane. He was sent to Italy and then on to Germany, eventually ending up at Stalag Luft III, southeast of Berlin, on April 4, 1943. Brickhill immediately became part of the camp's escape group. He worked as a lookout as well as digger on the "Tom" tunnel of the "Tom, Dick, and Harry" tunnels orchestrated by Roger Bushell's leadership. Brickhill worked on the tunnels a bit—but he was claustrophic, and once they got very deep/long, it sounded like he couldn't tolerate it, so moved to different tasks to help the effort. His background as a journalist helped him, and he worked as a forger, preparing documents for those who were going to escape. The men created a tiny printing press to increase their production of documents. Brickhill's claustrophobia also prevented him from taking part in the escape attempt.

His condition saved his life, and after the mass escape attempt, he was shocked when those who had been recaptured following the "Great Escape" were shot upon capture. With his background in journalism, Brickhill decided that he would document what had happened at Stalag Luft III. His mission was made more difficult by the rules of the POW camp dictating that prisoners were not allowed to write anything down, though they were allowed to write letters and postcards. Brickhill and a fellow prisoner, Conrad Norton, wrote down what they could remember of the Great Escape, as well as individual stories of the men inside the camp. They managed to hide these stories/papers from the German guards.

Once he was liberated, Brickhill returned to journalism by working in London before returning to Australia. After work each day, he rewrote the stories that he and Norton had written down. After obtaining a literary agent, Brickhill sold the stories of the Great Escape, and the book was published as *Escape to Danger* in 1946. Brickhill also sold his portion of the book on the Great Escape to Australian newspapers.

Brickhill was approached to write a historical account of Stalag Luft III escape, which he did, starting in 1949. Brickhill returned to England, where he wrote *The Great Escape,* which was published in 1950, as well as a book on the history of the 617 Squadron, *The Dam Busters,* which was published in 1951 and went on to sell over a million copies. Brickhill also wrote about British fighting ace, Douglas Bader, in *Reach for the Sky* (1954), which also sold well. Brickhill's books were optioned as movies, including *The Dam Busters* in 1955, *Reach for the Sky* in 1956, and *The Great Escape* in 1963. Although Brickhill did not participate in the Great Escape, his writings about the subject and firsthand knowledge of the men in Stalag Luft III added depth to the retelling of the story. His discussion of the demoralizing conditions and helplessness felt in his time in the German POW camp is compelling. Brickhill worked as a writer for the rest of his career, though none of his later works equaled the success of his early works. In 1969, he moved back to Australia. He died in April 1991 at the age of 74. Stephen Dando-Collins wrote a biography of his life in 2016.

Further Reading
Brickhill, Paul. *Escape to Danger* (with Conrad Norton). London: Faber and Faber, 1946.
Brickhill, Paul. *The Great Escape.* New York: Norton, 1950.
Dando-Collins, Stephen. *The Hero Maker: A Biography of Paul Brickhill: The Australian behind the Legendary Stories.* The Dam Busters, The Great Escape *and* Reach for the Sky. Sydney: Random House Australia, 2016.

Buchanan, Jessica, and Poul Hagen Thisted

Conflict: Terrorism
Captured: October 25, 2011
Rescued: January 25, 2012

As a young adult, Jessica Buchanan worked in many foreign countries, such as Honduras, South Sudan, Rwanda, and Kenya. She eventually moved on to Somalia, where she lived in the city of Hargeisa and worked as a teacher and for a nongovernmental organization (NGO) that taught young people the dangers of land mines and unexploded ordnance, which were ubiquitous in the region. Somalia was in a difficult situation politically, economically, and socially when Buchanan worked there, because the government had essentially ceased to function in many parts of the nation and warlords controlled portions of the countryside. An unofficial demarcation known as the Green Line separated territories controlled by Islamic extremists and the Somali government. The NGO that Buchanan worked for was the Danish Refugee Council, and this group held an organizational meeting near the Green Line, which was a safety concern. With extra security precautions in place, the NGO had personnel traveling in a three-car convoy to and from the airport, from North Galkayo to the south of the city, where the staff would hold the meeting.

Once the conference was complete, the group prepared to return north of the Green Line and to relative safety. The convoy of three vehicles arrived at the office, preparing for the passengers' departure, assuming that the security director would safely guide the procession out of town and back to the airport. Buchanan did not recognize the driver, but she ignored her concerns, assuming the security director or her Danish coworker, Poul Hagen Thisted, or others with more experience in the country, would object if something was amiss. Her assumption was faulty, as she learned shortly after departure. Ten minutes after leaving the conference, a large car blocked the convoy and armed men exited their vehicle, shouting orders and surrounding the car she and Thisted were in. The men were Somali pirates who forced Buchanan and Thisted into their car, and soon they were departing for the Somali countryside.

For the next three months, the Somali pirates threatened to kill Buchanan and Thisted or to hand the captives over to a militant Islamic group operating in the area. Both of the relief workers knew that this would probably result in a slow and terrible execution, which would be recorded on video and released with a political or religious message. The captives were denied food, which made them weaker and easier for the pirates to control. The pirates put pressure on the captives' families to raise money for ransom. Buchanan and Thisted spoke with their families a couple times and then only briefly, but it was proof that they were still alive.

Soon after the capture of Buchanan and Thisted, special agents from the Federal Bureau of Investigation (FBI), stationed in Africa and working on antiterrorism, took up the case. They quickly identified all of the local prison guards, and the FBI agents had a good understanding of the ways in which these various groups had organized the abduction. The captors' demands for an enormous ransom for the two aid workers would fund similar kidnapping operations in the future and guarantee a luxurious lifestyle in an economically depressed region. The pirates had begun negotiations, demanding $45 million, and after months of back and forth, had dropped their price to $18 million. This amount was still far too much for either of their families or nonprofit organizations to pay for their release. It seemed their talks had reached an impasse.

Even though the FBI was engaged with the case, leaders of the U.S. government and military were generally reluctant to step in to a hostage rescue mission on foreign soil. However, they would get involved if the situation met a number of conditions, and the primary condition was the imminent death of a hostage due to medical concerns or attempted murder. When negotiations broke down over the kidnappers' insistence that someone pay an unreasonably high ransom, U.S. officials determined that intervention was necessary.

On January 23, 2012, President Barack Obama ordered Secretary of Defense Leon Panetta to mount a rescue mission for the two relief workers. Because there was little time to mobilize, Panetta chose SEAL Team Six for the assignment. Leadership quickly formulated a rescue plan, utilizing the information the FBI had gathered, and on January 25, 2012, the conditions were favorable for the rescue attempt. It was a moonless night, the kind the special operators of SEAL Team Six desired because it gave them a decided advantage over adversaries who were not equipped with the technology held by the American soldiers. Each team member wore night vision goggles to function in the darkness and to prevent friendly-fire casualties, and each team member had an infrared device on his helmet. Anyone without that device was considered a hostile and treated accordingly. The mission was staged out of Djibouti, north of Somalia on the Horn of Africa. There, 24 members of SEAL Team Six boarded a C-130, flew to the vicinity of the hostages' location, and parachuted into the drop zone. The FBI had shared all they had for intelligence, including the location of Buchanan and Thisted and the number of hostiles guarding them. The jump and landing went as planned, and the SEALs were positioned a short distance away from where the captives were held.

The operators stowed their parachutes quickly and made their way toward the objective. Unaware of the impending rescue, Buchanan was awake and needed to leave her sleeping mat to relieve herself, but none of the guards would answer her because they were sleeping. Unbeknownst to Buchanan or Thisted, the SEAL team was very close by, surrounding the camp and very close to where Buchanan lay on her mat. The rescue team knew that guards ringed the prisoners at night to prevent their escape, and they exercised extreme caution in the close quarters.

Buchanan heard faint noises in the brush, like small rodents, and she lay still on her mat, unsure of what was going on. One of her captors awoke suddenly, jumped up, cocked his weapon, and then whispered insistently to his boss. This woke the others, and a number of other guards jumped to their feet and cocked their weapons as well. At that moment, the SEAL team shot down the standing captors, and the prisoners were quickly freed. Nine of the Somali guards went down almost instantly. After three months of captivity, Buchanan and Thisted were free.

The U.S. operators took the captives out of Somalia and returned to Djibouti. From there, they traveled to an American air base in Italy, where the captives received military treatment and Buchanan's husband met them. Buchanan was later interviewed on *60 Minutes;* she had returned with her family to the United States. As of this writing, Thisted continues in his work for the Danish Refugee Council.

Further Reading

Buchanan, Jessica. *Impossible Odds: The Kidnapping of Jessica Buchanan and Her Dramatic Rescue by SEAL Team Six*. New York, Atria Books, 2013.

"Navy SEALs Who Killed Osama bin Laden in Rescue of 2 Hostages in Somalia: Report," *Associated Press/New York Daily News,* January 25, 2012. www.nydailynews.com/news/world/u-s-military-raid-somalia-frees-american-dane-held-hostage-article-1.1011524.

Burns, Joe Lee

Conflict: Vietnam
Shot Down: July 20, 1972
Rescued: July 20, 1972

Joe Lee Burns was born June 8, 1941, in Peoria, Illinois, but spent much of his youth in the Fort Worth, Texas, area. His father had served in World War II and later worked for General Electric. Burns attended the Air Force Academy. Once on active duty, he joined the Black Panthers of the 35th Tactical Squadron. This group consisted of F-4D Air Force fighters. They were originally transferred for temporary duty from Kunsan Air Base, Korea, to duty in Southeast Asia, while stationed at Korat, Thailand. Ironically, the transfer occurred on April 1, 1972. Those in the squadron felt it was prophetic that their assignment began on April Fools' Day.

On July 20, 1972, Burns and the rest of the squadron prepared for a mission that included four flights of various aircraft that were equipped with assorted weapons needed for the unique targets on that particular mission. The objective was to destroy an underground fuel bunker, so many of the planes were carrying 500-pound bombs with delayed fuses. The plan was to drop the bombs, which then wouldn't explode until deep in the ground. The blasts would destroy the fuel containers and expose the fuel, and secondary attacks would light the fuel. Additionally, more planes in the squadron would provide air cover against enemy fighter pilots and surface-to-air missiles (SAM).

Twenty-four aircraft were to be involved in the mission, but problems started on the ground and several of the aircraft were not cleared for flight. One aircraft did get airborne but had to return to base because of mechanical issues. To carry out the mission, the first part of the plan called for the strike force to take off from their base in Thailand, and then rendezvous with tankers to refuel over the Gulf of Tonkin. Once refueled, the force would proceed to North Vietnam, and then on to the target. After the strike, the planes would fly out to Thud/Phantom Ridge, then south to refuel with the tankers again, and then return to base in Korat, Thailand.

Major Walt Bohan, call sign Caddy 1, was the mission commander, and Captain Joe Lee Burns, call sign Caddy 3, was the deputy mission commander. Just before hitting the tankers, Bohan's plane had mechanical difficulties and he had to return to base. At that point, Burns became the mission commander. After Bohan's departure from the formation, everything seemed to be going well, with little activity on the threat radar systems. Armed with the information from their intelligence briefings, Burns and the others in the squadron could easily identify the target and the attack commenced. Burns rolled toward the target at 500 miles per hour in a 60-degree dive, releasing his bombs at 14,000 feet, and then he pulled up hard to the left to avoid any antiaircraft fire. An antiaircraft artillery gun did fire at them from the ground, but the planes were not hit. The bombs and delayed fuses functioned as planned, and the fuel storage facility exploded, sending flames 1,000 feet into the air. Burns continued out of the area at about 500 feet above the terrain, trying to avoid further ground fire.

After radio checks with the other pilots checking on fuel status, Burns determined they were in good shape and continued out of the area. The plan was once they bypassed the next ridgeline, it would be time to turn away from a known surface-to-air missile (SAM) site and head away from the ocean. When Burns saw the water ahead of him once he cleared the ridge, he knew he had gone a ridge too far. The enemy gunners opened fire, and though he tried to accelerate out of the area, his plane was hit in the left engine. Burns and his copilot, Nelson, needed to get out over water before they could eject. Burns heard the radio chatter from his pilots telling him to eject immediately because the plane was on fire, but Burns went farther, past the coastline. By this point, most of the systems in the plane had failed or were failing, and Burns and Nelson initiated ejection from the aircraft.

Just past noon, Burns began the ejection sequence. They were four miles into the Gulf of Tonkin. He radioed for help after he released his parachute, sending out the Mayday signal, then landed in the water. Nelson landed about 100 meters away from him. Burns deployed a small lifeboat, crawling in and issuing another radio call, which was answered. He also was seen by a pilot who flew over and tipped his wings, indicated that the pilot had seen him. Shortly after, Burns received a radio communication that a search and rescue helicopter was headed to the site. To keep the enemy forces from trying to pick up the downed airmen, members of his squadron stayed in the area.

Burns and Nelson had been in the water for three hours before they heard the helicopter. One of the pilots told Burns they would be picked up in five minutes. The large navy helicopter, the navy version of the HH-53 Jolly Green Giant, was known as the MH-53 Sea Dragon. The crew picked up Nelson first, then came for Burns, who greeted the helicopter pilots by blowing them a kiss. The rescue jumper splashed next to Burns, making sure that he was okay and would not require medical assistance prior to loading onto the helicopter. Within minutes, both men were safely on board the helicopter.

Burns and Nelson were first taken to the USS *Long Beach*, a nuclear-powered destroyer, so that the navy medical team could check them out. They were met with applause and cheers. The ship's captain greeted them, and they were examined by the medical staff. Shortly after that, the pilots were transferred to the USS *Kittyhawk,* an aircraft carrier operating in the Gulf of Tonkin. The next day, they flew to Tan Son Nhut Air Base outside Saigon, where the men boarded a T-39 aircraft for the return flight to Korat, Thailand. There, they received a hero's welcome from their squadron. Joe Lee Burns continued his Air Force career for 27 years, finishing out his career at the Holloman Air Force Base, Alamogordo, New Mexico, and retired in Texas.

Further Reading

Burns, Joe Lee. "Interview with Joe Lee Burns." By Richelle Brooks. *Veteran's History Project.* Library of Congress, April 27, 2010. http://memory.loc.gov/diglib/vhp/story/loc.natlib.afc2001001.72186/transcript?ID=sr0001.

Burns, Joe Lee. "A Ridge Too Far: Shot Down by AAA and Rescued Off Haiphong," www.keytlaw.com/f-4/a-ridge-too-far/.

C

Cabanatuan Prison Rescue

Conflict: World War II
Captured: Various
Rescued: January 30, 1945

At the end of 1944, the Allies were advancing across the Pacific Ocean and liberating the islands of the Philippines, which the Japanese had occupied during World War II. The Japanese had captured many Allied prisoners, and the Japanese military high command ordered that no prisoners would fall into the hands of the Allied liberators. As the Allied forces approached the prison camp on December 14, 1944, near the city of Puerto Princesa, in the Philippine province of Palawan, the Japanese guards forced the 150 POWs into trenches during an air raid warning, then filled the trenches with gasoline and set it on fire. The guards shot the prisoners who tried to escape. Although several did make it into the woods, most of them were hunted down and killed; only 11 men escaped the slaughter. This incident gave urgency to the Allied rescue attempts throughout the Philippines.

One of those prison camps identified as likely to experience a reenactment of the Palawan Massacre was Cabanatuan Camp, where the Japanese held over 500 prisoners. Many of those held in the camp were American and Filipino soldiers who had been rounded up after the fall of Bataan. Even before the surrender, the soldiers were generally weak or sick. The Japanese had no idea how many soldiers had surrendered; there were many more prisoners than the Japanese army could support, and they executed many prisoners along the march from Bataan. For those who survived the trek to the prison camps, conditions only got worse as the Japanese provided little food or medicine, and the POWs were subjected to cruel punishments. Those who were too sick to work went to the medical clinic, not to receive treatment, but to die. The prisoners called the medical clinic "zero ward," as there were zero survivors.

As the Allies advanced closer to the prison camps, nobody knew when the Japanese would kill the prisoners, but many thought the time was drawing near. To prevent the slaughter of prisoners, a band of Army Rangers penetrated behind enemy lines, with a time frame of 72 hours to affect a rescue. The prisoners were well informed regarding the progress of the war, as some of them with electronics training were ordered to repair radio sets and had confiscated the primary components. With these spare parts, they built a contraband radio and kept abreast of the war news. Through these means, they had heard about the slaughter at Palawan, and they also knew that they could be next if the Allied forces got too close.

The prison camp lay 30 miles behind enemy lines. The American forces pushed closer to the camp, and U.S. Army officials knew they would have to send help

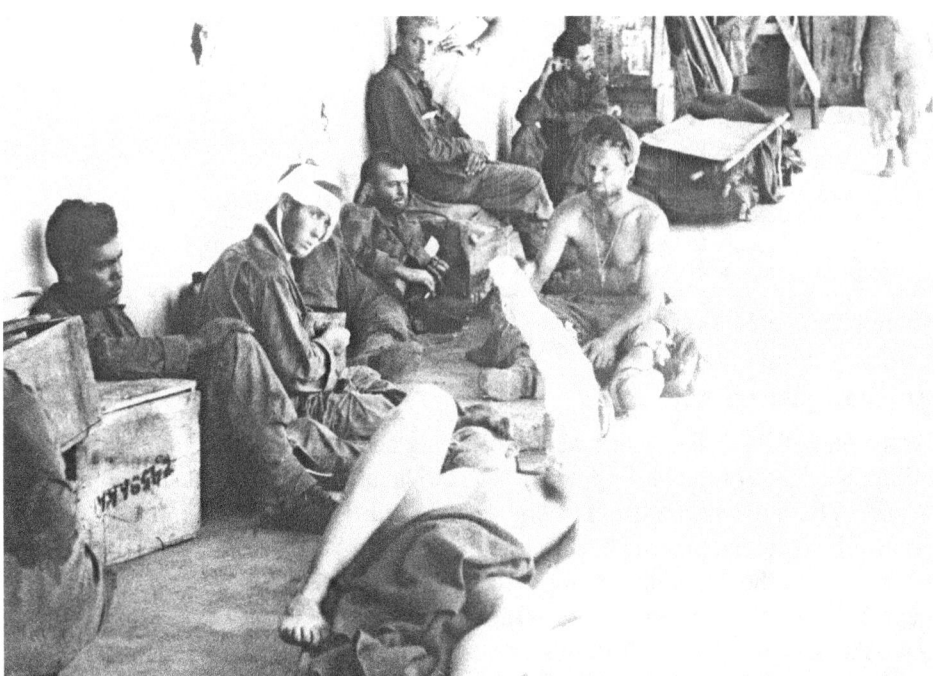

Conditions in the Cabanatuan POW camp were harsh, and many of those rescued needed extensive medical treatment. (National Archives)

quickly. Aware of the atrocity that had taken place earlier, the C and F Companies of the 6th Ranger Battalion, under the command of Lieutenant Colonel Henry Mucci, was ordered to liberate the camp at Cabanatuan. One hundred twenty-five Rangers left their lines at 2:00 p.m. with plans to arrive at the prison camp 12 hours later. Along the way, a number of other units joined the Rangers, including the reconnaissance unit known as the Alamo Scouts, and Filipino guerilla fighters. In total, the rescue force had about 450 soldiers.

The scouts informed Mucci that approximately 8,000 Japanese soldiers were now camped near the prison, which complicated their plans. Discussion followed this revelation, and it became obvious that the plan would have to wait for 24 hours until additional units could arrive. The odds against the small force successfully accomplishing their mission were too great. While the rescue unit waited, the Alamo Scouts crept close to the camp and gathered more information about the area, which helped to refine the plan. When the men crept closer to the camp, they discovered that the majority of the large Japanese unit had left, but about 800 Japanese soldiers were still resting near the camp. The guerillas set up machine guns between the Japanese and the prisoners to prevent the reinforcement of the Japanese guard force.

Local villagers were also instrumental in assisting the operation. They feared the presence of so many men would alert the local dogs, so they muzzled their dogs. Additionally, every villager in the local area brought their water buffalo and carts to an assembly point, anticipating the large number of sick and weak prisoners who would not be able to walk under their own power and to assist with the evacuation.

The attack plan called for C Company to crawl into position near the front of the camp and wait while F Company got into position at the rear of the camp. The Americans also used a P-61 Black Widow as a distraction. At 7:30 p.m. on January 30, 1945, F Company would initiate the attack by firing their weapons, but at the appointed time, there was no signal. One of the Japanese guards had spotted a soldier from F Company and sounded the alarm; then firing erupted from all around the camp. Many of the prisoners thought the feared massacre had started, but soon determined that the source of the shooting was their American comrades. The rescuers shouted for everyone to head to the main gate, and rescuers and prisoners helped the sick and weak to move in that direction.

The attack was such a surprise that few of the Japanese soldiers were prepared for the battle, and many prisoners made it out of the camp before an organized resistance was mounted. Most of the guards were killed in the attack. In only 30 minutes, all 513 POWs were evacuated. The line of prisoners, Rangers, guerillas, and Alamo Scouts stretched for over a mile along the jungle trail leading to American lines 30 miles away. Some hours later, the prisoners were returned to American control and within a week, they were on a ship bound for the United States, and then home.

Several films have retold the story of the raid, and many have included archival footage of the prisoners. The 1945 film, *Back to Bataan,* starring John Wayne, begins with the raid and actual footage of the survivors. In 2005, another film, *The Great Raid,* told the story as part of a large love story.

Further Reading
Breuer, William B. *The Great Raid on Cabanatuan: Rescuing the Doomed Ghosts of Bataan and Corregidor.* New York: John Wiley & Sons, 2002.
Rottman, Gordon L. *The Cabanatuan Prison Raid: The Philippines 1945.* Oxford, United Kingdom: Osprey Publishing, 2009.
Sides, Hampton. *Ghost Soldiers: The Forgotten Epic Story of World War II's Most Dramatic Mission.* New York: Doubleday, 2001.

Cavell, Edith

Conflict: World War I
Captured: August 1915
Escaped: Helped others escape Belgium

Born December 4, 1865, in Swardeston, Norfolk, England, Edith Cavell was a governess turned nurse who worked at the Fountain Fever Hospital in South London until 1907, when she went to Brussels to become a nursing instructor. She was known as a charitable person, someone with Victorian principles but who was not frivolous or prone to taking time for fun. From a very young age, she had a sense of social justice. Cavell was known for being a surrogate mother to the nursing students she helped educate, and for helping hundreds of men escape from the war and return to England.

Cavell was working at a successful nursing school in Brussels when war was declared in 1914. She was concerned when this occurred that Belgium was undefended. Germany invaded Belgium in August 1914 with 50,000 soldiers, and all

Germans were ordered to leave. She took student nurses and sent them out of the country, but Cavell felt compelled to stay and assist her supervisor, who was the president of the Red Cross in Belgium.

The Red Cross set up temporary hospitals, and the injured were treated there before being sent to prisoner of war camps. Cavell took in many wounded soldiers, and in November 1914, helped the first three, Sergeant Meachin, Colonel Boger, and Herman Capiau, escape. Cavell worked to get them out by providing guides, food, money, and clothing. Only Meachin got back to England out of the first group, but Cavell and her network became the hub of escape from Belgium, helping the "lost children," mostly British and French soldiers, get to the Holland border. Spies repeatedly tried to catch people involved in this network, but Cavell worked to conceal the network and continued to help hundreds of men in the coming months of World War I. She took them to Red Cross hospitals or private residences and used her connections to get them safely out of Brussels.

In a fragment of her diary from November 1914 to July 1915 survived, she outlined her network and how she orchestrated the handoff and raised money. Cavell was aware that she was being watched, but her desire to assist the soldiers overruled her sense of self-preservation. Some of the people she sought to help did not follow the rules of the rescue network, and this put her at risk. Cavell was a good nurse and a patriot, but she was not very good at being clandestine. Though her motives were good, she took risks that put her and those around her in peril. The nursing school was often searched, and finally, some in the network were caught.

In early August 1915, Cavell herself was arrested. Thirty-three others in the network were rounded up as well. When she was interrogated, she told the truth for some parts of her confession and fabricated other portions, primarily to protect those in the network. The second time she was interrogated, she signed written confessions, but she did not know what they stated because they were written in German. Cavell was put into a solitary cell and her trial set for October 7, 1915. Those outside of the network thought she would get prison time, and they did not react quickly to the news that she was on trial. By the time the British government realized that she was in danger, efforts to save her were too late. On her trial date, Cavell and 35 others, 22 men and 13 women, were tried over the span of 12 hours. Cavell's trial was first and lasted 10 minutes. She was sentenced to death at 4 p.m. on October 11, 1915, and her execution by firing squad was carried out the next morning. Cavell was 49 years old.

Cavell's execution was widely reported, though not all of the reports were factual; even so, her actions and execution made her well known posthumously across the world. Although some propaganda displayed Cavell as an innocent victim of a ruthless enemy, the reality was more complicated. The Germans had caught someone who was impeding their efforts, and the punishment was execution. However, their strict interpretations and execution of Cavell did not assist their efforts. Cavell's death was used effectively as propaganda to get more men to enlist, and stories, many mostly fiction, continued to circulate after her death.

Her remains were eventually brought back to England, and a service was held on May 19, 1919, at Norwich Cathedral. She is also memorialized by a statue in London at the National Portrait Gallery, near Trafalgar Square, as well as

During World War I, Edith Cavell helped Allied soldiers escape from German-occupied Belgium. Though her nursing position gave her some cover, the Germans executed her for her role in the escapes. (Library of Congress)

numerous other memorials in Canada, Australia, and Belgium. Several movies have been made about her life, and she has been memorialized in song and in verse. Her last words are noted as "But this I would say, standing as I do in view of God and eternity, I realise that patriotism is not enough. I must have no hatred or bitterness towards anyone."

Further Reading
Clowes, Peter. "Edith Cavell: World War I Nurse and Heroine," HistoryNet, June 12, 2006. www.historynet.com/edith-cavell-world-war-i-nurse-and-heroine.htm.
Hill, William Thomson. *The Martyrdom of Nurse Cavell: The Life Story of the Victim of Germany's Most Barbarous Crime.* London: Hutchinson, 1915.
Hoehling, A. "The Story of Edith Cavell," *The American Journal of Nursing* 57, no. 10 (1957): 1320–22. doi:10.2307/3461516. 1957.
Souhami, Diana. *Edith Cavell.* London: Quercus, 2010.

Charlie Company

Conflict: Vietnam War
Captured: Surrounded but not captured
Rescued: March 26, 1970

The U.S. military, all branches, has multiple units with fabled status. The 11th Armored Cavalry Regiment, also known as the Blackhorse Regiment, was one of those units. Begun as a horse cavalry unit in 1901, the regiment was motorized in World War II. In September 1966, the Blackhorse troopers were sent to Vietnam with a large force of equipment, munitions, and men. Because of the terrain and jungle, some thought this heavy unit would not fare well in Vietnam. However, the men of the Blackhorse Regiment fought for four years in Vietnam, in both large and small engagements.

One of the most remembered battles of the Vietnam War was the March 26, 1970, battle in a heavily canopied jungle area along the border of Cambodia and Vietnam. The 200 men of the Alpha Troop were called in to rescue another unit, which had stumbled upon a hidden North Vietnamese Army (NVA) base. The men of Charlie Company, approximately 80 soldiers, found themselves pinned down and surrounded by about 400 NVA troops. Early on the morning of March 26, the Blackhorse Regiment radio operators began hearing distress radio calls from the Charlie Company.

The Blackhorse Regiment captain, 25-year-old John Poindexter, made the decision to get to the Charlie Company. The Blackhorse soldiers were about four kilometers away, but they knew they were the only hope for the Charlie Company soldiers, as the dense overhead canopy prevented helicopters or other air support from coming in and targeting the enemy. The Blackhorse men averaged 20 years of age, and though most of the men in the Blackhorse Regiment considered themselves ordinary soldiers, their actions that day were anything but ordinary. After an extended eight-hour battle, the Blackhorse Regiment rescued Charlie Company. However, they were surrounded by thick jungle and knew more enemy soldiers were surrounding them. Rather than retreat, Poindexter decided to push forward into enemy territory, and this bold move allowed them to get the wounded out for medical care.

None of the men of the Blackhorse Regiment received medals for their actions. Thirty years later, John Poindexter was made aware that his award recommendations and even the battle records had somehow been lost. He worked for several years to ensure that his men's actions that day would be remembered. In 2009, President Obama awarded the Alpha Troop, 1st Squadron, 11th Armored Cavalry, also known as the Blackhorse Regiment, with the Presidential Unit Citation, which is given to entire military units for extraordinary heroism.

Further Reading

Keith, Philip. *Blackhorse Riders: A Desperate Last Stand, An Extraordinary Rescue Mission, and the Vietnam Battle America Forgot.* New York: St. Martin's Press, 2012.

West, Andrew. *The Boys of '67: Charlie Company's War in Vietnam.* Oxford, United Kingdom: Osprey Publishing, 2012.

Churchill, Winston

Conflict: Second Boer War
Captured: November 18, 1899
Escaped: December 12, 1899

Winston Churchill, born November 30, 1874, in Oxfordshire, England, is best known as the charismatic and strong-willed British prime minister, but many may not know his history as a military officer. Churchill joined the British army as a young man, and completed tours as a soldier in British India and the Sudan region, and as a civilian in Africa in the Second Boer War. Churchill was a renowned war correspondent, writing books about his experiences and the wars in which these occurred.

The Boer were a collection of German, Dutch, and Huguenot descendants that had first sailed to the Cape of Good Hope, on the southern tip of Africa, as early as 1652. They reluctantly submitted to British rule in 1806, but objected when the British outlawed slavery in 1833. Many left the colony and pushed their way to the north, wanting independence and isolation. The problem surfaced when the Boers discovered diamonds and then gold in their homeland, and the British government annexed the region. Inevitably, war broke out between the two sides and lasted from 1880 to 1881, but the British did not prevail; the Boers won the war. The British waited for their opportunity to take back the land, which came in renewed enthusiasm and commitment to a second war.

Some, including Winston Churchill, looked forward to participation in this conflict. Churchill had gotten out of the army at the end of 1898 because he believed his calling was to something greater in life than an army career. He was no longer a soldier, but when the Second Boer War broke out, he took a position as a journalist and attached himself to the British army in South Africa. He was 24 years old.

The Boers quickly gained the upper hand over the British forces in South Africa, before the bulk of the British forces could arrive and take part in the war. The British officer in command of the forces, Redvers Buller, decided to wait for additional soldiers before moving out of Cape Town. Buller had heard of a train traveling to the Port of East London where he could catch a ship to Port of Durban farther north, and from there he caught a train heading northwest to Natal, where the British were defeated at Dundee and a small outpost at Ladysmith. By the time Churchill had arrived in the Port of Durban, he learned that the British forces in Ladysmith

A young Winston Churchill while on campaign as a war correspondent during the Second Boer War in South Africa. (Library of Congress)

were cut off; nobody could get in or out. Undeterred, Churchill caught a mail train heading toward the front of the war, and in October 1899 he arrived in Estcourt, where there was an even smaller British garrison. Everyone in Estcourt knew the Boers would attack soon, long before Buller's army could provide relief to the British who were holding the garrison there.

The British had horses and bicycles to move about the countryside, but they also had armored trains. The Boers were reluctant to destroy the railroad tracks, which were necessary after the war, but the trains were fairly easy targets to ambush. Moreover, although the trains were armored, the routes were entirely predictable. Churchill knew that riding the trains was dangerous, but he was desperate to get close to, or into, Ladysmith. The Boers had planned to derail the train as it coasted down a steep incline, and once they had completed this portion of their plan, they surrounded the train. Churchill took charge of the situation, directing the men to push the damaged railcars off the tracks while mounting a defense. It was a gallant effort, but for naught. Many of the British soldiers were killed or wounded in the action, and the small force surrendered. The prisoners, including Churchill, were marched for the first part of the journey, and then rode a train to Pretoria, the Boer capital.

The prisoners taken that day rode into Pretoria on November 18. The Boers separated the officers and the enlisted, with Churchill going with the former. The enlisted soldiers were housed in a converted racetrack surrounded by barbed wire, with little in the way of shelter or sanitary conditions. The Boers put the officers in a red-brick building that was formerly a teachers' training college, newly surrounded by a tall iron fence. Although the Boers treated the British well, even kindly, Churchill was determined to escape from the prison. He came up with a plan for taking over the prisons of both the officers and enlisted, but senior leaders quickly put an end to that idea. Then Churchill discovered that two friends, Adam Brockie and Aylmer Haldane, had conceived of a plan to escape that involved just the two of them. Haldane was not keen to take the young journalist out with him. Churchill was not in good physical shape, the guards would notice him missing, and he had a tendency to talk too much. Although any of these shortcomings could cause problems during the escape attempt, in the end, the two men agreed to allow Churchill to join them.

The plan was to leave at dinnertime, when the guards were preoccupied. Haldane and Churchill made their way to the lavatory, where they could sneak to the fence. This night, however, two guards watched the building so long that the men had to give up. The following night they tried the plan again, and as before, the guards stood watching the building and they were unable to leave. They wandered back and forth between the lavatory and the barracks, looking for an opportunity. Suddenly, the two guards turned their backs to the compound and began chatting. This was Churchill's chance, and he quickly scaled the fence and waited for his two companions who had food, maps, and a plan. After waiting several minutes, Haldane came to the fence where Churchill waited. They could not get out, he said, the guard was growing suspicious. They talked about whether Churchill could get back into the compound, but the answer was no. Without any supplies, it was up to Churchill to escape on his own.

Churchill walked away from the prison and through the streets with the confidence of a man who belonged there. He was not confident about where to go next, but Portuguese East Africa seemed to offer the best option for staying out of a Boer prison and making it back to British territory. He found railroad tracks he thought would lead him in the right direction and followed them. He hopped aboard a train and settled in until dawn, when he jumped from the train and hid in a grove of trees. He was now about 70 miles into his journey, about a third of the way there. He had hoped to catch another train, but with his escape, the Boers had cut all train activity after dark, and he could not risk detection during the day. He was forced to walk at night.

Eventually, Churchill saw lights in the distance, and he thought they might be the bonfires of a livestock corral. As he neared the lights, he saw they were the industrial furnaces of a coal mine. He knocked on the door of the first house he saw, and luckily for him, the owner was British, and the one person within hundreds of miles who would not turn him over to Boer authorities. Churchill had rehearsed a story about being a Boer soldier in an accident, but he didn't need to convince the man that he was British. After a hearty meal, the Good Samaritan hid him in the coal mine, with a few other British in the area acting as conspirators. The darkness and solitary confinement began to get to Churchill after a few days, and those harboring him moved Churchill out of the mine and into an office aboveground.

The British hatched a new plan, which involved a local wool merchant's shipment of product to Portuguese East Africa in six railcars. Churchill would hide in a cavity created for him, passing the time with the food and whiskey his rescuers provided. The owner of the wool, Charles Burnham, went along for the ride to help ensure that Churchill made it to his destination. He was needed when an armed guard prepared to inspect the contents of the railcar, but Burnham invited the guard for coffee, an offer he quickly accepted. In the meantime, Howard had boarded a train going in the opposite direction, and he was surprised to learn that a man in the custody of Boer officials was accused of being Winston Churchill. Howard did nothing to rectify the misunderstanding. In the end, Churchill's patience paid off, and his train pulled into Ressano Garcia, the first train station in Portuguese East Africa. The train soon continued on to the next station, Lourenco Marques. Churchill knew he had to get inside the British consulate in Lourenco Marques before he would be safe. Unknown to Churchill, his good luck charm, Charles Burnham, was no longer on the train. Churchill sailed to Durban, where he learned that his escape had gained him notoriety. He stayed in the region, joining Buller's campaign, sending dispatches back to the *Morning Post* on the events in the war.

The rest of Winston Churchill's long career is more well known. He held several military appointments and honors, and he went on to serve as prime minister of the United Kingdom from 1940 to 1945, and 1950 to 1955. Books about his career as prime minister are plentiful, as are movies about his life, such as *Churchill* and *Darkest Hour* (both 2017), and dozens of television programs and documentaries have focused on him as well. He died in 1965 at the age of 90.

Further Reading

Manchester, William, and Paul Reid. *The Last Lion: Winston Spencer Churchill: Defender of the Realm, 1940–1965.* New York: Bantam, 2013.

Millard, Candice. *Hero of the Empire: The Boer War, a Daring Escape and the Making of Winston Churchill.* New York: Doubleday, 2016.

Code Name Bright Light

Conflict: Vietnam War
Captured: Various 1965 to 1971
Rescued: Various 1965 to 1971

From 1965 to 1971, the Joint Personnel Recovery Center (JPRC) worked in secret to recover prisoners of war in the Vietnam War. These groups, which included men from several branches of the service, were small and agile. Although the American military was adamant about not abandoning soldiers, the realities of the Vietnam War were not conducive to successful recovery efforts. The jungle canopy, weather, and guerilla tactics of the Vietcong intercepted or denied attempts to rescue POWs. The term "Bright Light" was generic for intelligence reports on POWs. The rescue teams used Bright Light intelligence to attempt to locate and rescue POWs in Vietnam and Laos. Although radio transmissions often were a source of reconnaissance information, flights were often more effective than ground missions.

Humane treatment of POWs by Communist forces was not the norm. Communist tactics included trying to convert prisoners to their ideology, torture to extract information about U.S. military efforts, and using the prisoners as propaganda. Prisoners who were released or rescued were often interrogated by the U.S. military after their release, to find out if the soldiers had stayed true to the code of conduct. Terrorist activity was high in and around Saigon, and in addition to soldiers, civilian contracts—mostly construction workers who were involved with bridges and roads—were captured as well. The turning point in U.S. POW policy came after two servicemen, Sergeant Kenneth Roraback and Captain Rocky Versace, were executed in retaliation for the execution of Vietcong terrorists. After this event, instead of notifying the Red Cross about POW deaths, the Vietcong destroyed the identification of any U.S. prisoners who were killed and buried those soldiers in unmarked graves. The JPRC instituted a reward program, offering $500 for the body of a U.S. soldier, and $5,000 for the return of a live POW. The unofficial motto of the JPRC was "Wheel and Deal and Bring 'em Home." Unfortunately, the JPRC was not extremely effective due to administrative issues, and even though their intentions were good, their efficacy was not. Although some POWs were released or rescued, none were directly related to the efforts of the JPRC. Senator John McCain, for example, was known to be a prisoner in the Hanoi Hilton, and yet he was not extracted. Unlike McCain, who survived a crash, about 40 percent of pilots died in the crash or were killed by enemy troops shortly after they crashed. Other pilots who were captured were sometimes hidden in caves or tunnels, and were moved often to avoid U.S. detection. The last American soldier returned by the Vietnamese was Captain Robert White, who was released in April 1973 from a prison in the Delta.

In addition to the JPRC, other units within the military also used Bright Light intelligence, including the Navy SEALs. The SEALs trace their heritage to World War II, when officials realized an organization was necessary to chart and to remove obstacles on enemy beaches. In 1962, the SEALs were created as two teams, one located on the West Coast and one on the East Coast. The name of the organization, SEAL, was created from the areas in which they operated: sea, air, and land. The teams were organized into platoons of 14 men, 2 of which were officers. The first platoons found their way to Vietnam in 1966, and working in swamps, jungles, and all manner of inhospitable terrain, the SEALs changed the terms of engagement. They were masters at camouflage and the art of the ambush. The enemy began calling them "the men with the green faces." They could sit in an observation post for days at a time, simply collecting intelligence.

Within a year of their arrival into Vietnam, the SEALs began conducting special missions to find and rescue American POWs held in South Vietnam. Although American pilots captured while taking part in Operation Rolling Thunder (the bombing campaign that was taking place against the north) were generally held in and around Hanoi, the Vietcong held American and South Vietnamese prisoners throughout South Vietnam. The conditions in the south were far worse than those the prisoners endured in the north, simply because the facilities were so primitive. The prisoners held in the south suffered from disease, malnutrition, exposure, and exhaustion. Given the situation, it was assumed that more men died while in captivity in the south than in the north.

The SEALs believed in never leaving a comrade behind and would proceed on a rescue mission as soon as planning allowed. They developed their own sources of information and continually honed their reaction time to quickly respond to reports on where the enemy held American POWs. In August 1970, a prisoner escaped the Vietcong and reported the position of the POW camp. On August 22, Lieutenant Louis Boink of SEAL Team Two, 6th Platoon, organized a massive operation to save the men located in that POW camp. Boink knew they had to act quickly, and his main concern was that the enemy would slip into the jungle and disappear, taking the prisoners with them. To prevent this, he coordinated with the Australian Air Force, who bombed the jungle paths to prevent their escape. As the SEALs moved into position, U.S. Army helicopter gunships opened up to the north and west of the camp, preventing the Vietcong's departure in that direction.

Unfortunately, when the Americans overwhelmed the camp, it was empty. The guards and their prisoners had quickly left the camp in the only direction left open to them, with the SEALs in hot pursuit. For hours, the SEALs chased the remnants of the prison camp. The enemy had discarded everything that might slow them down, including weapons and ammunition. With the help of Seawolf helicopter gunships and the five-inch guns from the USS *Sutherland,* the navy kept the pressure on the fleeing enemy. Finally, the SEALs came upon a group of 28 Vietnamese prisoners whom the Vietcong had abandoned in their flight. The Americans quickly called helicopter transport to evacuate the rescued prisoners. Unfortunately, no Americans were among the POWs rescued that day.

The SEALs were disappointed, as were the intelligence agencies operating within the country. Officials expedited handling and evaluation of any Bright Light material in hopes of finding actionable intelligence. When possible, this material was given to SEAL units in hopes of locating an American POW, and assets were constantly available for missions with short reaction times. Although a number of these missions resulted in raids on prison camps within the southern borders and resulted in the release of a number of allied prisoners, no Americans were ever located or released through the Bright Light operations.

Further Reading
Dockery, Kevin. *Operation Thunderhead: The True Story of Vietnam's Final POW Rescue Mission—and the Last Navy SEAL Killed in Country.* New York: Berkeley Caliber, 2008.
Veith, George J. *Code Name Bright Light: The Untold Story of U.S. POW Rescue Efforts during the Vietnam War.* New York: The Free Press (a Division of Simon and Schuster), 1988.

Comet Line

Conflict: World War II
Captured: 1940 to 1944
Escaped: 1940 to 1944

There were many resistance efforts during World War II, and the Comet line was developed in Belgium and France to help soldiers and airmen get back to Britain. The line started in Brussels and was organized by Andrée de Jongh, a schoolmaster's daughter who had grown up idolizing Edith Cavell. Like Cavell, de Jongh was also a nurse. De Jongh organized three main lines, all beginning in Brussels, where the men received food, clothing, and false papers. They were hidden in attics or cellars until they could be moved out of the city and escorted by a network of resistors who helped them move south through occupied France, into Spain, which remained neutral, and then home through Gibraltar, which was part of the British Empire. This particular route was over 1,200 miles long—600 miles through occupied France, and another 600 miles through Spain. Escapees were referred to as "parcels" or "children," and various teams were formed to work extensively through the region.

De Jongh, who was only 24 in 1940, worked with an extensive series of young escorts, very few of whom were more than 25 years of age. She also worked with the British Military Intelligence Section 9 (MI9), who provided support for the effort, including cash, as well. The Comet line helped more than 400 soldiers escape through to Gibraltar, and de Jongh escorted several groups, totaling over 100 airmen, through the Pyrenees herself. De Jongh swam the River Somme 11 times, and she had all Belgians on her team. The original *Planes, Trains, and Automobiles,* the escapees hiked, biked, swam, rowed, marched, and went in cars/wagons, from checkpoint to checkpoint, avoiding patrols. The network used Basque smugglers over mountains, and at the end of the line was Elvire de Greef, who was the mother of Belgium refugees.

By the end of 1942, the escape routes became more dangerous, with the Germans occupying much of the region. The Gestapo was looking for de Jongh, so she moved to France to work for a time, and her father took over in Brussels. When things became too heated for him, a Belgian aristocrat, Jean Greindl, took over leadership of the Comet line. From June to October 1942, 65 aircrew in 13 shifts got through the line and back to Britain. In January 1943, de Jongh was captured. After 21 interrogations, she only let slip one piece of information, that she was the leader of the group. She was sent to a concentration camp. The Comet line kept going, even though she had been captured. On October 20, 1943, eight of Greindl's men were caught and executed where Cavell had died. On March 28, 1944, Frederic de Jongh, her father, was shot. At that point, the Comet line stopped.

Some of the Comet line members were arrested and tortured. Some were executed; others were sent to prisons or concentration camps. Andrée de Jongh was eventually freed. She received the George Medal from Queen Elizabeth. She went on serving others, nursing lepers in Ethiopia. De Jongh died in 2007, in Brussels, at the age of 90.

MI9 records estimate that about 5,000 British and Americans were rescued by lines such as Comet during WWII. The Comet line also was the inspiration for the BBC television series, *Secret Army,* which ran from 1977 to 1979.

Further Reading
Neave, Airey. *Little Cyclone*. 2nd ed. London: Biteback Publishing, 2016.
Ottis, Sherri Green. *Silent Heroes: Downed Airmen and the French Underground.* Lexington, Kentucky: University of Kentucky Press, 2001.
Watt, George. *The Comet Connection: Escape from Hitler's Europe*. Lexington, Kentucky: University of Kentucky Press, 1990.

Cornelius, Elias

Conflict: American Revolution
Captured: August 22, 1777
Escaped: January 16, 1778

After the Battle of Brooklyn in August 1776 in which the British forces seized New York, about 1,000 Americans surrendered after their capture. They were not protected by international agreements on the treatment of prisoners, and their future was uncertain. Even referring to the captives as prisoners of war enraged the British officers, who had no respect for their adversaries and did not wish to give legitimacy to what they considered unmitigated rebellion. Once the battle was over and General George Washington and his men made their escape, over 3,000 men at Fort Washington in Manhattan also surrendered to the British. Colonial prisoners of the British numbered around 5,000 by the end of November 1776. Although some of the officers were allowed to find accommodations for themselves and to wander around town during the day, the British held common soldiers and some of the officers in a variety of churches, prisons, and sugar houses located throughout the city. The sugar houses were dirty warehouses where merchants kept sugar and molasses bound for refineries that the British had turned into makeshift prisons. They were huge buildings, but overcrowded and filthy.

The prisons were so full that there was no room for all of the captives, and due to overcrowding, the British transferred about 750 prisoners onto British navy ships that served as prisons. These ships were worse than the sugar houses and were crowded and filthy. The prisoners drank putrid water and fought with the numerous rats for the moldy bread they received as rations. The guards brought out the dead each morning, fastened a cannonball to the bodies, and threw them into the water. According to ship records, an average of a dozen prisoners died each night aboard ships, mostly from dysentery, typhoid, smallpox, yellow fever, starvation, and torture.

By the end of 1776, about half of the men taken prisoner only a few months before in New York were dead from disease and starvation. Just before Christmas, the British released about 1,000 of the sickest American soldiers. Most would not live through the winter, and the British officials assumed they could not assist General Washington because they were so ill. The British did not want to keep spending money on provisions to keep them alive. Even with these releases, a steady stream of captives kept the prisons filled past their capacity through the early years of the American Revolution.

Into these disastrous conditions Elias Cornelius, a Long Island surgeon's mate with one of the Rhode Island Regiments in the American Revolution, found himself captive. He became a prisoner when Tories ambushed his unit in August 1777 and turned him over to the British in New York. His fellow prisoners came to call him "Doctor" Cornelius. The British imprisoned him in Livingston's Sugar House, where his guard, a vindictive man named Walley, beat the prisoners and withheld the meager rations allotted each man. When Cornelius asked for paper with which to request a parole, Walley beat him and moved him to a notoriously brutal prison called the Provost, where he shared a cell with the famous revolutionary Ethan Allen.

Cornelius returned to the Sugar House and the charge of Sergeant Walley after a number of weeks in January 1778, and conditions were even worse than before. Most of the men were sick and dying, and soon Cornelius, who suffered from scurvy, developed a cough and fever, earning him a trip to the infirmary at one of the churches. Somehow, he and a few of his fellow patients managed to get their guard drunk and escaped into the dark night. He moved through the streets of New York, avoiding British soldiers as best he could. Eventually, a British soldier stopped him. Cornelius pretended to be drunk, fell down, and claimed he could not remember the password issued to anyone having business on the streets late at night. The soldier ordered him to remain until his sergeant showed up, but Cornelius talked the soldier into letting him go. Cornelius moved on, trying valiantly not to cough and give away his position.

Eventually, he made his way to the Hudson River where he hoped to find a boat to carry him to New Jersey. He searched for a boat while avoiding the notice of the guards. Unfortunately for Cornelius, he found no boat there, so he set out for the East River, but found no boat there either. He concealed himself in some bushes that night, then cold and hungry, he set out for the city that he had just fled to find shelter and food. He passed a number of British and German soldiers that he knew,

> **American Revolution POW Exchanges**
>
> At the outset of the American Revolution, British and colonial officials failed to negotiate an exchange of prisoners, and both sides retained combatants for extended periods ranging from weeks to years. One reason for the extended time was that the British routinely rounded up civilian noncombatants with the intent to exchange them for British soldiers and officers. Of course, the more this plan worked, the more civilians that the British took as prisoners of war.
>
> The British would sometimes parole an officer, or allow him to roam about New York City freely, but he had to provide his own food and lodging. He was honor bound not to flee or take up arms against the king until he was exchanged at some point in the future. However, the British refused to parole colonial officers early on, as they repeatedly broke their word not to fight against the Crown. Likewise, the British denied parole to common soldiers, who were thought to have no honor or moral reason to keep their word. When they escaped from the city and returned to their homes, General Washington ordered them back to New York to fulfill their commitment and to repair their honor and that of the army.
>
> There was limited enthusiasm to negotiate an exchange of troops early on, because the British mistreated the first prisoners taken in the war. General Washington would not consent to a trade of soldiers until later in the war. His argument was that the soldiers were in such poor physical condition that he was negotiating for men who would die soon after repatriation. Of the 5,000 prisoners taken at New York in the fall of 1776, half of them were dead by the end of December.
>
> Though General Howe, the British commander in New York, steadfastly denied any mistreatment of prisoners, American soldiers were not well tended to and did not fare well. Many of the soldiers kept in the British prisons died daily. The British paroled about a thousand prisoners at the end of the year, but most died shortly after their release of disease and the effects of starvation.

but none paid any attention to him. Exhausted, cold, and hungry, he knocked at the door of a house along his route and he met sympathetic colonials who fed and hid him until he recovered from his sickness. He moved from house to house, where friends fed and concealed him, until the point where he and several other escaped prisoners had accumulated an ax, a shovel, a musket, and ammunition. They ventured far into the woods and constructed a hut out of the trees, where they remained hidden for several weeks. Friends continued to supply food for them, until they stole a boat and the men made their way to Connecticut. From there, the men set out on foot to rejoin the American army encamped at Valley Forge in Pennsylvania.

Cornelius married after the war and had six children, including a son with his name who was famous in his own right as a minister and missionary among the Cherokee. Cornelius later wrote of his exploits during the Revolutionary War in a small booklet called *Journal of Dr. Elias Cornelius, A Revolutionary Surgeon.*

Further Reading

Burrows, Edwin G. *Forgotten Patriots: The Untold Story of American Prisoners during the Revolutionary War.* New York: Basic Books, 2008.

Cornelius, Elias. *Journal of Dr. Elias Cornelius: A Revolutionary Surgeon: Graphic Description of His Suffering while a Prisoner in Provost Jail, New York, 1777 and 1778.* Washington, D.C.: Tomkins and Sherman, 1903.

Cowra, Australia

Conflict: World War II
Captured: Various
Escape: August 5, 1944

The Cowra prisoner of war breakout was the largest attempted escape by prisoners of war in World War II. The Cowra POW camp was located near Cowra, New South Wales, Australia, and was used by Allied forces to hold Japanese prisoners. The area around the city of Cowra, which is located over 300 kilometers west of Sydney, was farmland. Just outside of Cowra, the Number 12 Prisoner of War Compound held over 4,000 military and civilian prisoners of war, including Japanese, Italians, Koreans, and Indonesians, during its use as a POW camp. Cultural differences caused issues between the Japanese prisoners and their guards, even though the POWs were treated fairly well, in accordance with the Geneva Convention. A riot in early 1943, at the Featherson POW camp in New Zealand, led to the tightening of security measures and POW camps throughout Australia, including Cowra. The authorities at Cowra installed machine guns, and the guards, who were mostly older or disabled veterans or those young men unfit for physical service, also carried rifles to guard the prisoners.

Because of the large number of Japanese POWs at Cowra, when leadership at the camp received notice that an escape was being planned, they moved all of the Japanese POWs, except for officers, to a camp in New South Wales. The Japanese government was notified of this impending move on August 4, 1944. That night, the Japanese POWs attempted a mass escape. About 2 a.m., a prisoner ran to the gates and shouted at the guards. After this, a bugle sounded, and more prisoners poured out of the buildings and began breaking through the wires in three large coordinated groups. One group was on the northern side of the camp, while the other two were on the western and southern sides. The prisoners had garnered weapons, including knives, clubs, and bats, and they used blankets thrown over the wires to aid in their escape. As they fled the compound, they set most of the buildings on fire.

Two of the sentries acted quickly after the escape began. Privates Ben Hardy and Ralph Jones tried to stop the exodus of prisoners, using their machine gun and firing into the crowds. The Japanese prisoners who had gotten over the barbed wire attacked them, stopping the machine gun fire. Before he died, Hardy disabled the bolt of the machine gun, which kept the machine gun from being used on the guards.

Estimates are that over 1,000 men tried to escape that night, with 359 prisoners of war who were successful in finding their way out of the camp. Most of the escapees were Japanese. Guards immediately went after the escapees, who had no transportation and little in the way of provisions. Some of those who escaped killed themselves rather than go back to Cowra. Within 10 days, all of the escapees had been killed, died at their own hand, or had been recaptured. Of those killed, 4 were Australian soldiers and 231 were Japanese soldiers. Another 108 prisoners were wounded. While the prisoners were outside of the camp, they harmed no civilians. The two privates, Hardy and Jones, were given the George Cross for their efforts in slowing down the escape. The Cowra Number 12 Camp continued in operation until 1947. The Cowra escape was the single largest escape attempt during World War II.

A large Japanese war cemetery is located at Cowra. Also, a Japanese garden was added to commemorate the location. The events were retold in many books, including Teruhiko Asada's *The Night of a Thousand Suicides* (1970), and guard Seaforth Mackenzie's *Dead Men Rising* (1975). A four-hour miniseries, *The Cowra Breakout,* was released in 1984.

Further Reading
Asada, Teruhiko. *The Night of a Thousand Suicides.* Sydney, Australia: Angus & Robertson, 1970.
McKenzie, Kenneth Seaforth. *Dead Men Rising.* Sydney, Australia: Angus & Robertson, 1975.

D

Dakota War of 1862

Conflict: Sioux Uprising of 1862
Captured: August to September 1862
Escaped: October 1862

The Dakota War of 1862, also known as the Sioux Uprising of 1862, occurred from August 17 to September 26, 1862, when the captives were rescued, or released, depending on the viewpoint of the person recounting the history. The final culmination, though, of this war, was the largest mass execution to take place in the United States, when 38 Sioux were hung along the Minnesota River in Mankato. This war precipitated the forced exodus of Native Americans from Minnesota, with the few who remained contained on small reservations.

Minnesota became a state in 1858, and its territories were new and open to settlement. As in other parts of the nation, many men were gone fighting the war, and military holdings at home were thin. Causes of the Sioux uprising are complex and varied, from loss of land, to delayed payments, to starvation. The treaties of 1851 and 1858, when the native population had been moved to reservations in much of the southwestern part of the state, had been broken multiple times. From Jackson, Minnesota, north to Montevideo, and east to New Ulm, groups of native warriors fought back against what they perceived as injustices against their people. Payments had been delayed, and food had been withheld, and loosely under the direction of Little Crow, attacks on settlers throughout the region began, from Lake Shetek to the Lower Sioux Agency to the full-scale assault on New Ulm. The Upper Sioux Agency, farther north up the river, was also attacked. Because so many of the natives were friendly, and many had taken to farming, it was difficult to always know who was fighting for what side. Men like John Other Day, who had become a farmer, fought on the side of the whites.

During these attacks, women and children were taken captive, such as Mary Schwandt, a girl traveling by wagon when they were set upon by natives. Mrs. Joseph R. Brown, a native woman, and her children, who were half white and half Native American, were captured as well. Mrs. Brown was personally cared for by Little Crow, who protected and hid the captives. The casualties of this uprising were significant, with about 400 whites killed and the number of Native Americans killed unknown. Chief Mankato was the only major chief killed in the battles over this six-week time frame, when he was hit by a cannonball at Wood Lake, which was a turning point for the war.

Three of the more receptive chiefs, Taopi, Red Iron, and Wabasha, began to exert more influence, and they took control of the captives after Wood Lake. Colonel Henry Sibley moved his troops up to where the captives were held, and worked to persuade the natives to release the prisoners. The 91 whites and 150 mixed-heritage people were released at first into Sibley's care, and over the next few days, 107 whites and 162 mixed-heritage people, 269 captives in all, were rescued. Most of these were women and children; some sources state that only one man was among those rescued. About 1,200 Indians were taken as prisoners, with many of them going to Fort Snelling in Minneapolis. About 300 were given a trial, though many said the proceedings were less than fair. President Abraham Lincoln commuted the sentences for many of those convicted, but did sign the execution papers for 38 Native Americans, who were hung in December in Mankato, in the largest mass execution in United States history.

Although many parties were taken captive, with numbers of over 250 in the totals, many small groups were also taken captive, and in at least one case, the rescuers were unexpected allies. On August 20, 1862, near Lake Shetek in southwestern Minnesota, Chief Lean Grizzly Bear and Chief White Lodge of the Southern Sisseton Dakota forces, who were usually north and west of the area, attacked nine families living near Lake Shetek. They had also been refused credit by the Indian agents, and many of the Sioux were starving. During the Lake Shetek raid, several captives were taken. One woman and a child escaped and made their way to Camp Release. Two other women and six children were captives of the Sisseton for nearly three months. Their release came near Mobridge, South Dakota, from an unlikely source, the Fool Soldiers. These young Lakota men, also Sioux and known as Teton Lakota, were dedicated to peace and at risk to their standing within the tribes, used food and other goods as ransom to rescue these captives who were later returned to their families. The Fool Soldiers were not hailed as heroes by the whites in the region; they were held at Fort Randall when they returned the captives, and some of them died while in captivity. As with other captives, not all of the women and children who were rescued went on to happy lives. Some were returned to their families and the events they had lived through were not shared again. For others, their families could not ignore what had happened to them, such as Julia Wright, who had a child after she was returned to her husband; he left her after she had given birth.

The captives and their stories were told and retold, with some claiming fair treatment by the Native Americans, and others claiming they feared for their lives for the five weeks they were held prisoner. Little Crow eluded capture for months, finally being shot when he was eating berries in a farmer's fence line. Thousands of natives were removed from Minnesota after the uprising, only returning in the later part of the 20th century. Two monuments to the rescue were erected, one at Montevideo and one at Lake Shetek; the former was dedicated in 1894, and the latter in 1925. These reconciliation events, widely attended by people in the region, were the beginnings of healing the rift between the people involved in these events generations earlier.

The events and stories of this conflict have become more prominent in the last 20 years in efforts to retell both sides of the conflict and better understand what happened. In addition to the many books and articles written about this event, several films and documentaries have also been created, such as *Dakota 38* (2012), an independent film shot and directed by Silas Hagerty that retells the story of the mass execution in Mankato, and *The Past Is Alive within Us: The U.S.-Dakota Conflict* (2013), a documentary that reviews the Dakota War and the relationship within the larger Civil War.

Further Reading

Brown, Curt. "In the Footsteps of Little Crow." *Star Tribune,* 2012. Minneapolis, MN. www.startribune.com/historical-narrative-of-a-dakota-chief-in-the-footsteps-of-little-crow/425712324/.

Carley, Kenneth. *The Dakota War of 1862: Minnesota's Other Civil War.* St. Paul, MN: Minnesota Historical Society Press, 1961, 1976.

Tolzmann, Don Heinrich. *German Pioneer Accounts of the Great Sioux Uprising of 1862.* 2nd ed. Little Miami Pub, 2002.

"US-Dakota War of 1862." Minnesota Historical Society. State of Minnesota. usdakotawar.org/.

Dengler, Dieter

Conflict: Vietnam
Captured: February 1966
Escape: Laos, July 20, 1966

Dieter Dengler was born May 22, 1938, in Wildberg, Baden-Württemberg, Germany. After watching Allied aircraft fly over his Black Forest town, Dengler knew he wanted to be a pilot. Surviving in war-torn Germany and assisting his family by scavenging what he could, young Dengler learned skills that would serve him well in his later life in America. A brash and risk-taking youth, his exploits as a navy pilot are legendary, and his story has captivated people for over 50 years. Eager to get to the front lines in Vietnam and fly missions, Dengler's journey from war-torn Germany to the naval station in California took grit and perseverance. After being deployed to Vietnam, his plane crashed after taking heavy fire on a mission in Laos. Dengler tried to escape several times, and was finally rescued after a 23-day escape attempt that followed six months of torture in a Pathet Lao prison camp. Dengler was the first captured airman to escape from a prison camp during the Vietnam War.

Dengler grew up in Germany during WWII, and after surviving bombings to his hometown, learned lessons in survival in the aftermath of those events. He made his way to the United States, determined to learn how to fly fighter planes. After living with his aunt on the East Coast, he earned an associate's degree and finally was accepted into the navy and was stationed in California. While he was in training, he not only escaped the capture simulations (his reputation legendary because he made 3 escapes in 12 hours), but he also made a survival kit, just in case he needed it once deployed to Vietnam. He kept his German identification, thinking he could perhaps convince captors that he wasn't an American, if he was shot down. When he could not requisition ponchos and mosquito nets, he made his own from scraps of materials. In this survival kit, he also added additional supplies, such as iodine capsules.

Dengler's SPAD was shot down over Laos during a highly secretive mission. Though the public knew the United States was at war in Vietnam, the missions in

A triumphant Lieutenant Dieter Dengler talks to the press about his escape from the Viet Cong. (Charles Bonnay/The LIFE Images Collection/Getty Images)

Laos were not discussed. Dengler's plane crashed after being hit by antiaircraft ground fire. Upon getting out of the cockpit, he destroyed his survival radio and hid most of his supplies. After evading capture during the first night, Dengler was captured by Pathet Lao, who didn't believe he was a German. He was shot at and tortured during the journey to a POW camp. He was tied to the ground at night, denied mosquito netting, and dragged through a village by a water buffalo after his captors tied him to the animal. Though he escaped once on this trek, he was recaptured when he had to retreat back down the mountain due to lack of water.

As with other POWs, Dengler was prompted to sign papers denouncing U.S. actions in the region, and he refused to do so. This earned him brutal beatings, one of which caused significant nerve damage in his arm, lasting for months. After arriving at the POW camp, Dengler immediately began planning his escape. Other prisoners in the camp—some Air America civilian pilots, some Chinese, and some Thai—were also involved in the escape attempt. They planned their escape for months, saving up food, loosening logs in the hut, and waiting for the rains. On June 29, 1966, they executed their plan, overtaking and killing most of the guards. The small group of prisoners split up. Duane Martin, another pilot, left with Dengler.

Both Martin and Dengler were very ill. They traveled for several days, eating the little food they had saved up and avoiding recapture until being seen by a village boy. A villager attacked them, killing Martin with a machete, but Dengler escaped. He was delirious, and finally he crawled onto a rock in the river. A pilot happened to see him when flying down the canyon, and they came back with a Huey to rescue Dengler, who by this point was down to 90 pounds, had liver damage, and was suffering from malaria and worms. Once back in U.S. care, the doctors estimated that he would have had a day or two to live, if he had not been rescued. Dengler was 28 years old and had been on the run from his captives for 23 days.

Charismatic and photogenic, Dengler did not shy away from the spotlight. His expansive personality had served him well during his capture and subsequent escape. His story has been told and retold in articles, books, and films, including the commercial movie, *Rescue Dawn* (2007). He worked as a commercial pilot after leaving the navy. Dengler developed ALS, and he committed suicide in February 2001 at age 62.

Further Reading

Dengler, D. "I Escaped from a Red Prison." *Saturday Evening Post,* December 3, 1966, pp. 27–33.

Dengler, D. *Escape from Laos.* San Rafael, California: Presidio Press, 1979.

Dengler, Dieter (interview). July 5, 2007, www.youtube.com/watch?v=IvhYWN3nW2E.

Fried, J. "Dieter Dengler Identified as the First American Pilot to Escape from North Vietnam in 1966." *Daily News,* July 28, 1966.

Henderson, B. *Hero Found: The Greatest POW Escape of the Vietnam War.* New York: Harper Collins, 2010.

Miles, D. (2007, June 20). "*Rescue Dawn* Tells True Story of Vietnam POW Rescue." American Forces Press Service, retrieved October 15, 2017, from www.af.mil/News/Article-Display/Article/126501/rescue-dawn-tells-true-story-of-vietnam-pow-rescue/.

Dramesi, John A.

Conflict: Vietnam
Captured: April 2, 1967
Escaped: Several, but recaptured

John Dramesi, born February 12, 1933, was from Philadelphia, Pennsylvania. He earned an Air Force commission through Rutgers University and served as a forward air controller (FAC) with the 4th Infantry Division in Vietnam in 1966. Once his tour on the ground as an FAC was over, he transitioned back to flying F-105D aircraft, moving from his base in Japan to one in Thailand. Dramesi's squadron officially provided cover for rescue operations throughout Southeast Asia, but more often, they functioned as strike aircraft for CIA operations in Laos.

Dramesi taught survival techniques and prison camp training for the air force, and he is one of the few to successfully escape POW camp training, including the punishment box at Stead Air Force Base. In 1966, he went to Vietnam, where he flew the F-105D Thunderchief, unofficially nicknamed "Thud." The Thunderchief was a workhorse of an aircraft, valued by operations planners and their crews for their ability to fly low and fast. At low altitude, the aircraft was vulnerable to a wide variety of antiaircraft artillery fire, ranging from large-caliber machine guns to missiles, particularly around important points such as the capital city of Hanoi, or high-value targets such as port facilities. The air force lost nearly half of all F-105 Thunderchiefs ever produced, over 400 in all, shot down over North Vietnam.

On April 2, 1967, Dramesi climbed into his aircraft as he always did, for what would be his 59th mission. The plan was to hit a truck park with 10 aircraft, each carrying over 4,000 pounds in bombs, and then to move in on secondary targets using the M61 Vulcan cannon. The bombing run went off without a hitch, but flying toward the secondary targets, Dramesi flew into a wall of high explosive rounds coming up to meet him from hidden antiaircraft artillery positions. As his cockpit filled with smoke, he ejected from the aircraft.

Like all U.S. servicemen and women, Dramesi had studied the Code of Conduct; he knew he was to evade capture, if possible, and what to say if he was captured. A tough kid who had grown up in South Philadelphia, his background as an athlete on the football field and as a former wrestler had helped him hone the skills that made a good pilot. He was smart and had speed. However, ejection from a rocket-propelled ejection seat in a plane at 500 miles an hour is a violent experience; he lost consciousness when he ejected and woke standing on the ground. Dramesi moved to higher elevation, thinking this was where the rescue helicopters would most easily find him. His wingman had called in his position and rescue was on the way, but he would have to fend for himself until they arrived. He put his experience as a FAC to good use, directing A-1 Skyraiders against the enemy that had shot him down and now sought to capture him, but his luck ran out when he was shot in the leg. He had not seen the enemy approaching, and then he was captured.

The enemy soldiers moved him out of the area as quickly as possible, carrying him due to his injuries. One leg had a bullet in it, and the other he had injured when landing after the ejection. The guards fashioned a hammock for him, carrying him at night from village to village along his route to a permanent cell. His legs felt much better after a few days, but Dramesi pretended they were still injured. He knew he wanted to attempt an escape and wanted his captors to think he was incapable of movement, giving him an edge. After suffering his first ordeal by torture, he resolved to leave his guards soon, and he saw his chance after several days. He had escaped twice from instructors at his U.S. Air Force Survival School. Finally, Dramesi got his chance, slipping out of the hut in which he was held, and he moved several miles away before guards discovered his absence. He heard the clanging of a gong and then hid in a cesspool of raw sewage when guards approached, but they did not find him and continued their search elsewhere. He moved east, hoping to somehow link up with elements of the Seventh Fleet in the South China Sea, but he was discovered a short distance from the shore. A mob surrounded him, beat him, and waited for soldiers to arrive and put him back on the path to occupying a prison cell. His captors kept moving him from village to village, and when he couldn't walk, they carried him. He didn't receive much in terms of medical care. The captors tried to get him to sign something, and when he wouldn't, he was beaten. He was interrogated several times, beaten, and put in holding cells or holes.

Dramesi was moved to Hoa Lo Prison, which is better known as the Hanoi Hilton. He was tortured for eight days, then taken to a small cell where his legs were put into wooden stocks. A rat in the cell acted as his sentinel; Dramesi would know when the guards were approaching when the rat scurried off. After a month, Dramesi finally received medical attention for his initial wounds, as well as for those received from the beatings and the stocks. He and a roommate were moved to another prison camp, Pha Phim Cu Loc Prison, which was known as the Zoo. In 1967, 120 were prisoners there. They were isolated from each other and punished if they spoke to one another.

Though Dramesi saw other prisoners try to escape, be captured and taken back to the Hanoi Hilton, he and eight other men still worked on an escape plan. Prisoners were rotated at the camp, making it difficult to formulate an escape. Dramesi waited for another opportunity and encountered Ed Atterberry, a crew member aboard an RF-4C, who was shot down in August 1967. Atterberry agreed to escape with Dramesi, and the two planned extensively, collected information and materials for disguises, and began to save the peanuts from their food allotment. They agreed to leave during a rainstorm to help them overcome the electrical fence and to conceal their movement while among the guards. Once they left the prison, which was quite a feat in itself, the men planned to head down the Red River, then steal a small boat to proceed down the river. Eventually, the naval fleet in the South China Sea was the objective. In May 1969, they attempted their escape. They were caught in a thicket in a churchyard and returned to the prison camp. Atterberry was so badly beaten that he died just eight days later on May 18. Dramesi endured 38 days of torture and was down to 100 pounds before he was deemed to have received enough punishment for his attempted escape.

Dramesi and many others endured a period of torture after his attempted escape, but treatment of the prisoners generally improved between 1969 and 1970. Men were allowed to live in large communal rooms and communicate freely, and talk returned to escape, with prisoners forming an escape committee. The leader of the escape committee did not want to endanger the men who were left behind or the men who might try to escape, and he made the seemly impossible caveat of having the escape plan approved by the military hierarchy in the United States. Through highly classified and covert means, it was possible to communicate with the higher command in the Pentagon. The men got a message to the military hierarchy, asking to escape and communicating their plan. They acquired a detailed map of the area and again they assembled information, supplies, and materials. Because of the sensitive nature of the communications, approval came in a unique way. An SR-71 Blackbird, the fastest aircraft known to man and relatively immune to air defense, flew over Hanoi at a designated time and sped through the speed of sound, creating a sonic boom heard throughout the city.

On May 10, 1970, Dramesi managed to get a note out that he was going to make another escape attempt. The plan for Operation Thunderhead, as the POW rescue was called, was a largely navy-run plan that involved SEALs, ships, and helicopters that would pick up the escapees as they became known to their rescuers. Everyone trained for their piece of the operational mission. The plan called for SEALs to stand watch over the expected route of the POWs after being brought to enemy shores by the USS *Grayback,* a submarine constructed in the 1950s but relegated to service with the special operations forces. Almost immediately, the plan went off script when the current between the submarine and the island was much stronger than expected. It ended up draining the batteries of the SDV (SEAL Delivery Vehicle) used to ferry the men. The SEALs followed the current out to sea, where a helicopter picked them up and transferred them to a U.S. Navy ship.

Despite the setback, the plan was still going forward to rescue the POWs; the operators wanted to get back to their submarine and continue the mission. A helicopter took the men out to the location of the submarine and dropped them into the water, a technique called "casting" that was undertaken at speeds less than 20 miles per hour and no higher than 20 feet. The height and speed were much higher than the maximum allowed; two of the four men were injured and two had gone missing. The situation became much worse when the men discovered that they were not near the submarine, but near another SDV that also failed to make their objective due to mechanical issues. It sank to the bottom of the sea. The men managed to communicate with a search and rescue helicopter that came to pick them up, and they found the two missing SEALs. One man was found alive, but the officer in charge of the team, Lieutenant Melvin "Spence" Dry, was dead. He had hit a piece of floating debris in the sea when he leaped from the helicopter, which killed him. Spence was the last SEAL killed in action in Vietnam.

Despite the effort and sacrifice, Operation Thunderhead was not successful. The senior leadership inside the camp had forbidden the escape committee from leaving the prison. The senior prisoner in the camp ordered the escape committee to stand down. Dramesi was finally liberated on February 12, 1973.

Further Reading

Dockery, Kevin. *Operation Thunderhead: The True Story of Vietnam's Final POW Rescue Mission—and the Last Navy SEAL Killed in Country.* New York: Berkeley Caliber, 2008.

Dramesi, John A. *Code of Honor.* New York: Norton, 1975.

Rochester, Stuart, and Frederick Kiley. *Honor Bound: American Prisoners of War in Southeast Asia 1961–1973.* University Park: Illinois: Naval Institute Press, 2007.

Dunkirk: Operation Dynamo

Conflict: World War II
Captured: May 24, 1940
Rescued: June 4, 1940

In late May 1940, nearly 400,000 Allied troops were stranded on the coast of Flanders, France, near the French port of Dunkirk, and pinned down by Hitler's forces. By June 4, 338,000 men had been evacuated to England. This massive evacuation was a turning point in World War II. This withdrawal of the Allied soldiers, codenamed Operation Dynamo, was also considered a miracle due to the large number of British and French troops rescued in a very short time. The quick decision and nearly impossible organization of ships and manpower to rescue the soldiers was an effort by Churchill and the Brits to save the core of the British army.

In the weeks before the Dunkirk rescue, the Germans were moving into position in France. The French leaders had all but disappeared from the battlefield in their homeland, blowing up bridges as they retreated. The British, who had gone to France to shore up economic sanctions against the Germans, now found themselves stranded. The French leader called Churchill on May 15 and told him they were defeated. The Allied forces had a pocket of soldiers near Dunkirk; the British Expeditionary Force (BEF) and two French armies, and nearly all Belgians—nearly a million soldiers were protecting the flank and pulled back. Refugees were everywhere, and some of the Germans pretended to be refugees or women to get through the enemy lines. The Allied forces managed to stay 10 to 15 miles ahead of the Germans and were mostly holding them off.

However, a series of miscommunications led to further retreat. The French General Gaston Billotte came up with the evacuation idea on May 18. Billotte went to Lord John Gort's command post, but again, communications broke down between the parties. Churchill wanted to send troops south and link the British and French forces. But Belgians were also a part of forces, and they were unclear what to do. Unfortunately, Billotte was killed in an accident, and the replacement options for leadership were not great.

Gort took charge. He went north with two divisions, and he had a plan to get to Dunkirk, and then home to England. Churchill had modest plans for the rescue, hoping to get 20,000 to 30,000 men rescued. As these operations unfolded, many were skeptical, and even Churchill admitted that he thought only a miracle could save the British and other Allied forces. Luckily for Churchill, the Germans also suffered from communications issues, and on May 25, when the Germans were only 10 miles from Dunkirk, German leaders asked Hitler to reverse his course, and he refused. The men of the 1st and 2nd Panzer Divisions of the German forces chased the British soldiers into Dunkirk.

The Allied forces at Dunkirk would need the navy's help in getting back to England, and the British sent every ship they had, even steamers, to help with the convoy. Churchill ordered the planning for the evacuation on May 19, with a plan to use Calais, Boulogne, and Dunkirk. They initially hoped to get 2,000 soldiers out a day.

Twenty-four miles west of Dunkirk, Calais was being held by the Brits who worked to slow down the Germans. The garrison held for a day with only 3,000 British men and 800 French troops, but then they had to surrender. Forty-six of the men swam out into the breakwater, where a British ship picked them up.

At this point, the British had 36 ships lined up in Dover, mostly ferries. On May 21, 1940, they updated the plan, had 30 ferries, and intended to get 10,000 soldiers out every 24 hours. Originally, they thought to send ships to the three ports in pairs. By the next day, May 22, that plan had changed again, because they realized they could only get to Dunkirk. Vice Admiral Bertram Ramsay, working out of Dover Castle, organized the delegation. In Dover Castle, underneath the castle were multiple rooms used for meetings. Because the team worked out of the Dynamo Room, the rescue effort became known as Operation Dynamo. Admiral Lionel Preston was the director of the British Navy's Small Vessels Pool and was also engaged in the planning.

On May 23, a large collection of ships—barges, skoots, channel dredges, ferries, navy patrol boats, battleships, and small ships—all showed up at Dover. These vessels were moored in the Thames estuary, and then armed with machine guns if

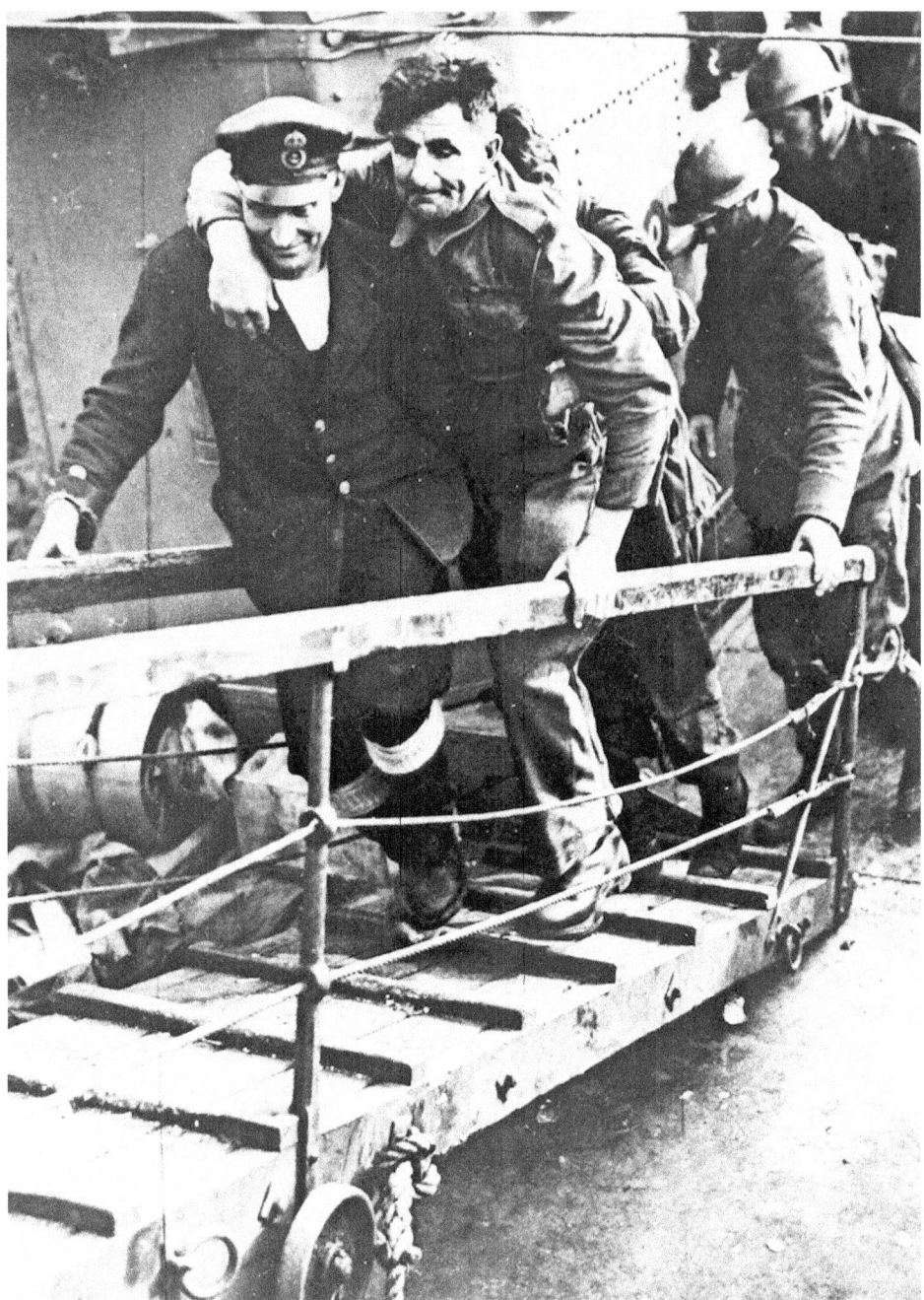

One of the saved soldiers from the "Miracle of Dunkirk" in early June 1940. (Paul Popper/Popperfoto/Getty Images)

possible. Meanwhile, the BEF blew up bridges and towns behind them near Dunkirk to slow down the Germans. The Germans ran bombing raids on Dunkirk, and the Royal Air Force stayed back. On the morning of Sunday, May 26, 1940, at 6:57 p.m., Operation Dynamo was officially launched. The goal was to keep the escape route open long enough to get as many people out as possible.

The boats began to arrive in Dunkirk, but there were not enough, and communication was sent back to Admiral Ramsey that more were needed. The first ship on May 26 picked up 1,420 troops and was attacked by gunfire and shells. A normal 3-hour trip took 11 and a half hours, because the rescuers had to take a longer route, avoiding a direct path. Sometimes the shelling was so intense that the boats had to turn back. On May 27, there was yet another communication error, with a false report that Dunkirk had fallen. After the report was noted as not true, the vessels started moving again, and the leadership also commandeered an additional 200 private vessels. Volunteers were plentiful, but many had little or no training in handling ships. One older officer who was retired had been on the *Titanic;* he owned a yacht and made trips across to Dunkirk, picking up 30 soldiers at a time.

During this time, King Leopold III of Belgium resigned, and this action put the rescue at additional risk. Although Leopold did not know about the Allied efforts, his actions had an immediate reaction. More people came into Dunkirk, and Allied leadership were determined to save as many as they could. On May 27, about 9,000 soldiers were evacuated, and on May 28, nearly 18,000 more were rescued. The soldiers waiting to be rescued were surprisingly orderly as they waited their time to leave Dunkirk. The German navy did their best to intercept the rescue ships, using S boats and torpedoes. They hit several rescue ships, and three ships went down. Starting on May 29, the Allied commanders pulled the larger destroyers as they were needed elsewhere, and started using smaller ships on May 30. The rescuers continued to make voyage after voyage, often putting more rescued soldiers on ships than they were rated to hold. From May 29 to May 31, over 90,000 soldiers were evacuated. One problem that came to light was that very few French soldiers were being evacuated, and Churchill remedied this by ordering that more French were to be rescued effective immediately.

The Royal Air Force fighters were also engaged, and the rear guard fought to keep the Germans back. The German infantry was now in Dunkirk, and thousands were captured. June 1, a day that is recorded as clear and bright, brought air attacks by the Germans that disrupted rescue efforts. When ships were sunk, fuel leaked into waters, causing an issue for others who tried to swim to safety. Soldiers from one ship that went down were picked up, only to be sunk on the second ship. Soldiers on land watched as Germans bombed the ships, and they could do nothing but hope the Royal Air Force could hold them off.

As of June 1, eight days in to the rescue mission, 39,000 British and 100,000 French were still trying to get out of the situation at Dunkirk. By June 2, 338,000 Allied troops and 170 dogs had been rescued. The seaway, or mole, was used to send troops out as far as possible. Each night, the soldiers were evacuated off the mole for their safety. On June 3, the commanders sent in every vessel they could, with over 100 small craft joining in the mission. It took a long time to get everyone loaded, and at 3:30 a.m., the last ships pulled away from Dunkirk. On June 4, they made one last run to pick up additional French soldiers. Dunkirk fell at 10:20 a.m. on June 4, 1940. Approximately 30,000 to 40,000 French POWs were left behind, but only a couple of dozen British soldiers were still in Dunkirk.

What has often been called the Miracle of Dunkirk was truly an extraordinary effort. Not only was the sheer number of over 338,000 soldiers rescued impressive, but so were the number of ships utilized, the bad weather, the lack of extended effort by German forces to stop the ships, and the limited German Luftwaffe attacks on ships moving between England and the shore at Dunkirk.

Upon return to England, some of the soldiers slept 36 hours. Churchill had hailed the mission as a miracle, and the British press expounded on that idea. The story of Dunkirk has been told in a half dozen films, including two films, *Dunkirk* and *Darkest Hour,* released in 2017. Dozens of books and hundreds of articles have been written about this mission and seemingly superhuman rescue effort.

Further Reading

Boyle, David. *Dunkirk: A Miracle of Deliverance.* CreateSpace Independent Publishing Platform, 2017.

Korda, Michael. *Alone.* Liveright, 2017.

Lord, Walter. *The Miracle of Dunkirk: the True Story of Operation Dynamo.* New York: Open Road Media, 1982.

McCarten, Anthony. *Darkest Hour: How Churchill Brought England Back from the Brink.* Harper Perennial: Media Tie, 2017.

McKay, Sinclair. *Dunkirk: From Disaster to Deliverance—Testimonies of the Last Survivors.* ReadHowYouWant, 2015.

Ramsey, B. H. "The Evacuation of the Allied Armies from Dunkirk and Neighbouring Beaches". *London Gazette,* July 17, 1947. London: His Majesty's Stationery Office: 3295–3318. www.ibiblio.org/hyperwar/UN/UK/LondonGazette/38017.pdf.

Sweeting, Adam. "Dunkirk: The Soldiers Left Behind." *The Daily Telegraph,* May 21, 2010. www.telegraph.co.uk/culture/tvandradio/7750005/Dunkirk-the-soldiers-left-behind.html.

East German Escapes

Conflict: East Germany, 1945–1988
Escaped: Multiple

In the four decades from 1945, when the German Democratic Republic (GDR) first drew a line within Germany, to 1989, when the Berlin Wall came down, millions of people escaped from East Germany. Estimates are that approximately 4 million people found a way out of East Germany, in most cases on foot, to escape the political issues and living conditions. The East Germans decided what professions people had as well as where they could live. For many, the lack of housing or food from the collective agricultural policies factored in people's desire to leave the country. Although a few people also emigrated from West Germany to the eastern side of the Berlin Wall after its construction in the early 1960s, this was an anomaly to the large numbers of East Germans who were seeking to escape. From 1945 onward, those who tried to escape were to be shot on site, and mines and traps were used to stop those seeking to leave East Germany. This wall was a tangible piece of the Cold War and Iron Curtain, but escapes from East Germany also took place across water as well.

Peter Döbler was one of the fearless who attempted to escape East Germany via the Baltic Sea. He left from the beach at Kühlungsborn, which was an unobtrusive spot. He took with him identification papers, a compass, a bit of chocolate for energy, and very little else. He had planned his route carefully, knowing where the buoys and shipping channels were. He planned to swim 28 miles in 26 hours, but he was picked up in West German waters after 20 hours. He went on to become a doctor in West Germany. He was one of approximately 900 to swim away from East Germany and to find freedom elsewhere. It is estimated that over 5,000 attempted escape via this route. Some used surfboards; others used motorized underwater propulsion devices to aid in their escapes. It is unknown how many drowned in their attempts.

Although the escapes via water were impressive, another interesting caveat of these escapes are those of the East German athletes who strove to leave their country. The governmental control was extreme, and athletes were political pawns. Entire teams, such as the football (soccer) team in 1950 moved to West Germany so they could compete. Track stars also left the country. Some returned only when their families were threatened with harm. The Olympics were another venue for escape, and from 1956 to 1964, many athletes left East Germany for good. Though athletes were generally under surveillance, many outside of the GDR worked to help them escape.

The Berlin Wall has now been down longer than it stood upright, having been down since 1990. The 96 miles of concrete barrier seemed to come down quickly, but a unified Germany was not nearly as quickly brought about. The millions of people who moved through the border, all of those across the world who have heard

Co-author David W. Mills visits the Berlin Wall in December 1989. Here, he shakes hands with an East German border guard through the wall. (Author's collection)

the phrase "Checkpoint Charlie," the name of the most well-known Berlin Wall crossing point, know that escape from East Germany during those times was anything but simple.

Further Reading

Braun, Jutta, and René Wiese. "'Tracksuit Traitors': Eastern German Top Athletes on the Run." *The International Journal of the History of Sport* 31, no. 12 (2014): 1519–34, doi: 10.1080/09523367.2014.922549.

Döbler, Peter. "The Lone Swim." In *Great Escapes.* Pleasantville, NY: The Reader's Digest Association, 1977.

"Escape into East Germany Not Blocked by Wire, Mines." *The Associated Press,* July 7, 1963.

Fischer, Marc. "'Let There Be Light': The Fall of the Berlin Wall and How Fear Dies." *Washington Post,* February 5, 2018. www.washingtonpost.com/news/retropolis/wp /2018/02/05/and-let-there-be-light-the-fall-of-the-berlin-wall-and-how-fear-dies/ ?utm_term=.8d0965e460ce.

Olterman, Phillip. "Surfboards and Submarines: The Secret Escape of East Germans to Copenhagen." *The Guardian,* October 17, 2014. www.theguardian.com/cities/2014 /oct/17/surfboards-and-submarines-the-secret-escape-of-east-germans-to -copenhagen.

Eichmann, Adolf

Conflict: World War II
Escaped: 1940
Captured: May 11, 1960

Adolf Eichmann, born in Solingen, Germany, on March 19, 1906, was one of the most notorious war criminals of World War II. He was not a soldier, but he was an efficient administrator who organized the systematic execution of millions of people, particularly Jews, during the Holocaust. He escaped justice following the war, moving frequently and often changing his name. Jewish organizations and the U.S. Army Counterintelligence Corps pursued him following the conflict. He succeeded in migrating to Argentina and living there under an assumed name with his wife and three children, who joined him from Germany.

Though Adolf Eichmann was born in Germany, he spent much of his early life in Austria. The normality of his early life contradicted the man he would become, when he was known as the architect of the Holocaust. He completed high school, then entered the Linz Higher Federal College for Electrotechnology, Engineering, and Construction, and took a job working with his father at a company that built electrically powered trams. Growing bored with this position, he moved on to sell wireless receivers, which were new on the market in the late 1920s, and then to sell various products for the Vacuum Oil Company. He disliked this occupation as well, and was actually relieved when the company had to cut back on staff and let Eichmann go as the only unmarried man on the sales force.

After leaving business, in 1932, he got involved in politics and joined the Fascist Party and the Schutzstaffel (SS) after meeting an old friend at a political rally. The friend, Ernst Kaltenbrunner, was a lawyer from Linz and later one of 24 defendants who went to trial for war crimes at Nuremberg following the war. Although Eichmann was apathetic about his responsibilities in the business world, he thoroughly embraced the Nazi ideology. He joined the Deutschland Battalion, composed of Austrians, but was hoping to work on the administrative side. He soon secured a position in Berlin, working in a department that watched the Freemasons and their organizations within the nation. Soon, he found his true calling working in a new agency being formed, the Jewish Department, where he was in charge of reviewing literature written by or about Jews. By all accounts, he was diligent in carrying out his duties and fanatically dedicated to the Nazi cause.

Eichmann's specialized knowledge of Jews made him the logical choice to head up the Jewish Department in Austria when Hitler annexed that nation in 1938. In sum, his job was to get as many Jews out of the nation as possible, which he did by calling in wealthy and influential Jewish citizens to meet with him. In his office, Eichmann outlined for his guests the organized abuse and mistreatment he envisioned for Jews in the coming years. He encouraged them to leave the nation immediately, but he would only sign their emigration papers if they contributed large amounts of money to get the poorer Jewish citizens to emigrate as well. Although Germany managed to get 19,000 Jews to leave Germany, Eichmann convinced over 50,000 to leave Austria. Eichmann's model was introduced throughout the Reich in January 1939. When Germany invaded Russia in the summer of 1941, execution squads followed the Germany army, and by the summer of 1942, the "final solution to the Jewish question" was national policy. The eradication of all Jews, in addition to others the Reich deemed undesirable, was the task of dedicated Nazis such as Adolf Eichmann. Throughout the war, Eichmann organized the logistics of the Holocaust, including the transportation of those sent to concentration camps.

Eichmann's work eradicating European Jews continued through December 1944, when the threat of Russian forces made him move out of Budapest. In 1945, Eichmann began to have concerns about what would happen to him after the war. He

Adolf Eichmann was one of the main architects of the Nazi plan to murder millions of Jews. He was tried and executed for war crimes in Israel in 1962. (Israeli Government Press Office)

knew that the Allied forces would not understand his work, and he would likely be tried as a war criminal if he were caught. In April 1945, Eichmann fled into the Austrian mountains. His initial plans, to take Jewish hostages and negotiate his safe passage or start a resistant movement, both fell flat. It was too late in the war for negotiations, and there was not enough support for a resistant movement. Eichmann met up with other Nazi officials, and he made preparations for his family to get out of the country. His wife and children were met by Americans. Eichmann was eventually apprehended by an American patrol near Ulm and sent to several prisoner of war camps. He pretended to be other people, including Otto Eckmann and Otto Heninger, knowing that if his true identity were known, he would be treated harshly.

Eichmann found it difficult to keep his identity hidden, and he began looking for ways to escape the country. Groups of Jewish people walked through Allied POW camps on a regular basis, looking for those who had harmed their people. Also, news agencies were reporting that he was in a POW camp and had listed his aliases. He knew he had to escape, and left the POW camp with forged papers, as Otto Heninger. He moved to Prien, in Bavaria, and then on to Celle in northern Germany, where he worked as a lumberjack for several years. He was focused on saving money, knowing that he would eventually need to get out of the country.

Eichmann's partners in the SS testified against him at the Nuremberg trials, sharing details about his actions and appearance. Eichmann's appearance was distinct, and his thin dark blond hair and gold dental work gave him away, as did his bow-legged stature. With these details, Simon Wiesenthal, a survivor of Mauthausen, began tracking Eichmann and other Nazi war criminals, with the aim of bringing them to justice. Wiesenthal worked diligently to find clues to Eichmann's whereabouts, searching his parents' home, his ex-wife's home, and even tracking down Eichmann's nine mistresses. One of them kept a photograph of Eichmann, who had been fanatical about not being photographed.

By the spring of 1950, Eichmann knew that Wiesenthal and others were getting closer to finding him. Exactly how Eichmann escaped to Argentina is laden with conspiracy theories. It is true that he stayed in convents while moving across Germany and through Europe. Eichmann then purchased a ticket on a ship headed to Argentina, and the Argentinian consulate issued him a visa for some reason. The exact connections that Eichmann had are unclear, but he did manage to get papers and get away from the continent.

Eichmann and his family lived in Argentina for several years. He let his guard down as the years went on, and he was seen in Buenos Aires in 1953 and beyond. This information was shared with Israeli intelligence, and in 1960, after others came forward with information about Eichmann, the Israelis sent commandos to capture him on May 11, 1960, and took him to Israel to stand trial. Eichmann was held for nine months as evidence against him was gathered and organized. Eichmann's trial was held from April to August of 1961. On December 15, 1961, Eichmann was sentenced to death, and he was hung on June 1, 1962.

Eichmann's life is well documented in books, including *The Capture and Trial of Adolf Eichmann,* by Charles River (2015), *Hunting Eichmann: How a Band of Survivors and a Young Spy Agency Chased Down the World's Most Notorious Nazi* by Neal Bascomb (2010), and *Eichmann in Jerusalem: A Report on the Banality of Evil,* by Hannah Arendt and Amos Elon (2006). Several films and documentaries have also been released, including *The Man Who Captured Eichmann* (1996), *Eichmann* (2007), and *Operation Finale* (2018).

Further Reading

Aharoni, Zvi, and Wilhelm Dietl. *Operation Eichmann: The Inside Story of History's Most Notorious Manhunt Told by Its Chief Investigator.* New York: John Wiley & Sons, 1996.

Aharoni, Zvi, and Wilhelm Dietl. *Operation Eichmann: The Truth about the Pursuit, Capture and Trial.* London: Arms and Armour, 1997.

Bascomb, Neal. *Hunting Eichmann: How a Band of Survivors and a Young Spy Agency Chased Down the World's Most Notorious Nazi.* Boston: Houghton Mifflin Harcourt, 2009.

Fields, Kenny Wayne

Conflict: Vietnam War
Captured: May 31, 1968
Released: June 2, 1968

Kenny Wayne Fields, a navy pilot who had grown up in West Virginia, Kentucky, and Ohio, may have the record for being one of the few pilots shot down on their first flight mission. Fields was just two months into his deployment and had recently arrived on the USS *America,* a new aircraft carrier, and was ready to fly his Navy A-7 Corsair over central Laos. Fields was a 27-year-old full lieutenant with 6 years of aviation experience. His call sign for his Corsair was Streetcar 304.

In Vietnam, one of the U.S. military tactics was to take out bridges and disrupt the flow of equipment and supplies. Streetcar 304's (Fields') job was to take part in a multi-aircraft attack and bomb barges and an underwater bridge. As the pilots approached the target, they took heavy fire from ground artillery, and Fields made his first pass without getting hit. When the unit made their second run, Streetcar 304 flew directly into tracer fire on his second run, and he was on his outward climb when he was hit by ground fire.

A large section of the wing dropped off, and when Fields lost control of the plane, he ejected. His first flight was 34 minutes long. Once on the ground, Fields knew he could not stay put and ran for cover. He was surrounded by enemy soldiers and was shot at several times. Within a couple of hours, his squadron came back and bombed the enemy, who were continuing to shoot at the planes. During this friendly fire, there were several times when bombs landed close to where Fields was hiding. He avoided patrols and managed to keep from being captured. He had a small battery-operated radio, and he knew there would be search and rescue. But he also knew that he was deep in hostile enemy territory. And he knew if downed pilots were not rescued in the first hour, the odds of them being captured went up drastically.

Fields spent three days and two nights in hiding, working to avoid enemy patrols in the pitch darkness. He could only use his radio sparsely, both because of the patrols in the area, and because of limited battery power. On his second day on the ground, he again nearly was killed when U.S. bombers were sent in to shut down the ground fire. Weather also worked against the search and rescue teams, and Fields was frustrated when they called off the rescue attempts for the day. Fields understood the enemy tactics of trying to use his rescue as bait to bring in more aircraft, which they would ultimately try to shoot down. This limited his ability to call in reinforcements, due to the danger they would be put in.

> ### Vietnam Escapes
>
> One of the most difficult places from which prisoners tried to escape was Vietnam. The most common prisoner in that conflict was a pilot or other member of a flight crew who had been shot down over enemy territory. The prisoners were most often tall and Caucasian, making it almost impossible to blend in with the local population. Someone with those features would immediately raise the alarm from the local population and literally be noticed at a glance. Additionally, prisoners usually did not speak the language, and the infrastructure within North Vietnam did not lend itself to escape. There were few trains or ships that a prisoner could hide aboard, and no opportunity to develop a network of safe houses to hide prisoners and move them along the way to friendly lines.
>
> The prison systems themselves also denied the opportunity to escape. Many prisoners were held all over North Vietnam; there was no centralized prison system until after the failed Son Tay raid in 1970. It was easy for guards to keep their eyes on one or two prisoners. Once all prisoners were consolidated at the "Hanoi Hilton" after Son Tay, then other considerations took priority. The first factor was that prisoners were kept one or two to a cell, making it difficult to communicate escape plans. Prisoners used Morse code to communicate between cells, a slow and inefficient communication method. Prisoners were also poorly fed and were beaten frequently, so they lacked the strength to travel very far.

On the third day, search and rescue began again, and the bombs were once again too close. He tried to get the bomber to change his course or abort, but the bomber dropped his bomb and the bomblets were headed right for Fields. Though he ran and attempted to bury himself in the ground, he took several hits to his back and legs. Fields saw a sniper in a tree trying to hit the chopper, and he did what he could to stop him. Finally, the helicopter pilot saw him and they lowered the basket to pick him up, nearly 40 hours after he had been shot down.

A little over an hour later, he was back on the USS *America* and was headed to the medic for treatment. Fields had taken a dozen hits and had pellets still embedded in his flesh. He had malaria and needed surgery to remove more pellets, but eventually went back to service. He had to be recertified to land on aircraft carriers before he could return to flying missions.

When Fields was shot down, he was not even two months into his deployment, and he'd left his pregnant wife and two young children just 52 days before his first run. He was able to see his wife and children after his rescue. Fields flew 186 more sorties/combat missions, clocking over 3,350 flight hours and 475 successful aircraft carrier landings. He went on to be a successful businessman and author.

Further Reading

Carroll, B. "Streetcar 304 Returns to Combat." *USS America Museum Foundation,* February 23, 2011. ussamerica-museumfoundation.org/library/fields.html.

Fields, Kenny. *The Rescue of Streetcar 304: A Navy Pilot's Forty Hours on the Run in Laos.* Annapolis, Maryland: Naval Institute Press, 2007.

Flight 181: Mogadishu Hijack 1977

Conflict: Terrorism
Captured: October 13, 1977
Rescued: October 18, 1977

Lufthansa Flight 181 took off from the island of Majorca in the Mediterranean Sea bound for Frankfurt, Germany, on October 13, 1977. The Boeing 737-200 carried 86 passengers and 5 crew members, and the flight was unremarkable until the aircraft approached the southern coast of France. At that point, a man and a woman in the first-class cabin rose to their feet and screamed at the passengers to put their hands up. When the chief stewardess, Hannelore Piegler, went into the first-class cabin to investigate the commotion, one of the hijackers hit her hard across the face. Moments later, two more terrorists demanded the passengers in the economy section put their hands up as well. The attackers had two handguns and six hand grenades, which were not difficult to take on board given the security measures at that time.

The leader of the terrorists, Zohair Akache, went forward to the flight deck to inform the captain, Jurgen Schumann, and copilot, Jurgen Vietor, that the flight plan had changed. Akache removed Vietor from the cabin and forced him into a passenger seat, then informed the captain that the aircraft should head for Rome. When the flight touched down at the Rome airport at 3:45 p.m., German authorities were aware of the situation. The terrorists were members of the Popular Front for the Liberation of Palestine (PFLP), and they relayed their demands to the control tower. They wanted the release and safe passage of PFLP prisoners held in Germany and Turkey, and the payment of $15 million. The terrorists threatened that all of the hostages aboard the plane, and another hostage taken a month earlier, Hanns Martin Schleyer, would be killed if the demands were not followed.

Once the situation was clarified, the German government took the lead because the aircraft was of German origin. The German chancellor alerted the GSG 9, a police special unit formed after the disastrous attempt to rescue the Israeli athletes taken hostage during the 1972 Munich Olympic Games had failed. The unit commander was Colonel Ulrich Wegener, a highly trained officer who had witnessed the tragedy of the Munich games, and who had trained with the most renowned antiterrorism units in the world, including the British and Israeli special operations forces. One of the GSG 9's primary missions was aircraft assault, which seemed a likely course of action to resolve the incident. In the meantime, the terrorists demanded that the Italians refuel the plane, which they did. The plane took off from the Rome airport at 5:42 p.m.

The hijackers took the plane to Cyprus, where the GSG 9 commandos hoped to resolve the situation. However, Cyprus officials would not give permission for an assault on their soil, and the plane was quickly refueled and took off again, this time bound for the Middle East. The plane landed and refueled in Bahrain, then traveled to Dubai. With the plane sitting on the runway with its doors open in Dubai, authorities learned of four hijackers wearing Che Guevara T-shirts. After refueling again, the plane took off for Oman in the United Arab Emirates, but authorities blocked the runway, refusing them permission to land. Next, the hijackers ordered the plane to Aden, in Yemen, which also refused permission for the plane to land and had also blocked the runway. There were airstrips parallel to the main runway that were not blocked, however, and a low-fuel situation forced the pilot to land on one of them. The Yemeni military surrounded the plane once it came to a stop. Authorities announced that the plane would be refueled, but would have to take off again. However, the rough landing on the secondary runway required that the pilot inspect the landing gear, and the hijackers agreed. Once down, however, Schumann simply walked across the runway to the control tower and asked for help. The authorities ordered him to return to the plane, especially once the terrorists began shouting over the radio. The pilot returned to the aircraft, only to face an enraged group of criminals and their kangaroo court. Without explanation, the leader of the terrorists, Akache, shot the pilot in the head.

Conditions on the plane were deteriorating. When the plane ran out of fuel, the air conditioning system could not run. The toilets backed up, and the pilot's body, which the terrorists had placed into a storage compartment in the rear of the plane, began to smell. By this time, the Yemeni authorities wanted the plane gone and agreed to refuel it. As the only remaining pilot, Vietor got the plane ready to fly, and then took off. Once in the air, the terrorists ordered the pilot to Mogadishu, Somalia. Somali authorities denied the plane permission to land, but they did not block the runway with vehicles. Vietor landed on the Mogadishu airfield. It was just after 6:00 in the morning on October 17.

Once on the ground, the hijackers commanded to know the status of their demands, but German officials had no information. Unless the prisoners were released by 3:00 p.m. the hijackers threatened, they would blow up the plane and everyone on it. The situation was reaching its climax, as the GSG 9 unit head left for Mogadishu shortly after the hijacked plane touched down in that city. The unit had not arrived by 2:30 p.m., however, when terrorists began pouring alcohol over the heads of passengers. An extension was desperately needed by German authorities, and a quick-thinking individual in the control tower provided the necessary relief, telling the terrorists exactly what they wanted to hear: the prisoners were all released and were on their way to Mogadishu to meet their comrades. The hijacker's deadline to execute everyone was extended long enough to allow for their supposedly released comrades to fly from Germany to Turkey, and then to Somalia. The new deadline was 1:30 a.m. the next morning. The GSG 9 unit arrived by 7:00 p.m., and the president of Somalia had given permission for them to end the hostage crisis.

The GSG 9 team had about 60 highly trained members and two British Special Air Service (SAS) liaison officers, and they were assisted by a large number of Somali soldiers and police. The unit commander, Wegener, selected 28 GSG 9 officers and the 2 SAS soldiers for the assault force, and he determined that everyone in the force would carry only pistols. The plan was simple: get as many soldiers into the aircraft as quickly as possible, with the element of surprise, and take out the hijackers. The 737 had six entrance points, two at the front, center, and rear of the aircraft, with large doors on the port side of the craft and smaller doors on the starboard side.

The assault plan was as follows. First, the assault team would approach the aircraft from the rear, where the hijackers had no line of sight. They would use special ladders to reach the six entrances, and they would operate in pairs as each team entered the aircraft. The main assault area was the teams operating in the center of the aircraft. They would enter quickly, using the emergency exit panels on the outside of the aircraft. The pair entering from the port side would fight their way up to the front of the aircraft, killing or incapacitating any terrorists in the economy section. The starboard pair would clear to the rear of the aircraft, while the teams at the front and rear of the plane would also gain access and support the main effort of the central teams. The only adjustment to the plan was made once the team was on the ground in Mogadishu. They enlisted the help of the tower personnel to talk to the terrorists during their preparations, distracting them, and the Somali police would start a bonfire, visible through the cockpit windows, to draw the attention of the hijackers to one location.

At 1:00 a.m. on October 18, the team formed up and moved toward the aircraft, unnoticed by the hijackers as they crossed the 700 meters to the plane. The assault teams formed up under the plane in the predetermined points and waited. The planned discussions from the tower began, followed by the bonfire being set in front of the plane. With everyone in position, Wegener gave the code word to start the operation: *Feuerzauber* ("Fire Magic"). The assault team went into action. Two stun grenades went off near the front of the plane, and the assault teams opened the emergency panels and began their attack.

The first members entered the aircraft and proceeded toward the cockpit. Almost immediately, they encountered one of the female hijackers, Suhaila Sayeh, who was hit and incapacitated by her wounds. The lead terrorist, Akache, began firing his weapon and hit one of the GSG 9 members in the neck, though his injuries were not life threatening. Another terrorist holding two grenades appeared out of the first-class cabin, and he was shot in the head. He dropped the grenades, whose pins were pulled, and they exploded under one of the seats. Miraculously, only two passengers were injured in the blasts, primarily because the weapons were not military grade. Akache appeared in the economy cabin and fired off a few rounds at the rescuers. He was hit by five rounds and eventually died of his wounds. Three terrorists were down, and quiet enveloped the plane.

The GSG 9 members began evacuating passengers from the plane, and once everyone was safely off, the soldiers realized that one of the hijackers was missing. They proceeded back into the plane, now empty of hostages. The final terrorist, Hind Alameh, was discovered hiding in one of the aircraft lavatories when she cracked the door and began firing at the soldiers. One of the GSG 9 men fired into the wall. She fell out of the lavatory, dying of her injuries a short while later. Seven minutes after the assault began, it was over. The hostages were taken to the control tower to receive medical attention, and then passage was arranged to get them back to Germany. Three out of four hijackers were killed; Suhaila Sayeh survived her wounds. The other death was that of the pilot and captain, Jurgen Schumann. The airplane for that flight is currently being restored for an exhibit scheduled to open in 2019. Two German films were made about this event, *The Death Game* (1997) and *Mogadishu* (2008).

Further Reading
Davis, Barry. *Fire Magic—Hijack at Mogadishu*. London: Bloomsbury Publishing, 1994.
McNab, Chris. *Storming Flight 181: GSG 9 and the Mogadishu Hijack 1977*. New York: Osprey Publishing, 2011.

Flight 571: Tel Aviv Hijack 1972 (aka Operation Isotope)

Conflict: Terrorism
Captured: May 8, 1972
Rescued: May 9, 1972

By 1972, terrorists understood the power of hijacking aircraft and getting a worldwide audience for their message. Prior to 1972, terrorists had focused on Jordanian targets, but after 1972, they switched their attention to Israel. However, they were not able to land telling blows against the state on the West Bank and the Gaza Strip. They targeted Israelis outside of the nation itself and brought a new level of terror to the international scene. They executed Israeli government officials, hijacked Israeli aircraft, and sent letter bombs to various targets throughout Europe. These actions brought them greater exposure to the international media.

On May 8, 1972, the Belgian Sabena Flight 571, with British pilot Reginald Levy, was en route from Brussels, through Vienna, and on to Tel Aviv. Twenty minutes after they were in the air after taking off in Vienna, the hijackers entered the cockpit. The four terrorists were members of the Black September Organization, which was a Palestinian terrorist group. They had pretended to be passengers on the flight, posing as married couples. The two men and women were heavily armed with guns and explosives. Captain Levy let the passengers know that they had "friends" on board, but he did not tell the hijackers that his wife was also a passenger on the plane.

Entry into the cockpit and taking over the plane was fairly simple in the 1970s. As was common in those days, the cockpit door was open to the rest of the plane, and this allowed the men to walk to the front of the aircraft without attracting much notice. Once at the cockpit door, they drew their weapons and took control of the flight. Of the 90 hostages on board, 67 were Jewish. Before the plane landed, the terrorists moved the Jewish hostages to the back of the plane. They forced Captain Levy to land at Ben Gurion International Airport in Tel Aviv. After landing, the hijackers made their demands. Similar to other cases, they demanded the release of others of their belief system—in this case, 315 convicted Palestinian terrorists who were in prison in Israel. The terrorists stated they would blow up the plane and kill all the passengers if their demands were not met.

Captain Levy sent a coded message to the Israelis, asking for help. Defense Minister Moshe Dayan and Transport Minister Shimon Peres, who would later become the president of Israel, negotiated with the hijackers. Dayan ordered the lead negotiator from the Israeli secret service, Victor Cohen, to engage the terrorists in long and tedious discussions of their demands. Nobody intended to meet those demands, and the objective was to tire the terrorists through frustration and lack of sleep while they got the rescue plans under way. At the same time, they set in motion a rescue

> **Hijackings**
>
> Aircraft hijackings began soon after the advent of commercial flight, with the first one occurring in 1931, and a large number of them occurring in the 1970s at the height of terrorism. Hijackers used the plane as a weapon, the passengers as currency with which to barter, and the event as a way to spread the word about their cause to an international audience. Sometimes the hijacking involved the plane being commandeered in flight, and other times, the hijacking occurred before the plane left the runway. Most often, the pilot and copilot were forced to fly to a neutral location, where the hijackers would demand the release of political prisoners, request money to fund their efforts, demand that a grievance be rectified, or ask for some other type of political concession. Governments sometimes tried to negotiate settlements with the hijackers, but the demands were usually not ones that could be met, often being outside of the government's control. Crew members received special training to deal with these situations, as did military special forces, the goal being hostage release without casualties. With airport security changes in the last decades, fewer hijackers have taken over flights for political purposes.

operation, code-named "Operation Isotope." Captain Levy talked to the hijackers, trying to keep things calm on the aircraft, while they waited.

The group went through numerous rehearsals of the rescue plan, using an identical Boeing 707 located elsewhere at the airport. Meanwhile, Cohen kept the terrorists up all night with his lengthy negotiations; the hijackers again demanded the release of 315 Palestinians kept in Israeli jails, and Cohen kept asking for the release of hostages. Finally, he convinced the terrorists to allow the Israelis to examine the bombs they claimed to have on board. They wanted to verify that they were real. The hijackers complied, sending Levy out to meet with the government officials carrying a sample of the explosives. While there, Levy told the Israelis all he could about the hijackers: there were four of them, two men and two women. Levy gave their descriptions, and the pilot confirmed that there were no seats near the emergency exits on the plane.

Levy returned to the interior of the aircraft and told the terrorists that Moshe Dayan had agreed to their terms. The Israelis would fly the 315 prisoners to Cairo, Egypt, where Flight 571 would meet them and where the hijackers could free the hostages. First, however, they had to repair the aircraft, which the pilot said had suffered a severe malfunction upon landing. They convinced the hijackers that the plane's hydraulic system was not working correctly, and that the technicians were needed to repair that system before they could leave.

The actual rescue operation began at 4:00 p.m. on May 9, 1972. Sixteen Israeli commandos, known as the Sayeret Matkal, disguised themselves as El Al technicians and approached the aircraft. The group was led by Ehud Barak and Benjamin Netanyahu, both of whom were future Israeli prime ministers. Once up close to the aircraft, they stormed in, killing the two male hijackers and taking the two women hijackers into custody. Three passengers were wounded, and one, Miriam Anderson, later died. The entire rescue operation took 90 seconds. Netanyahu was wounded when a bullet passed through one of the hijackers and lodged itself in Netanyahu's bicep.

After the failure of the hijacking and the swift Israeli response, the terrorists of the Black September group were determined to execute a daring international incident that would humiliate the Jewish state. They set their objective as the 1972 Munich Olympic Games, where 11 Israeli athletes would lose their lives in one of the most daring kidnappings, and botched rescue attempts, in history.

Further Reading
Klein, Aaron J. *Striking Back: The 1972 Munich Olympics Massacre and Israel's Deadly Response.* New York: Random House Trade, 2007.
Levy, Reginald. *From Night Flak to Hijack: It's a Small World.* Gloucestershire: History Press, 2015.

Fort Stanton

Conflict: World War II
Captured: Various
Escaped: November 1, 1942

Fort Stanton is located on Bureau of Land Management (BLM) land in south-central New Mexico. The fort was originally opened in 1855, and the military used the base to fight against the Mescalero Apache Indians. During the early part of Civil War, the fort was given over to Confederate forces, and the buildings were badly damaged. The fort was retaken by Union forces under Kit Carson's command in 1862 and after the Civil War, was rebuilt. Black soldiers were station there in the 1880s, and they were responsible for pursuing Geronimo and other Apache bands. When the fort was decommissioned, it served as a Merchant Marine tuberculosis hospital, a World War II internment camp, a school, and a prison.

During World War II, Fort Stanton housed an internment camp for German detainees, because when the camp opened in January 1941, World War II had not started yet, and they could not be considered prisoners of war. Fort Stanton was originally an old army post from post-Civil War times, and once the German prisoners arrived, they actually rebuilt the facility, which resembled a small town more than a prison. Most of the early German prisoners were on the crew of the SS *Columbus,* a German luxury liner that was sunk about 400 miles off the cost of Virginia in December 1939. About 400 Germans were detained at Fort Stanton, and the U.S. Border Patrol ran the camp, not the army or other military branch. The remote location was considered ideal because it was so isolated yet with a hospital in proximity.

Life for detainees at Fort Stanton was pretty simple when they first arrived in January 1941. Because the fort was still being rebuilt, the Germans were given a role in the construction of the barracks and supporting structures, including a kitchen, dining hall, laundry, bathrooms, and officers' quarters. There were also gardens and a swimming pool for recreation. Because World War II was not yet under way, the Germans had unprecedented freedom within the internment camp, including leaving the immediate area. However, once Hitler declared war on December 9, 1941, the Germans were not allowed to go in to nearby Capitan or walk in the mountains. The German soldiers, who had thought they would be able to go home sooner rather than later, found themselves in an encampment where guard towers and fences now kept them from leaving the area at all. Life changed considerably for them after the attacks at Pearl Harbor and German declaration of war.

Before the successful escape, a few men in the internment camp had tried to escape but were unsuccessful, whether they tried to go over the fence, simply walk out the gate, or dig a tunnel. Any who did get outside the fence were quickly recaptured. Because of the desolation and topography near the camp, as well as the distance to Mexico (over 100 miles south), there was not anywhere to go if the prisoners did escape. Even so, nearly a year after the declaration of war, four of the German sailors successfully escaped Fort Stanton on November 1.

During the night of November 1, 1942, Bruno Dathe, Willy Michel, Hermann Runne, and Johannes Grantz snuck out of the camp and headed south. They planned to go to Mexico. However, they were discovered missing the next morning, and the guards and local police led a concerted effort to find the men and bring them back to the prison. The men were spotted in a canyon not far from the internment camp, and word was sent back to the commander of the forces looking for the men. On November 3, the men were found about 14 miles from the camp, inside the Lincoln National Forest. The 25 men trailing the escapees rode up to them on horseback, and there was a shoot-out, where one of the Germans was wounded in the exchange. All four were captured and taken back to Fort Stanton.

Fort Stanton is now a state monument and museum. To date, there are over 80 historic buildings located on the fort, including some built as early as 1855. Only a small number of the buildings are fully renovated and preserved, including the museum and administrative offices. There is also a Merchant Marine cemetery near the site, with rows of white crosses in the fashion of other national cemeteries.

Further Reading
McBride, James J. *Interned: Internment of the SS* Columbus *crew at Fort Stanton, New Mexico 1941–1945*. Santa Fe, New Mexico: Paper Tiger, 2003.
Ryan, John P. *Fort Stanton and Its Community: 1855–1896*. Yucca Tree Press, 1998.

G

Garros, Eugene Adrien Roland Georges

Conflict: World War I
Captured: April 1915
Escaped: February 1918

Roland Garros was born in France on October 6, 1888, and was a fighter pilot during World War I. He began flying at the age of 21 and gained experience with monoplanes, competing in European air races. Garros set an altitude record (12,960 feet) in September 1911, and a year later, regained the record by going to 18,410 feet. In 1913, he made the first nonstop flight across the Mediterranean Sea, traveling from the south of France to Tunisia. In 1914, he joined the French army when World War I started. Garros was erroneously reported to have been involved in the first air battle in war history, with reports detailing that he had flown into a Zeppelin and the pilots as well as he had been killed. However, he was alive and in Paris, and the entire story had been false. The first Zeppelin was not shot down until June 1915.

Garros did have a direct impact on early warfare when he helped solve issues with forward-firing machine guns. Though he is not credited with the engineering and eventual manufacturing of an interrupter gear, a synchronization device eventually credited to Anthony Fokker, Garros's crude manufacturing of materials to create a metal deflector attached to propeller blades was a workable prototype. In April 1915, Garros shot down the first aircraft by a fighter firing through a propeller. He had a total of four shoot-downs; to be an ace, a fighter needs to have shot down five. Although Garros has often been called the first ace, he did not achieve that honor.

Also in April 1915, Garros either had mechanical issues or was shot down by ground fire near Flanders when he was trying to bomb a train, and he landed his plane on German-controlled land. The gas line had probably been hit, and as trained to do, Garros set the plane on fire. German soldiers on the ground saved the plane and captured Garros. Because his airplane glided in and wasn't destroyed, the German engineers, including Fokker, were able to study his modified propeller. Even though Fokker had reportedly been working on the design for some time, the change in design of the interrupter gear greatly improved the German's ability to shoot down Allied aircraft.

Once in the Scharnhorst prisoner of war camp in Magdeburg, Germany, Garros began thinking of ways to escape. He sent messages back to France, and he received a package with a map hidden in the hollow handle of a tennis racket, which began his association with the sport. Also in the POW camp with Garros was pilot Anselme Marchal, whose German was better than that of Garros. In February 1918, three years after his capture, Garros and Marchal put on German officer uniforms that they had made and walked out of the camp. The two pilots did their best to remain unnoticed in the town and made their way to the Netherlands, from there to London, and finally back to Paris. Although Garros was offered a position with the air force that would keep him off the front lines, Garros wanted to get back in his plane. Later that year, in October, he died when he was shot down near Vouziers, Ardennes. World War I ended just a month later. Garros died one day before his 30th birthday.

Garros is remembered throughout Paris, and several buildings, including a tennis center built in the 1920s, are named after him. That tennis center still hosts the French Open, and the tournament is officially called the *Les Internationaux de France de Roland-Garros* (the "French Internationals of Roland Garros"). An airport is named after him, and Peugeot even commission a Roland Garros's limited-edition car.

Further Reading
Driggs, Laurence La Tourette. *Heroes of Aviation*. Little, Brown, and Company, 1918.
Gershkovich, Evan. "Who Was Roland Garros? The Fighter Pilot behind the French Open." *New York Times,* June 10, 2017. www.nytimes.com/2017/06/10/briefing/roland-garros-facts-french-open.html.

Giraud, Henri Honoré

Conflict: World War II
Captured: August 1914 and May 1940
Escapes: October 1914 and April 1942

Henri Giraud was born in Paris on January 18, 1879. He is one of the few who served in both World War I and World War II, and perhaps the only man to make escapes during both of those conflicts. After graduating from military academy in 1900, Giraud joined the French army and served in North Africa, commanding Zouave troops, until he was sent back to France in 1914. He then went on to serve in World War I.

As a captain in World War I, Giraud was injured and captured during a bayonet charge during the Battle of St. Quentin in August 1914. Though he was left for dead on the battlefield, he was captured soon after when it was discovered he was still alive. He spent two months in German captivity at a camp in Belgium, where he recovered from his injuries. During this time, he prepared for his escape, and he initially escaped and traveled with a circus for a time. Then, with the help of Edith Cavell and her network, Giraud escaped back to the Netherlands and eventually back to France. After World War I, Giraud continued to serve, including stints in Istanbul and Morocco.

Just over 25 years later at age 61, five-star General Henri Giraud was fighting near Le Catelet, France, on May 10, 1940, when he was again captured by the Germans. During his long military career, Giraud had honed his knowledge of German tactics and was not surprised when they took him to Königstein, a prisoner of war camp on a cliff face with guarded entrances. They knew Giraud's status and capabilities, but they did not think he would be able to escape from Königstein. For two years, Giraud looked for ways to escape, learning German and memorizing the area around Königstein as well as a map that he had confiscated. Because of his rank, Giraud was given some privileges, such as daily walks and packages from home. Though it took him two years, he managed to smuggle in the supplies he needed for his escape through those packages, including rope, copper wire, and other items. Though he wore his uniform, he removed the embellishments and had a nondescript raincoat that he planned to wear over the top to conceal his identity.

On April 17, 1942, Giraud climbed down the 150-foot cliff face at Königstein. For any man, climbing 15 stories is impressive, but Giraud was 63 when he made his escape. He made it to the base, shaved his mustache, and put on a hat and raincoat as he headed away from the camp. The escape consisted of two parts. First, at a prearranged time and place, he met a young man who had clothes and papers for him. This meeting had been arranged by Giraud's wife, and because of her efforts, Giraud was able to leave that meeting and be transformed into a businessman with a new identity. Part 2 of the escape was a bit trickier. Giraud got on a train, avoiding the Gestapo, and bluffed his way through checkpoints. He crossed the border into occupied France. He made it through even though guards were stopping anyone over 5 foot 11. Giraud was six foot, and he knew they were looking for him. He got back onto the train and headed for the Swiss mountains. Eventually, he ran into Swiss guards on the mountain trails and they helped him escape back into France. In 1914, Giraud had sent a telegram to his wife when he escaped during World War I, and he sent the same one on his second escape in World War II. "Business concluded excellent health affectionately Henri."

Giraud's military career was still not over. In October 1942, he was summoned to assist in North Africa. Because the Germans wanted him dead, Giraud had gone into hiding. The Allies got him out of France by submarine. Giraud would serve in North Africa for two years. Eisenhower, Roosevelt, and Churchill all worked with Giraud. He continued a long career as a leader and diplomat. Giraud retired in 1944 and died a decorated military hero in 1949.

Further Reading

Echternkamp, Jorg, ed. *Germany and the Second World War.* Oxford: Clarendon Press, 2014.

Painton, Frederick C. "The Elusive French General." *Great Escapes.* Pleasantville, NY: The Reader's Digest Association, 1977.

Roussel, Meg. "Escape Artist: General Giraud." The National WWII Museum, April 17, 2012. www.nww2m.com/2012/04/escape-artist-general-giraud.

South, John. "You Can't Hold Me: General Henri Giraud Escapes the Germans in Both World Wars." War History Online, January 15, 2016. www.warhistoryonline.com /guest-bloggers/henri-giraud-escapes.html.

Glazier, Willard W.

Conflict: Civil War
Captured: Initial capture in 1863
Escaped: Multiple unsuccessful; successful 1864

Few Civil War survivors have the history of Willard Glazier or took the time to write as thoroughly about those adventures. Born in rural Upstate New York in

1841, he went to a normal school in Albany and taught school for two years. In 1861, with some friends and classmates, he enlisted and was placed in the 2nd New York, also known as the "Harris Cavalry" regiment, because he had a horse. Lieutenant Glazier was first taken prisoner in Virginia in October 1863, when his horse was shot from under him. He was knocked unconscious and laid in the mud until he woke up and was taken first to the Warrenton Jail, then to Libby Prison in Richmond.

Willard Glazier, Civil War brevet general, spent months in several Confederate prisons, including Andersonville. (Chaiba Media)

Glazier details the diseases known to frequent prisoner of war camps, such as scurvy, pneumonia, and chronic diarrhea. He sent messages out of Libby Prison by way of buttons, hat linings, coat linings, and shoes. Between sections of the building was an intricate series of keyhole communications, through holes in the floor, and the prisoners helped each other watch for guards so messages wouldn't be intercepted. Some of the guards could be bribed; others could not. Some prisoners played dead to be taken out of the prison, but the guards soon figured this out, and watched the living as well as the dead.

Glazier's first escape attempt was from Libby Prison, where Glazier and other prisoners created a tunnel in the basement of a building, hiding it in a small, unoccupied room. They accessed the room with a short ladder that they confiscated from the guards. They hauled the dirt out in slop barrels, using an old trowel and half a canteen to scoop out the material. The space was very small, where only two could work at a time, and they labored for several weeks. One hundred fifteen men escaped through the tunnel one February night, but 48 of them were caught. Glazier had not gotten out that night.

Not long after that, he was transferred to several other prisons, including prisons in Georgia, Charleston, and then Columbia, South Carolina, where he made his first escape. Here, Glazier had also helped with tunneling, and this time, he successfully left the prison through that tunnel. However, he was recaptured after several weeks and was sent to Sylvania, Georgia. He escaped from there in December 1864, finding his way back home because he had fulfilled his service. In February 1864, Glazier reentered the army and served with the 26th New York Cavalry, staying with that regiment until the end of the war. He was not captured again. In 1867, he achieved the rank of brevet captain for his service.

Glazier wrote about his escapes in *The Capture, the Prison-Pen, and the Escape,* which he wrote in 1865, and which sold over 400,000 copies. His text is written in the genteel style of the age, but his attention to detail and memories of his incarcerations are vivid and engaging. Glazier doesn't spend many words discussing the volume of deaths in the war, except for those recorded at Andersonville (13,000 recorded) and an estimate of how many died in rebel prisons (81,000).

Glazier discusses where the main rebel prisons were located, providing details on the following:

- Libby, Richmond, Virginia
- Castle Thunder, Richmond, Virginia
- Danville, Pittsylvania County, Virginia
- Belle Isle, in James River, near Richmond
- Macon, Georgia, known south as Camp Oglethorpe
- Savannah, Georgia, known south as Camp Davidson
- Andersonville, Sumter County, Georgia, known south as Camp Sumter
- Millen, Burke County, Georgia, known south as Camp Lawton
- Charleston, South Carolina
- Columbia, South Carolina

- Blackstock, South Carolina
- Florence, Darlington County, South Carolina
- Salisbury, Rowan County, North Carolina
- Raleigh, North Carolina
- Goldsboro, North Carolina
- Charlotte, North Carolina
- Tyler, Smith County, Texas
- Cahawba, Dallas County, Alabama

After the war, Glazier traveled, explored, and wrote. In 1875 and 1876, he rode from Boston to San Francisco on horseback, and he was captured by hostiles near Skull Rocks, Wyoming Territory, but made his escape. In 1881, he made a canoe voyage of 3,000 miles, from the headwaters to the mouth of the Mississippi. Glazier was a colonel of a provisional regiment of Illinois Infantry during the Spanish-American War. And from 1902 to 1903, he explored the uncharted Labrador Peninsula and discovered a river that now bears his name. Glazier died in 1905. He was 64 years old.

Further Reading

Glazier, Willard W. *The Capture, the Prison Pen, and the Escape: Giving a Complete History of Prison Life in the South.* New York: United States Publishing Company, 1868.

Glazier, Willard W., and Hudson Brother. *Heroes of Three Wars: Comprising a Series of Biographical Sketches of the Most Distinguished Soldier.* Charleston, SC: Bibliolife, 2010.

Grimson, George

Conflict: World War II
Captured: July 15, 1940
Escaped: Multiple, February 1944

George Grimson was born in October 1915, and he grew up in South West London, the son of a plumber and his stay-at-home mother. His father died when Grimson was in his early 20s, and he joined the Royal Air Force (RAF) in 1938, to support his mother and his siblings. He trained as a radio operator and a gunner, serving in RAF Squadron 37 and Vickers Wellington bombers at the outbreak of the war. His combat service was relatively short. Grimson was a wireless radio operator, and his plane was shot down on July 15, 1940, during a raid on Hamburg and Bremen. Grimson and one other man survived, bailing out of the bomber before it burst into flames.

Grimson was captured by the Germans, who sent him to a number of camps: Stalag Luft I, Stalag VIII-B, and back to Stalag Luft I, before he settled into a more or less permanent assignment to Stalag Luft III. Grimson was a habitual escaper who, in his frequent bids for freedom, possessed skills and attitude that defied logic.

Grimson learned German and spoke it without an accent, and his self-confidence and bluster were assets in his multiple escape attempts.

Grimson had twice escaped from German prison camps by impersonating German officers, although the Germans subsequently recaptured him, after which Grimson's most daring episode began. Grimson disguised himself as a Luftwaffe enlisted man, wearing a blue jumpsuit, Luftwaffe cap—an RAF cap dyed to look like the German hat—and a leather belt. He carried a bag full of electrical wires and a fake electrical meter, and he also had fake identity papers hidden in his clothes. He borrowed a ladder from the prison theater and then approached the perimeter fence, looking every bit the part of the German electrician tasked to inspect the camp's telephone lines.

Grimson approached the guard tower, pointed to the lines, and got permission from the guard to begin his work. He started his project a distance from the main gate, pretending to work to lull the guards into a false sense of security. He worked his way around the perimeter until he approached the portion of the fence that separated the prison camp from the German camp, and then dropped his test meter outside of the prison camp wires and near the German fence. He cursed, looked up at the guard in the tower, who gave him permission to retrieve his meter, and then made his way through the fence. When the timing was right, he made his way into the area of the camp reserved for the Germans and out to the main gate, where he bluffed his way out of camp. Once outside the camp, he discarded the overalls, revealing a plain suit that he had gotten from the escape committee. His civilian clothes mimicked what the Gestapo wore, and he even bluffed his way aboard a train that was headed toward the Baltic Sea. The Germans eventually discovered his identity on the train, and this time shipped him off to the prison camp at Heydekrug.

Most prison camps had escape committees, an organization charged with providing prisoners civilian clothing, money, and identity papers that would assist them in their attempts to flee Germany. Grimson had engaged the help of that committee to get out of Stalag Luft III. The escape committee at Heydekrug realized that they could only do so much to prepare a prisoner for his flight, and that once they exited the camp, no assistance was available. The escape committee proposed that one man should escape for the sole purpose of assisting other prisoners once they made their way out of camp. The escape committee selected George Grimson for that role.

In February 1944, Grimson walked out of the camp gates dressed as a German prison guard. Once outside the camp, he worked tirelessly to help other prisoners to get back to England. Several of the prisoners did make the entire trip successfully, thanks to Grimson, who traveled around the countryside establishing contacts and building an escape network. Then, without notice, Grimson disappeared. He failed to contact anyone associated with escape activities following the discovery of several British sympathizers working inside the prison camp who assisted the escape committee. Some of these men were trusted Poles, others were Germans who hated the Hitler regime, and all were tortured before their executions and undoubtedly revealed information on Grimson's activities. Most likely, the

Germans arrested Grimson around the end of April and executed him shortly thereafter.

Further Reading

Bishop, Patrick. *The Cooler King: The True Story of William Ash, the Greatest Escaper of World War II*. NY: Overlook Press, 2015.

Carroll, Tim. *The Great Escape from Stalag Luft III*. New York: Gallery Books, 2005.

H

Hambleton, Iceal "Gene"

War: Vietnam
Shot down: April 2, 1972
Rescued: April 14, 1972

Iceal "Gene" Hambleton, a native of Illinois born on November 16, 1918, was a career military man. He served in the last years of World War II, though he did not participate in combat in that war. He stayed in the Air Force Reserve and was brought back to active duty in the 1950s. Hambleton flew 43 sorties during the Korean War without incident. In the 1960s, he worked on air force projects, mostly in the ballistic missile area. In the late 1960s, he commanded a squadron at Davis-Monthan Air Force Base in Tucson.

It was no surprise that Gene Hambleton also flew in Vietnam. He was the navigator of an EB-66, electronically sweeping an objective area before a squad of B-52s would arrive and dropped their payload. At 53 years old, he was older than the average pilot to fly combat missions, but with the North Vietnamese Easter Offensive of 1972 that saw three divisions cross the demilitarized zone in force, everyone, regardless of age, was shuffled into the rotation. It was a routine mission from the start, and Hambleton wondered if he would return to the air base in time to play nine holes of golf, his favorite sport.

The surface-to-air missile that hit Hambleton's plane was a complete surprise, with the pilot having little time to evade the projectile before the explosion killed everyone aboard except Hambleton, who ejected from 30,000 feet. As he descended toward earth and dangled under his parachute, Hambleton spotted a forward air controller (FAC) that he contacted while descending. The pilot was Captain Jimmie D. Kempton, flying a light twin-engine turbo prop aircraft named the OV-10 Bronco, who told him to find cover once he hit the ground. To secure Hambleton's position, a number of A-1E aircraft spread mines all around him. After the A-1Es had dropped the mines, two UH-1B Cobra gunships and two UH-1H Huey passenger transport helicopters tried to rescue him. Enemy fire destroyed one Huey and damaged one of the Cobras, forcing them to pull back.

Hambleton dug a hole to hide in and covered himself with leaves and other vegetation. As luck would have it, Hambleton landed near one of the busiest routes the North Vietnamese used in their drive south. He had attracted a lot of attention from the Communist soldiers who swarmed around his position but kept their distance, as aircraft circling near his hideout continued to drop scatterable mines between the pilot and the Communist soldiers. A rescue helicopter tried to make it to him on the second day, but the antiaircraft fire was too intense. It broke off when it took a round in the engine, trailing smoke all the way back to base.

Throughout the ordeal, various aircraft and FACs took turns watching over Hambleton, including an F-4 Phantom with a crew consisting of Captains William Henderson and Mark Clark, son of the famous World War II general of the same name. The Vietnamese hit the aircraft with a surface-to-air missile, forcing the crew to bail out. Henderson was captured almost immediately, and Clark was now on the ground and evading capture, just like Hambleton.

For five days, Hambleton waited in his hole for the helicopters to try another rescue attempt. The air force had suddenly found itself with a number of other downed aviators to rescue in addition to Hambleton and Clark. When the air force launched another rescue mission, five men died when their big Jolly Green Giant helicopter was hit with antiaircraft fire.

After the destruction of the Jolly Green Giant helicopter and the death of its crew, air force officials decided against another helicopter extraction. Instead, they opted to exfiltrate Hambleton from his position and move him toward the river, which was two miles away. The problem with the plan was that between Hambleton and the river lay several villages and many enemy soldiers, all of whom Hambleton had to avoid. Air force officials and Hambleton's former golf partners came up with an ingenious solution, which was to use the layout of many golf courses, which Hambleton had memorized as a golf fanatic, to communicate by radio without the enemy understanding the plan. The FAC communicated the specific hole from the specific golf course, from which Hambleton could determine the exact direction and distance to travel, a technique that got Hambleton around enemy positions and occupied villages. The first nine holes were designed to get Hambleton from his hidden position to the river, and the last nine holes would get him down the river.

Hambleton left his position after eight days, moving through a corridor in the minefield surrounding him that the F-4s had made in one of their last passes. He was exhausted, hungry, and thirsty, but he knew he could not risk the lives of more aircrews to come get him, and his capture was imminent if he remained in his position much longer. Traveling only at night, Hambleton made good time and had little difficulty until a Vietnamese man with a knife surprised him and tried to kill him. The men fought until Hambleton got the advantage on the stranger and killed him. Though shaken, the incident motivated Hambleton to continue. By the time he reached the river, he could hear North Vietnamese soldiers who were searching for him, having discovered that he was no longer hiding.

Hambleton entered the water and found a railroad tie that supported his weight, which he then used to help him navigate down the river. He rode the railway tie for the last nine holes, until he arrived at a small cove in the river. After several hours, U.S. Navy SEAL Thomas Norris and a Vietnamese Commando Nguyen Van Kiet arrived in a sampan they had stolen, loaded Hambleton aboard, and began to make their way back to friendly lines. Three times they detected enemy soldiers waiting for them, and in the last instance, a tank with a 76-mm gun was trained on the river, waiting for them. The FAC called in orbiting fighters that bombed the enemy positions, allowing the small party to proceed. Twelve days after he was shot down, the rescue team met up with the helicopter crew from a Jolly Green Giant, which took everyone back to the air force base in Thailand, with the exception of Hambleton, who was taken to the hospital at Da Nang in South Vietnam. The air force medically retired him due to injuries he received during the ejection process.

Hambleton was awarded several medals for his service, including an Air Medal, the Distinguished Flying Cross, the Meritorious Service Medal, a Silver Star, and a Purple Heart. His story was told in the book *Bat 21,* which was also made into a movie in 1988. Hambleton died in 2004 in Tucson, Arizona.

Further Reading
Anderson, William C. *Bat 21.* New York: Bantam, 1980.
Whitcomb, Darrel D. *The Rescue of Bat 21.* Annapolis, Maryland: Naval Institute Press, 1998.

Hamill, Thomas—Civilian Contractor

Conflict: Iraq
Captured: April 9, 2004
Escaped: May 2, 2004

In May 2003, coalition forces had begun Operation Iraqi Freedom, the ground war to overthrow Saddam Hussein, and by April 2004, large-scale combat operations were mostly over. Small-scale combat operations were just beginning, however, when groups of militant fighters joined together to oppose the American occupation of Iraq. Logistics convoys presented easily identifiable targets to the remaining insurgents. More and more often, ambushes directed at convoys and improvised explosive devices (IEDs) detonated under vehicles became the tactics of choice. As combat operations continued, the situation required more and more logistics personnel. Civilian contractors began to come into Iraq, which freed up soldiers for combat operations. One of those civilian contractors, Thomas Hamill, arrived in country during the fall of 2003.

Thomas Hamill grew up in Noxubee County, Mississippi, and lived there with his wife and family. He worked many jobs to provide for his family and to keep the family farm operating. To supplement his income and to serve his country, Hamill took a job driving a fuel truck in Iraq in late 2003.

Hamill had started as a truck driver, then worked his way up to assistant convoy commander and then convoy commander. He was in charge of the convoy driving trucks to provide fuel to the American forces, going to Baghdad International Airport that day, Good Friday, April 9, 2004, which was the one-year anniversary of the capture of Baghdad. Hamill was in charge of the trucks, but 1st Lieutenant Matt Brown was in charge of the soldiers accompanying the fuel trucks. The convoy departed about 10:00 a.m., and things seemed to be going along normally until Hamill noticed that there was far less traffic than normal, and vehicles began to swerve off the highway as if avoiding some obstacle. Hamill knew something was about to happen, but he could not turn the big truck around because of the guardrail in the median.

The insurgents first attacked a truck in the rear of the convoy, but soon the entire convoy was under fire. All of the drivers accelerated, trying to outrun the attack, but they were unable to do so. One of the soldiers radioed that there was a truck on fire on the road ahead. The insurgents had planned the ambush well. Hamill slowed his truck to a stop, and he knew the situation was dire. Hamill did not know it then, but five drivers and two soldiers were already dead. The convoy veered off the road through a hole in the guardrail, and onto another road. Hamill had just grabbed his satellite-linked computer to send a warning to his headquarters when a bullet ripped through the cab of the truck and hit him in the arm. He tied a sock around the wound and gave his radio to the driver, hoping to call for help. The attack continued, and trucks began to explode, either because the fuel they were hauling ignited or because their truck took a direct hit from a rocket-propelled grenade. As Hamill's truck approached a burning truck, they realized that they could not pass it. The fuel leaking from their vehicle would ignite.

Their truck was not only leaking fuel, but the engine had been hit and was not functioning properly. They stopped and got out of the vehicle and were separated. Hamill got down on the ground and tried to crawl to safety, but his right arm was useless. Almost immediately, he was captured by one of the gunmen and two young boys. A crowd gathered around him, and one of the men hit Hamill with the butt of his weapon. A car pulled up and four men jumped out, shoved Hamill into the vehicle, and then sped off. Most of Hamill's time was spent moving from place to place, with a variety of guards. His captors attempted to treat his wound, which was serious and continued to bleed for days after his capture. The captors performed surgery on the arm and removed much dead tissue, in addition to routine medical care such as keeping the wound clean. They treated him well overall.

Hamill's first attempt to escape came after 15 days of captivity. His guards had left him alone for a day and a night, and in the meantime, a man and his two sons tried to break into the hut where his was held. In trying to break in, the man had almost broken open the door, but fled when he realized an American was held there. The next morning, Hamill heard the sounds of helicopters approaching and forced the door open. He ran outside to signal the helicopters, but they did not see him. When two helicopters flew by later, Hamill again tried to signal them by waving his shirt. One helicopter wobbled back and forth as a "hello" but did not stop. When his guards returned, they knew that the door had been opened. They moved Hamill several times, he was told, because patrols regularly inspected houses. Guards also shackled him every night, not because they feared he would escape, but in retaliation for the treatment of prisoners at Abu Ghraib.

After 23 days of captivity and numerous moves, the guards transported Hamill to a new location. The new hut where he was imprisoned had no door. His captors placed a piece of sheet metal over the opening, then pushed a board up against it. The first morning in his new location, Hamill fell asleep after breakfast, but he awoke to the sound of a diesel engine outside. He managed to push the metal door aside just enough to see outside, and saw a Humvee and several five-ton army trucks. American soldiers were walking beside the vehicles. Hamill pushed with all his might against the door, but it was firmly wedged in place. He managed to slide it to one side, creating a hole just wide enough for him to slip through. The soldiers were a half mile away, and Hamill started running in their direction. He took off his shirt and waved it at the men, both to show that he was not armed and to attract their attention. His rescuers were 40 members of the New York National Guard, who evacuated Hamill to a secure base, then the military transported him to Germany, where he was hospitalized for treatment from his incarceration and gunshot wound. Hamill received medical attention, called his family, and was eventually evacuated to Germany for further medical treatment. His wife met him in Germany, and they returned to the United States together. Throughout his ordeal, Hamill credited his faith in God as the reason he survived.

Further Reading

Dakss, Brian. "Thomas Hamill on His Iraq Escape." CBS, October 10, 2004. www.cbsnews.com/news/thomas-hamill-on-his-iraq-escape/.

Hamill, Thomas, Paul T. Brown, and Jay Langston. *Escape in Iraq: The Thomas Hamill Story*. Accokeek, MD: Stoeger Publishing, 2004.

Harrer, Heinrich

Conflict: World War II
Captured: September 3, 1939
Escaped: May 10, 1944

Heinrich Harrer, the son of a postal worker, was born on July 6, 1912, in Huttenberg, Austria. Harrer was an Austrian mountaineer, skier, geographer, and author. In 1933, at age 21, Harrer joined the Sturmabteilung (SA) and then the Schutzstaffel (SS) a month later. He was given the rank of sergeant, and the next month became a member of the Nazi Party. Harrer was involved in sports and studied geography at the University of Graz. In 1935, he was chosen to be on the alpine skiing team at the 1936 Winter Olympics. Harrer did not have the chance to participate with the team because of a conflict in their instructors' status. The Austrian alpine skiing team boycotted the event in protest. In 1937, Harrer competed in the World Student Championships, and he won the downhill event.

Harrer was an expert mountaineer, and he wanted to be on a Himalayan expedition. He convinced a friend, Fritz Kasparek, to climb the north face of the Eiger in the Bernese Alps in Switzerland. The peak is a little over 13,000 feet, and the ice field, known as the White Spider, had caused many to fall to their deaths. Bernese officials had prohibited people from climbing the vertical wall because it was so dangerous. Even so, when Harrer was finished with his course work in July 1938, he and Kasparek went to the Eiger and planned for their climb. In the midst of their ascent, they met up with another team, Ludwig Vörg and Anderl Heckmair, who were German. The four of them worked together for the rest of the ascent, and because Heckmair was the most experienced climber, he led the expedition. Avalanches, rock slides, and poor weather hampered their climb. Even though they were caught in an avalanche as they climbed the White Spider, they persisted and reached the peak on July 24, 1938. Their achievement brought them notoriety around the world. The climbers met with Adolf Hitler and were photographed with him.

A year later, in 1939, Harrer joined an expedition in India to climb the Diamir face of the Nanga Parbat. The team, including Friedel Sattler and Peter Aufschnaiter, wanted to explore if any additional avenues to reach the peak. After a relatively short time, they concluded that there were indeed additional paths to the summit. By

August, the men were in Karachi and looking for passage home. Due to delays, three of the men tried to head to Persia first, but they were intercepted by British soldiers and taken back to Karachi. War was declared in India on September 3, 1939, and the four men were taken to a detention camp near Bombay. They were then transferred to Dehradun, where they were held with over 1,000 other prisoners.

Harrer and the others contemplated escape routes, deciding that Tibet or Burma would be their best option. Harrer and the others tried to escape several times, and they were recaptured many times before they successfully escaped. Harrer and six others all escaped at once, with five of them dressed as British officers, and two as native workers. They walked out of camp to freedom. From there, two caught a train to Calcutta on to Burma. The other five walked toward the closest border. One, Sattler, gave up on May 10, and the remaining four escapees, included Harrer, entered Tibet on May 17, 1944. They had crossed the Tsang Chok-la Pass, which peaks at 19,350 feet. Harrer's mountaineering skills were definitely in demand on the trek through the pass. Harrer and Aufschnaiter traveled to the capital city in Tibet, Lhasa, arriving there on January 15, 1946. Records show that in 1948, Harrer worked for the Tibetan government as a translator and photographer. Harrer met the 14th Dalai Lama, and the two became friends. Harrer was the Dalai Lama's tutor in English and Western customs.

After spending seven years in Tibet, Harrer traveled back to Austria in 1952. He wrote about his experiences and published several books, including *Seven Years in Tibet* (1952) and *Lost Lhasa* (1954). *Seven Years in Tibet* was extremely popular, and a best seller in the United States in 1954. The book was translated into 53 languages and sold more than 3 million copies. This book was also made into a film, once in 1956 and again in 1997, in which Brad Pitt starred as Harrer. In 1952, after returning to Austria, Harrer was cleared of any involvement in war crimes. Harrer recanted his involvement in the Nazi Party as a youthful mistake.

In the later years of his life, Harrer continued to explore, traveling to Alaska, the Andes, Africa, and the Amazon, where he traveled with the former king of Belgium, Leopold III. He continued to climb, and wrote more than 20 books, including those mentioned previously. He was also an exceptional photographer. He completed more than 40 documentary films and founded a museum with his name in Huttenberg. Harrer died in January 2006 in Friesach, Austria. He was 93.

Further Reading
Harrer, Heinrich. *Seven Years in Tibet*. London: Hart-Davis and the Book Society, 1953.
Harrer, Heinrich. *The White Spider: The Story of the North Face of the Eiger*. New York: Harper Perennial, 2005.

Holzminden: The First Great Escape

Conflict: World War I
Captured: Various
Escape: July 23, 1918

The Holzminden camp was a prisoner of war camp for British officers. At any given time, about 500 officers were held there, as well as another 100 prisoners who were

Former British prisoners who escaped the Holzminden POW camp during World War I, from left: Second Lieutenant Kennard, Major Gray, and Lieutenant Blair. The three traveled 200 miles through the Netherlands and back to Britain. (Popperfoto/Getty Images)

designated as servants to those officers. Located in Lower Saxony, the camp opened in September 1917 and closed in December 1918. The site was originally a cavalry barracks that had been built in 1913, and consisted of two four-story barrack blocks. The basement included solitary confinement jails. Holzminden is well known because it was the location of the largest prisoner of war escape of World War I in July 1918. Twenty-nine British officers escaped through a tunnel, and 10 of them made their way back to Britain. Charles Rathbone, born February 17, 1886, in Trieste, Italy, was the senior British officer in the Holzminden camp and one of the most notable of the escapees.

Life for prisoners at Holzminden, even though they were officers, was difficult and harsh. Mistreatment was arbitrary, and prisoners were beaten or killed without provocation. Although officers generally had better conditions than other prisoners of war, Holzminden was considered the worst of the worst POW camps. Kommandant Karl Niemeyer was cruel and vindictive, and even his wife was known to frequent the camp and mete out punishments at will. Capital punishment was often given with no provocation.

As with most prisoner of war camps, food was a valuable commodity, and because of the economic blockage, Germans had little food available for their citizens and even less for prisoners of war. Prisoners were allowed to get packages from home, and the Red Cross also provided additional support where possible. Some of the prisoners ate what they received, and others used their rations to barter with guards. In some instances, the prisoners ate better than their captors. Even

---

World War I Prison Camp System

The Germans captured 4,480 members of the Allied Expeditionary Force (AEF) during World War I. A surprisingly small number of those soldiers, 44, tried to escape during their captivity. Several of the men tried to escape a number of times, tormenting their captors and risking their lives during each attempt. Of the 44 escapees, 6 made it back to Allied lines. A smaller percentage of British POWs tried to escape, given that 190,000 British soldiers were prisoners but only about 500 tried to escape. This is a surprisingly low number, given that the British were involved in the war for many more years than the Americans were. About the same number of French soldiers as British tried to escape from their prison camps. The Germans captured 500,000 French soldiers during the war, and only about 1,000 made an escape attempt. Apparently, once French were safely out of the war, they were content to wait it out for the duration of the conflict, figuring that they would be released when the war was over.

Most of the soldiers who tried to escape were officers, not because they were brave or foolish in proportionally higher numbers than the enlisted men, but the Germans treated the two groups differently. German society was highly sensitive to class structure, a fact reflected in their prison system. The officers and enlisted were immediately separated upon capture, and the enlisted were forced to perform manual labor each day, while the officers were not. Additionally, the officer camps were less crowded, and offered such comforts as canteens where food and beer or wine were available. They also had theaters and recreation facilities, including the ability to take leisurely walks around the outside of the prison camp. Because the enlisted soldiers had none of these amenities, they lacked the time and resources to plan an escape.

though life at Holzminden was harsh, the prisoners played sports, put on concerts and plays, and had access to reading material.

Given the conditions, it is not surprising that many of the officers attempted to escape from the camp. Whether they tried cutting through fences or masquerading as guards, or in the case of one man, reportedly masquerading as a woman, many were able to escape. Unfortunately, most were recaptured in a short time. Like many other prisoners of war, the officers at Holzminden began work on an escape tunnel in late 1917 that would be used in the largest mass escape in World War I. The tunnel took roughly nine months to complete, and on the evening of July 23, 1918, the officers queued a list of over 80 officers who would escape, and went to the hidden entrance under a staircase and began the trek underground out of the camp. However, the 30th man became stuck in the tunnel. The first 29 escaped, and 10 of them made their way to the Netherlands. Colonel Rathbone was relatively fluent in German, and he made it to the Dutch border in five days by traveling by train and bluffing his way through checkpoints.

The city of Holzminden was also home to the Holzminden internment camp, a pair of large camps that housed men in one and women and children in the other. At one time, as many as 10,000 Belgian, French, Polish, and Russian nationals were held in these internment camps. This camp was separate from the prisoner of war camp. The escape from the prisoner of war camp at Holzminden was memorialized in film, both as a fictional story of the escape in *Who Goes Next?* (1938), and prior to that, as *The First Great Escape,* which was produced by National Geographic (2014).

Further Reading

Bascomb, Neal. *The Grand Escape: The Greatest Prison Breakout of the 20th Century.* September 25, 2018.

Cook, Jacqueline. *The Real Great Escape: The Story of the First World War's Most Daring Mass Breakout.* Random House Australia, 2013.

Durnford, H. G. *The Tunnellers of Holzminden.* London: Cambridge University Press, 1920.

Hoover, Robert

Conflict: World War II
Captured: February 9, 1944
Escaped: April 1945

Robert Hoover, born January 22, 1922, began bagging groceries in the 1930s to pay for flying lessons at the local airport. He turned his hobby into a passion and a career, flying for most of his life. When he joined the military, he was destined to fly bombers because of his height, but switched places with another pilot who did not share Hoover's dream of flying fighters. He spent the first part of the war assembling and testing new airplanes in the North African Campaign, all the while begging for a transfer that would allow him to fly combat missions. Shortly after he got his wish, he was shot down and taken prisoner. He attempted to escape numerous times, until he managed to steal a German plane and fly to friendly lines.

Hoover had dreamed of flying combat aircraft all his life, but when he got to Africa, the Army Air Corps put him to work testing aircraft that was shipped to the continent in crates. Someone had to put them together and see if they flew correctly. Hoover had an almost unnatural ability to fly anything with very little introduction to a new aircraft. He could climb into the cockpit, start up the plane, and take off. His pilot skills were so good that his supervisor would not let him transfer out of the unit. However, he was determined not to spend the war testing aircraft, and he longed to get into the fight. When he met up with a friend who was commanding a fighter squadron, Hoover asked to join his outfit. Although it took several months to work out the transfer, he continued in his unit, completing tasks such as transferring a B-25 to another base. After landing, Hoover was standing near the operations tent when a two-star general struck up a conversation with him. Not one to let an opportunity pass him by, Hoover explained that he was an outstanding pilot who could fly any aircraft and that he longed for combat duty. He asked the senior officer to intervene in his transfer. It wasn't long before the transfer order arrived for Hoover to join a combat unit, but still the officer would not let him go, arguing that his skills were too important to the war effort to simply have him killed flying combat. Eventually, Hoover's superior allowed him to join the 52nd Fighter Group. It was September 1941.

Days after arriving at his unit, the commanding officer asked Hoover to take a Spitfire, the British workhorse plane, and show the other pilots what it could do. His performance was flawless. His demonstration gave fellow pilots great confidence in the aircraft. Hoover quickly moved up in the squadron to positions of increased responsibility. He was a flight leader by February 9, 1944, flying missions off the French and Italian coasts, looking for German transport vessels. On that particular day, his flight of four Spitfires carried belly tanks to increase the range of their aircraft, which allowed the pilots to stay aloft for longer periods of time. In the event the flight encountered enemy aircraft, the pilot could jettison the extra belly tanks. The planes were too heavy to duel German fighters with the tank attached. When four German FW-190 aircraft appeared, Hoover pulled the D-ring in the cockpit to release the tank, but the ring came off in his hand. The tank stayed connected to the undercarriage of Hoover's Spitfire. Hoover managed to bring down one of the enemy aircraft before his engine took a number of direct hits and exploded. He managed to turn the aircraft upside down, open the canopy and release the shoulder straps, and slide out of the airplane. His parachute worked correctly, and he landed in the water and waited for rescue. Unfortunately, a German ship arrived first and pulled him out of the Mediterranean Sea. He was now a prisoner of war.

Hoover followed the code of prisoners, and he attempted to escape from his German captors a number of times. His first jail cell had metal bars covering the window, and he removed several of them and eased through the opening. He dropped down from the window into the middle of a number of guards, several of whom had German shepherd dogs that attacked him. After his first escape attempt, he was transferred to another prison by train. In his second escape attempt, he asked to use the latrine aboard the railcar, got inside, closed the door, and then kicked out the small window. He squeezed through the opening and fell to the ground where the snow was several feet high. The guards immediately detected his absence and stopped the train. They recaptured Hoover after only a few minutes. Undeterred, he tried again, again asking to use the latrine, but when he entered the room, he did not close the door completely. When the guard was distracted, he crawled out of the bathroom and out an exit door. Once outside, he limped to the gates of the compound. At first, no one seemed to notice him, but when Hoover did not reply to the German guard, he was captured again. After this attempt, he was placed on a train bound for another prison camp, the infamous Stalag Luft I prison camp on the Baltic Sea.

One of the first prison camps in Hitler's Germany, Stalag Luft I was actually a series of camps placed together, each of which was surrounded by 10-foot-high barbed wire. Barbed-wire walls and guard towers with mounted searchlights surrounded the entirety of the camp. The guards boasted that no prisoner had ever escaped from the camp, but this presented more of a challenge to Hoover than a deterrent. He took advantage of the only opportunity to get outside the wire without getting shot when he volunteered for the coal detail. When the group of prisoners loaded a wagon with coal for use in their barracks stoves, Hoover had the other prisoners cover him with coal in the storage shed, and darkness helped to hide the fact that the detail was missing one prisoner on the way back into camp. When he thought the area was clear, he moved with stealth out of the shed, then ran as fast as he could down the dark road, and ran right into a guard. Hoover's latest escape attempt cost him two weeks in solitary confinement.

In April 1945, the situation in Germany worsened as the Soviets closed in on Berlin and other major cities. Nobody wanted to face the Soviet army, including Germans, because they were considered unpredictable. Additionally, Allied prisoners were concerned that the German population of fanatical SS troops might slaughter the prisoners as the end of the war drew to a close. Hoover and two accomplices were desperate to get out of camp and planned their escape. The guards were preoccupied as the Soviet army moved ever closer, and a fight staged by the prisoners provided the distraction necessary to let the three of them simply sneak past the guards and out of the prison camp. They walked along roads, stole bicycles and rode for a while, always west and away from the Soviet troops, now ubiquitous throughout the German countryside. They observed numerous executions and other atrocities, more determined than ever to escape the vicinity. Along the way, one of the German women they met handed Hoover a small pistol, to be used in self-defense against the Russians. She was terrified to be caught with it.

Hoover and escapee Jerry Ennis came upon a Luftwaffe fighter base, overflowing with aircraft but with relatively few ground crew in the area. One of Hoover's close friends in the prison camp had flown captured German fighters in England before he too was shot down. Hoover knew the Focke-Wulf 190 very well, and with his experience flying a wide variety of aircraft, he knew he could fly it if he could get it off the ground. They found a plane with full fuel tanks, then pointing the gun at a mechanic, asked for assistance in getting the plane's engine started. Though Jerry Ennis decided to take his chances on the ground, Hoover took off in the plane, flying along the coastline until he was sure he was in Allied-occupied Holland, then landed the plane in a plowed field. A group of Dutch civilians with rakes and pitchforks approached, believing that he was a German pilot and meaning to do him harm. Hoover convinced them that he was an American, and the mob of angry demonstrators softened, glad to help him find the Allied lines. Robert Hoover was a free man after 16 months of incarceration.

Hoover left military service in 1948, but he never left flying. He had a successful career flying for a number of aircraft companies after the war, testing their latest fighter designs. Once the planes had passed qualifications, he taught military pilots how to fly the new aircraft. Chuck Yeager selected Hoover to fly in the chase plane when he broke the sound barrier in 1947, and Hoover flew an F-16 as the chase plane on the 50th anniversary of the flight. Jimmy Doolittle, a pioneer in the field of aviation and a military leader, called Hoover "the greatest stick and rudder man who ever lived." Hoover also spent decades as one of the premier acrobatic pilots in the United States. Hoover was inducted into the National Aviation Hall of Fame in 1988. He retired from the air show circuit in 1999, and his last piloted flight was in 2003. A documentary about Hoover's life, *Flying the Feathered Edge: The Bob Hoover Project,* was produced in 2014. Hoover passed away October 25, 2016, at the age of 94.

Further Reading

Collins, Bob. "Bob Hoover, One of History's Greatest Pilots, Dead at 94." Minnesota Public Radio News, October 25, 2016. blogs.mprnews.org/newscut/2016/10/bob-hoover-one-of-nations-greatest-pilots-dead-at-94.

Hoover, Robert. *Forever Flying: Fifty Years of High-Flying Adventures, from Barnstorming in Prop Planes to Dogfighting Germans to Testing Supersonic Jets*. New York: Pocket Books, 1997.

1

Iran Hostage Rescue Attempt: Operation Eagle Claw

Conflict: Iran Conflict
Captured: November 4, 1979
Rescue attempt: April 24–25, 1980

On November 4, 1979, militant students took over the American embassy in Tehran, Iran. This hostage situation pushed the United States into an international crisis that lasted 444 days, until the radical government in Iran chose to release the last of the Americans held hostage. Earlier in 1979, rebels in Iran overthrew Shah Mohammad Reza Pahlavi. He had been allowed access to medical care in the United States to treat cancer, and those in power in Iran were demanding that he be returned to stand trial for crimes committed during his reign. The U.S. government did not comply with the Iranian demands to return the shah, and when the militants took hostages in the American embassy, the U.S. government saw this as a violation of international diplomatic immunity.

Almost immediately after the militants stormed the embassy, the orders came from the highest levels of American government to begin planning the rescue of the 52 American hostages. An operation of this size and scale had only been attempted a few times in America's history, and those attempts did not turn out well (Son Tay prison raid and Mayaguez rescue attempts, for example). Even so, the military moved ahead with planning a rescue of the hostages while the diplomatic crisis played out on the international stage.

One of the factors that hampered the rescue attempt from the beginning was the fact that no command and control headquarters existed to manage multiservice antiterrorist operations, and an ad hoc organization was put together for this particular crisis. Components of the task force were led by people who had never worked together, including an army general in command of the entire organization, an air force commander in charge of fixed-wing assets, a marine commander focused on helicopter resources using navy and marine pilots and crew, and an army commander who controlled the ground forces. To make matters worse, the Iranians held the hostages somewhere in the middle of an enormous metropolitan city that was completely controlled by hostile forces and a long distance from any Allied operational bases.

The commander determined that the only feasible plan to take control of the hostages required a unit of Delta Force operators to force their way into the buildings of the American embassy, where the militants presumably still held the hostages. The only way to get the Delta Force into the area was by helicopter, which required the establishment of an operating base in the Iranian desert. Fuel was the limiting factor for the helicopters, and a refueling site was established. Operational limitations further dictated that the rescue and refueling operations could not take place on the same night due to the limited hours of darkness. The leadership had determined that all facets of the operation must take place at night to reduce the possibility of detection and operational failure.

The final plan involved many components. Three MC-130 aircraft would carry in the Delta Force operators, combat controllers, and a contingent of Rangers for security operations. They would leave the island of Masirah, off the coast of Oman, for the initial rendezvous site in the Iranian desert, which had the code name Desert One. Three EC-130s carrying fuel bladders would also depart for Desert One from this island location. Once the six aircraft reached their destination, they would assemble a refueling point for the helicopters, with Rangers providing local security. At this point, two of the MC-130s would depart. The eight RH-53D helicopters would fly in from the USS *Nimitz,* which was operating off the coast of Iran, and arrive at the refueling point. Once their tanks were full, the helicopters would load the Delta operators and fly to a hide site where they would wait to begin the rescue mission the following night. The remaining C-130s, with the Rangers, would return to Masirah.

On night two, four MC-130s to carry the Delta operators and rescued hostages, along with four AC-130 gunships to provide fire support during the rescue operation, would depart for Manzariyeh Airfield, an abandoned site that was perfect for rescue purposes. Operatives had purchased trucks to get the Delta operators into the city. Once the hostages were safely in the possession of the rescue force,

Wreckage of an American helicopter after a collision with a refueling plane during the aborted attempt to rescue hostages from Iran in 1980. (Bettmann/Getty Images)

helicopters would land on the embassy grounds or at a nearby soccer field to extract everyone. The helicopters would then fly to Manzariyeh Airfield, where two C-141 cargo aircraft would fly everyone out of the old airfield.

Because of operational security concerns, the separate forces had not come together to practice the entire rescue plan. Some of the portions were rehearsed, but not all. Secondly, the helicopter pilots had not practiced flying using night vision devices prior to the mission, though they seemed to do well in training. This was one of the smaller known issues, and several additional factors would have become apparent had the entire plan been rehearsed. One of these factors was major, as in the fact that the army helicopters could not communicate with the different radios used on the air force aircraft. These communication issues would prove to be problematic.

At 6:00 p.m. on April 24, the first MC-130 took off from Masirah, headed for the Desert One base. Within an hour, the last of the C-130 aircraft had departed the island base. At 8:30 p.m., and then again at 9:00 p.m., the lead C-130 aircraft flew through a tremendous sandstorm. The pilot tried to contact the helicopters that had taken off from the USS *Nimitz* at about the same time as the fixed-wing aircraft, but communications systems were not functional. At 9:00 p.m., a blade warning light flashed on the instrument panel of one of the helicopters, leading the crew to abandon it. They were picked up by another helicopter. Two helicopters were separated from the other seven by the sandstorms, and one developed instrument problems and turned back to the USS *Nimitz*. By the time all of the helicopters showed up to the refueling point at Desert One, the operation was down to six aircraft, the bare minimum to complete the mission. As the helicopters refueled, one of them experienced a hydraulic pump malfunction. The HH-53 had two pumps in the hydraulic system, so it was able to fly, but the senior aviator determined that it was not safe to operate. The mission was now down to five aircraft, below the minimum number required to perform the mission. The plan was aborted.

The situation turned from bad to worse when one of the helicopters lifted off. Its blades sliced into one of the C-130 aircraft carrying aviation fuel, the two aircraft burst into flames, and ammunition from the helicopter began to explode. Airmen tried to avoid the fireball, but three helicopters received extensive damage and were abandoned. Eight U.S. servicemen died inside the damaged aircraft. Two helicopters remained undamaged: the one with the bad hydraulic pump and the last helicopter that was not refueled. The crews had to abandon all helicopters at the Desert One site. The crews then boarded the three remaining C-130 aircraft for the flight back to friendly lines.

In the aftermath, government officials and the American people wanted to understand why the operation had failed. A commission headed by retired Navy Admiral James L. Holloway determined that the operation failed because of overly strict operational security that precluded a full-scale rehearsal. A more thorough rehearsal might have revealed the difficulty of maneuvering helicopters and fixed-wing aircraft near each other, as well as the communication difficulties between the pilots of different military branches. The lack of communications equipment that would allow the pilots to talk to members of the chain of command were not available, so each pilot pulled his aircraft from the mission without input from those in charge of the operation. It would take the U.S. military years to overcome the calamity that was the failed rescue attempt.

In the years that followed the disastrous Operation Eagle Claw, special operations forces and the U.S. military as a whole improved operations and coordination in the areas of command and control, communication, aircraft employment, training, and funding. Finally, the creation of the Joint Special Operations Command gave the different services the ability to train and communicate between groups, negating some of the fatal flaws seen at Desert One.

Although this mission failed and the hostages were not rescued during the attempt, the hostages were eventually all released, with the majority being released in January 1981. Many books have been written about this attempt, and the story has also been told in film, including the portion about those who evaded being taken hostage. All of the U.S. State Department and CIA employees taken hostage were eventually awarded the State Department Award for Valor, a now obsolete award, which was given for actions while under threat of physical attack or harassment, or an individual act of valor or exceptional performance.

Further Reading
Bowden, Mark. *Guests of the Ayatollah: The Iran Hostage Crisis: The First Battle in America's War with Militant Islam.* New York: Grove Press, 2007.
Kiper, Richard L. "Delta Force at Desert One." In *Great Raids in History: From Drake to Desert One,* edited by Samuel A. Southworth. New York: Sarpedon Publishers, 1997.

Izac (Isaacs), Edouard

Conflict: World War I
Captured: May 1918
Escaped: August 1918

Edouard Isaacs was born in Cresco, Iowa, on December 18, 1891, and served in the U.S. Navy during World War I. His father had emigrated from Alsace-Lorraine, and his mother's family was heavily German. He changed his name to Izac after visiting France and learning that his surname was originally spelled IZAK. Izac attended the United States Naval Academy and graduated from there in 1915. He later served in the United States House of Representatives (California) and received a Medal of Honor.

Izac's original assignment was on the USS *Florida,* and he transferred to the troop transport the USS *President Lincoln* in July 1917. The *President Lincoln*'s first voyage was in October 1917. In May 1918, the *President Lincoln* was attacked by a German submarine, the U-90, and the ship sank. Izac was taken prisoner, held at first on the submarine that had attacked his ship. Izac was well treated on the submarine and even ate with the officers, describing how they played cards together in the evenings. The U-90 cook was exceptional, and captain informed Izac that he would not fare as well once he was in a true prisoner of war camp. Rather than head past England, the submarine's captain headed north, through the Arctic

Circle, then through Norway, Denmark, and Sweden, on the way back to Germany. Izac contemplated escaping, as he had a life preserver, but the opportunity did not present itself.

After they arrived in port, Izac was taken on shore and placed in a barred room. He was given basic toiletries and allowed to have a bath the following day. Soon he was on board a destroyer and headed for a prisoner of war camp in Wilhelmshaven, and the treatment and rations changed dramatically for the worse. Wilhelmshaven was a heavily fortified city, and escape initially seemed impossible. Izac was then taken to the prisoner of war camp at Karlsruhe. About 200 officers were held at this camp.

Izac focused on gathering information about the enemy as he was transported to Germany and at the various locations. Once at Karlsruhe, he began to review his options for escape, knowing he was about 100 miles from the Swiss border. He determined that once free, he could make the trip in about 15 days. Before that could occur, he was moved by train to another camp. Izac watched for an opportunity to escape, and eventually, pushed himself through a window and fell outside the train. The guards immediately saw him go out, and they stopped the train. Izac was badly injured in the fall, and he was recaptured. He was beaten for trying to escape and spent several days in a cell in Villingen.

About three months after he had been taken captive, Izac and another American did manage to escape from Villingen. After his first attempt that ended so poorly, Izac was determined to make it out on his second attempt. The Russian officers in the camp had tried to tunnel out so often that Izac planned to use an unconventional route of escape. The guards were on notice and raids were conducted often of the barracks. Izac and three other American aviatorsescaped from the barracks over a man-made bridge and past the fence. Though the guards saw them and fired at them, none of the men were hit. They had established a rendezvous point, and once Izac got there, he waited for the other men to show up. Willis met him at the meeting place, and they made their way to Switzerland, about a week after they escaped from a German prison camp in the middle of the night. Izac and Willis traveled through the mountains, ate what they could find along the way, and swam the Rhine River not far from the German sentries. Though he and Willis were separated in the river, they both made it safely to Switzerland.

Although Izac shared his information with commanders when he made it to London, the war was virtually over, and the information wasn't seen as useful at the time. Izac returned to the United States in November 1918, and he was awarded the Medal of Honor in 1920. His war injuries were significant enough that he retired in 1921, and he moved to San Diego, California, where he worked as a newspaper writer until 1928. Izac became interested in politics and ran for election in 1934, 1940, and 1944. He was elected as a Democrat and served in Congress from 1937 to 1947, when he lost a reelection effort. Because of his experiences in World War I, in 1945, Izac traveled with other senators and congressmen to review the sites of Buchenwald, Dachau, and other recently liberated concentration camps. Izac wrote about the experience, sharing his experiences with other senators, in a report entitled, *Atrocities and Other Conditions in Concentration Camps in Germany.* This work was published in May 1945.

Izac eventually relocated to Virginia, where he died in 1990. He is buried at Arlington National Cemetery, and he was the last living Medal of Honor recipient from World War I at the time of his death. His autobiography, *Prisoner of the U-90* (1919), tells the story of his capture and escape.

Further Reading
Isaacs (Izac), Edouard V. *Prisoner of the U-90.* New York: Houghton Mifflin, 1919.
Izac, Edouard Victor Michel. *The Holy Land—Then and Now.* Springfield, Massachusetts: Vantage Press, 1965.

J

Jensen, Agnes

Conflict: World War II
Crashed: November 8, 1943
Rescued: March 21, 1944

Agnes Jensen was born on December 3, 1914, in Stanwood, Michigan, and was part of a medical unit as a flight nurse in World War II. On November 8, 1943, a C-53 Skytrooper aircraft carrying 30 American military personnel, including 13 nurses, 12 medical technical sergeants, a corporal catching a ride back to his unit, and 4 members of the flight crew, left on a mission from Sicily to Bari, Italy. The medical personnel were headed to pick up wounded soldiers from field hospitals close to the fighting to the north, and then bring them back to hospitals where further treatment and recovery could begin. Unfortunately, the weather was only minimally acceptable for aircraft flight. Bad weather the previous two days had caused missions to be scrubbed. The crew was anxious to get into the air, as they knew the wounded soldiers lying in poorly equipped hospitals desperately needed more care than what could be found inside the combat zone. The flight crew finally decided it was acceptable to take off, believing the next storm was far enough away that they could complete their mission safely. Only a short time into the flight, however, the weather turned much worse and the plane veered significantly off course, over German-held territory. Antiaircraft fire from the Germans, the loss of radio communication, and a lack of fuel forced the flight crew to crash-land in a muddy field of corn stubble in what they discovered was Albania, a German-occupied nation.

The 30 Americans all survived the crash, and they quickly organized to escape the region. A group of Albanian partisans met the plane and helped get the survivors on their way because German soldiers were nearby and moving toward the crash site. Jensen and other members of the crew gathered as many supplies as they could carry and went with the Albanian villages to safety. After several hours of walking, they were taken to a small house deep in the woods and sheltered there from the elements. After resting overnight, the Albanians and Americans discussed escape plans. Eventually, they decided that the Albanians would help the Americans get to the town of Berat, where they were certain they could find additional Allies to help get the Americans out of the country.

After walking for several days, the Americans and their Albanian guides made it to Berat, where they were welcomed as liberators. They broke into smaller groups of twos and threes, and each of the groups went with a host family who provided food and shelter. The Albanians were proud of their city, and they took time to share important sites and talk about ways to fight back against the German occupation.

The crash survivors could do little to immediately help the villagers, but they promised to share their plight with the American chain of command once they were back at American bases.

The Americans enjoyed several days of rest and recovery in Berat, but then they were awakened one morning by the distinct sounds of bombing. The Germans continued to bomb the town, and the Albanians provided a truck to get several of the Americans outside of the area. They stopped a few miles out of town to regroup, and only 17 of the 30 crash survivors had made it to the vehicle and gotten out of town. Though these 17 were concerned about those left in town, they had to continue on. They knew that if they went back to town, the Germans would be searching the area for them. The 17 Americans and the Albanians with them abandoned the truck and the road, moving into the woods. After several hours of walking, they came to a small village. This time, the 17 Americans stayed together and did not split up into small groups.

The Americans left the village the following morning, and some of the Albanians remained with the group as guides. A few hours into their journey, they encountered a band of Italian soldiers who joined them. The Italian soldiers in Albania had joined Allied forces after Italy left the Axis side. At this point, the group of Americans and Albanians, now joined with the Italian soldiers, had turned into a several-hundred person multinational force. Later that day, the Albanians and Italians fought against a German unit they encountered. The nurses in the medical unit treated those who were injured in the skirmish, doing their best to treat their wounds sufficiently enough that the group could keep moving toward the border.

By Wednesday night, just three days after the Sunday morning attack on the town of Berat, the group of 17 Americans continued to move, looking for food and supplies. Many of the people who lived in the houses they had stopped at while traveling had been too poor to feed them. They finally reached a village where enough people had resources to share a meal with them. The locals also shared good news: a group of American soldiers had been in the village only two days before the escapees, and the locals told them which direction the American soldiers were headed. The crash survivors were reenergized, and they left at dawn the following morning to try to catch up. At the next village, the group of 17 learned that the guide for the other group of 10, Steffa, was actually loyal to the Germans, and they feared that the smaller group would be turned over to the enemy. Additionally, three nurses were still unaccounted for after the attack in Berat.

Two days later, the larger group of 17 caught up to the smaller group of 10. They had taken refuge in an old hospital. Although the suspected German loyalist, Steffa, acted strangely, the group did not accuse him yet, waiting to see what he would do. Steffa offered to continue to help them get to the British units in the region, and he claimed he could help the Americans get out of the region by plane with the British. Although the group doubted Steffa's claims, they sent out a runner to find the British troops. For the next few days, they moved cautiously, staying ahead of the Germans in the area. The Americans even doubted Germans were in the area, though they did not have enough facts to dispel what Steffa told them.

As a group, they moved in the general location of where they though the British were camped, but the mountains between where they were and where they needed to be were a problem. As they traveled up the side of the mountain, the weather worsened, with rain turning to snow the higher they went. Finally, after half a day, they descended and the conditions did improve. In a small village, they were met with news from the runner, who had indeed found the British location. The runner had specific directions for them, with instructions to travel to the village of Lovdar, where they would meet a British officer, Smith, at that location. In verifying travel routes with the locals, they knew they had another week of travel, over the mountain, to get where they could rendezvous with the British troops.

The Americans made their way into the village of Lovdar on December 1, 1943, and the British officer who had contacted them, Captain Victor Smith, was there to greet them. Smith had orders to keep the Americans safe, get them to the Albanian coasts, and from there, the group would be evacuated by sea. The group rested for a few days, and then they followed the British officer into the mountains to where his headquarters were located. The snow and cold caused difficulty for the Americans. Once at the headquarters, they rested again, and then on December 8, they left for the Albanian coast. British Lieutenant Gavin Duffy was their guide for this part of the journey.

This portion of the escape journey was not much easier, and at one point, the group passed a large, flat area that the Italians had previously used as an airfield. The American pilots in the group suggested that U.S. forces could send in a transport there and get them out. The British were not sure it would work, but they did radio out the message, seeing if it was possible. The American pilots agreed to try, and returned a message that they would send a plane on December 29 at 1:00 p.m. German forces were in the area, but the Americans would try to extricate the group by air if they could, knowing it would be difficult at best. The crash survivors and British escort assembled near the field, but when the U.S. aircraft came into the area, the Germans were too close, and Lieutenant Duffy could not give the signal to land. Though the two C-47 transport planes had 18 fighter planes along for security, they made two passes through the area, looking for a signal, before being forced to turn around and head back to Italy. The American survivors on the ground were deflated but not defeated, and they refocused on the next leg of their journey, getting to the coast.

Nothing on this trip had been easy to date, and the journey to the coast was not much better. The weather was cold and the snow made the trek difficult for the tired and hungry members of the party. Though they stopped at villages as they moved toward the coast, most of the locals had very little to eat and not enough to share. Additionally, the fighting between the Albanians and Germans also slowed them down, sometimes causing them to stay put for several days at a time. On January 6, 1944, the group finally met with American Captain Lloyd G. Smith, an intelligence officer, whose mission was to get the group out of the country. At this point, the guide, Steffa, finally departed from the group. Though the Americans had been suspicious about his loyalties, he had not put them in harm and had gotten them to relative safety before leaving them. Jensen gave her flight wings to Steffa to pass along to his son, who had admired them and thought Jensen was a pilot.

The group had two days of travel left, and on January 8, 1944, they got to the coastline, where they met up with a group of British officers. That night, the American survivors were put on a boat and after noon the next day, docked in Bari, Italy, two months and 800 miles away from where the group had started out. The Americans were sent to the local base hospital, where they received food and medical attention. They also were debriefed on what they had learned during their journey.

After getting the 27 American survivors settled in Italy, Captain Lloyd Smith returned to Albania to try to find the last three nurses. They had stayed in Berat after the initial attack, and when the Germans took over the town, they stayed with a family for several months, learning to speak Albanian to blend in. Captain Smith helped coordinate an escape for them. He had the nurses dress in Albanian attire, and with papers that included their pictures, the women were able to ride by car most of the way to the coast, though they did have to walk the last distance. They met Captain Smith at the coast on March 19, 1944. The following day, an Albanian yacht took the last three nurses to Bari, Italy, as well. By March 21, 1944, the last of the 30 Americans were returned to Allied control.

Agnes Jensen's diary of their travels was taken from her upon the group's return to Italy, but later on, she requested the diary back from the U.S. War Department and received it after the war. Though she did write about her experience in *Albanian Escape: The True Story of the U.S. Army Nurses behind Enemy Lines* in 1999, she was concerned that the Albanians who had helped her and the others would be retaliated against for helping the American survivors. Jensen died on May 3, 2010, and is buried in Arlington National Cemetery in Virginia.

Further Reading

Mangerich, Agnes Jensen. *Albanian Escape: The True Story of the U.S. Army Nurses behind Enemy Lines.* Lexington: University of Kentucky Press, 1999.

Taylor, Judith. "Odyssey to Freedom: Remembering a Daring Escape from Behind Enemy Lines." Air Force Medical Service, November 8, 2013. Air Force Medicine. www.airforcemedicine.af.mil/News/Article/582964/odyssey-to-freedom-remembering-a-daring-escape-from-behind-enemy-lines.

Joseph, Dilip

Conflict: Terrorism
Captured: December 5, 2012
Rescued: December 9, 2012

Dr. Dilip Joseph knew his nonprofit work training health care workers in Afghanistan carried risks, but he had been to the war-torn country nine times in four and a half years, and he had managed to avoid issues with the Taliban, even though he traveled to clinics and other sites within noted war zones, training medical workers to deal with casualties. On Joseph's 10th trip in country, however, his luck changed, and on December 5, 2012, he found himself facing down the Taliban.

Joseph gave several interviews after his fateful 10th trip into Afghanistan, and the details of his capture emerged from his retelling. He was en route from Kabul to a very rural area. On this trip, he was traveling with Afghan colleagues who spoke Pashto, the local language, which Joseph did not speak. When they had completed their work that day, they had lunch at a local police chief's house, where talk turned to the changing security concerns in the area. Looking back, Joseph feels he should have recognized the warning signs, but he did not at the time. When he and his two interpreters headed back to Kabul, they were stopped on a mountain road by a gunman. As their car stopped, other gunmen emerged from the area. Because Joseph is Indian, he did not look much different from the other men he was with, but when the gunmen started going through his backpack, they found his American passport. At that point, Joseph knew his situation was precarious. An American hostage was valuable.

From the road, the gunmen took Joseph and his colleagues up into the mountains. They hiked for over nine hours, and though Joseph tried to converse with the men, to tell them he was there to help the people in the region on a humanitarian mission, they did not engage with him. They rested briefly, then continued hiking into the night. The kidnappers made their demands from a remote shack, calling in to authorities that they had an American hostage and they wanted $300,000 for him. They threatened to kill Joseph and his Afghani friends if the money wasn't immediately brought in. Joseph was given the opportunity to call the office in Kabul and tell them about the kidnapping and ransom request. By the second day, they no longer had cell service.

During this lapse in communication, the captors asked Joseph more about his life, including his work and family. One of the captors, a young 19-year-old man, shared some of his life experiences with Joseph as well. Joseph was 39 years old at the time, and he found out that the young man's father had been imprisoned for the last 14 years. This boy had only known his father for a short time, and even then, his father had been fighting with the insurgency. Joseph began to understand how this young man could end up with an extremist group, due to his upbringing and circumstances.

For four days, the gunmen negotiated for the release of the hostages, but they were not making progress and split up the group, removing Joseph from his translators. Joseph was afraid that this change would not end well for any of them, concerned that they would be killed. During the fourth night, Joseph heard noises outside his small room. He could also hear gunfire. A man broke down his door, but he was hit by gunfire. Another man called out to him, and Joseph recognized them as Americans. Joseph called back, and then they swarmed the shack, taking out the members of the Taliban, including the young man who had befriended Joseph.

The men were members of the Navy SEALs, and specifically, of SEAL Team Six. The rescue took just a few moments, and they waited for the helicopters to arrive for the extraction. The first man who had been shot, 28-year-old Petty Officer First Class Nicolas Checque, had died. The helicopters took them to a nearby military base. Joseph was relieved to find out that his Afghan friends had also been rescued.

Further Reading
Joseph, Dilip, and Jim Lund. *Kidnapped by the Taliban*. Nashville, Tennessee: Thomas Nelson, 2014.
"Taken by the Taliban: A Doctor's Story of Captivity, Rescue." *All Things Considered*. NPR, October 12, 2013. www.npr.org/2013/10/12/232759605/taken-by-the-taliban-a-doctors-story-of-captivity-rescue.

Kilpatrick, Ralph

Conflict: Korean War
Captured: July 1950
Escaped: October 1950

Sergeant Ralph Kilpatrick, originally from Phoebus, Virginia, had strong survival instincts, even when the odds were stacked against him. Kilpatrick disappeared from his unit, C Company of the 19th Regiment, 24th Infantry Division, in July 1950. The Korean War was in the very early days of the conflict, and the lines were fluid as battles were fought to secure the border between north and south. Kilpatrick's unit was surrounded in the Battle of the Kum River near Taejon, about halfway between Seoul and Pusan. Although many of his fellow soldiers tried to flee when their unit was overtaken, Kilpatrick had hurt his ankle and could not run. He managed to survive by playing dead when a North Korean soldier inspected his body, and then he eluded capture from behind the enemy lines for 77 days, while he attempted to reconnect with his unit.

In the early days of the Korean War, the unexpected invasion of the North Koreans south of the agreed-upon border made the U.S. troops scramble to take up defensive positions and stop the offensive attacks from the north. During an intense battle in mid-July, the fighting went on for a number of days as the North Korean troops came closer to their position, effectively surrounding the American unit. Finally, the lieutenant in charge told his men to make a run through enemy lines and try to link up with the rest of the 24th Division. Kilpatrick, with his badly sprained ankle, knew he would not make it to the 24th Division, and he and another soldier decided to stay and fight as long as they could, defending their position as long as possible. Eventually, though, enemy soldiers rushed them, and Kilpatrick lay in the trench, motionless, hoping they would think he was dead. The other soldier tried to flee, but the North Koreans shot him and left him for dead. Even when a North Korean soldier jumped down into the ditch, lifted Kilpatrick's head by the hair, and stared into his eyes, Kilpatrick did not blink or flinch. He knew his safety depended on the enemy soldiers believing he was dead. His performance was convincing, and the North Koreans moved on. Kilpatrick tried to help his friend who had been shot, staying with him and providing as much first aid as he could, but the other soldier died the next day.

Shortly after the death of his friend, Kilpatrick gathered supplies, including a carbine and 200 rounds of ammunition, and then moved away from their position and into the hills, living off the land for the next two and a half months. He had to be diligent in watching for enemy patrols, as the North Koreans sent many units into the area looking for any American survivors of their attacks. Kilpatrick developed a sophisticated camouflage system, and even though the North Korean patrols often passed within a few feet of his position on several occasions, he was able to avoid being captured. In addition to living in a cave and avoiding being seen there, Kilpatrick also was treated well by a South Korean family who was nearby. The family was not sympathetic to the North Korean offensive, and they often gave Kilpatrick food to eat when they could. Kilpatrick was careful not to visit them often, as he knew that repetitive patterns and being seen with them could get both him and the family into trouble. While on his own, Kilpatrick ate bean sprouts, cucumbers, melons, and any rice he could find, faring better than many who were behind enemy lines.

Over the next two months, Kilpatrick continued to live off the land and avoid North Korean patrols, making contact with several sympathetic South Korean families, who in turn got word to U.S. forces that an American soldier was behind enemy lines. Eventually, Lieutenant William Patch, a fellow Virginian, got word and sent a note to Kilpatrick through the South Koreans. The note stated that the area between Kilpatrick and the main unit was clear, and to just walk out of the hills. Kilpatrick was not as confident, as he feared a North Korean ambush. Lieutenant Patch sent the messenger back in, with another note and the offer of fresh American cigarettes if he would come down to the camp. With a full beard, but overall in good condition, Kilpatrick was reunited with his unit. Kilpatrick had been 220 pounds when the battle began, and was 175 pounds after his 77-day ordeal ended. Asked how it felt to be back, the understated Kilpatrick replied simply, "It feels good."

Further Reading

"77 Days Behind Enemy Lines: Sergeant Returns to the Land of the Living." *Corpus Christi Times,* October 2, 1950.

Appleman, Roy E. *South to the Naktong, North to the Yalu: United States Army in the Korean War.* Washington, D.C.: Department of the Army, 1998.

L

Larive, Etienne Henri "Hans"

Conflict: World War II
Captured: October 1940
Escaped: October 1940 and August 1941

Hans Larive was born in Singapore on September 23, 1915, but he returned to the Netherlands as a young man and joined the Royal Netherlands Naval College at the age of 19. He graduated in 1937, and was commissioned as an officer in August of that year. In 1940, the Germans attacked Holland, and his ship, the *Van Galen,* was commissioned into the fight. The destroyer had to maneuver a narrow waterway, and she was unwieldy. German fighter pilots bombed the ship and sunk her.

Upon capture, the officers were told that if they gave their word that they would not fight against the Germans, they could leave. Larive and 60 other officers refused to do so, and they were then transported to German prisoner of war camps. Larive was sent to Oflag VI-A, located in Soest, Germany, and he escaped from there in October 1940. He headed toward the Swiss border, where he was caught near Singen. The arresting Gestapo officer pointed out to Larive just how close he was to crossing the border, and Larive later used that information to help others cross out of Germany and into Switzerland.

Larive and other Dutch POWs were sent to Oflag VIII-C, where two officers again escaped. After that, the Dutch officers were sent to Oflag IV-C, which was in the town of Colditz. The castle, originally developed in the late 11th century, sat upon a large hill and was difficult to reach. The Germans had used it as early as 1933, when they housed political prisoners and others considered "undesirable" in Colditz. In 1939, the Nazis used the castle as a prisoner of war camp. Because of its location on the hill and sheer rock face, it was fairly simple to add more security measures, turning the site into a high-security camp for those prisoners considered dangerous. Though Oflag IV-C was considered the most secure of the German prisoner of war camps, it also had the record of most successful escape attempts.

The escape attempts of Dutch officers, including Larive, were organized by Captain Machiel van den Heuvel. On August 15, 1941, Larive's escape was organized to occur while a rugby game was underway. Another officer created a diversion, cutting a hole in the barbed-wire fence and getting caught, gaining the attention of the guards. Larive and Francis Steinmetz hid under a manhole cover, waiting until dark to sneak out of the castle. About a month later, two more Dutch officers also made their way out of the castle in this manner. Larive and Steinmetz traveled by train, heading back toward the Swiss border. They made it to neutral Switzerland on August 18, 1941.

Because Switzerland was neutral, Larive and Steinmetz had to remain there until false papers could be provided to get them out of the country. Larive made it back to London in December 1941. In March 1942, Larive went back into active service, commanding a torpedo boat, an *MTB 203*. He held that post until he gained a senior officer appointment, in which he was in charge of all the Dutch motor torpedo boats. When the Dutch torpedo boat service was ended in 1944, Larive moved on to the Dutch Naval Press Agency MARVO. He stayed in that appointment until he left the Dutch navy in 1946.

After the war, Larive went to work for the Royal Dutch Shell Company. He wrote about his experiences of Colditz in his 1950 wartime memoir entitled *Vannacht varen de Hollanders* ("The Dutch Sail Tonight"), later published in English as *The Man Who Came in from Colditz,* a take on the film, *The Spy Who Came in from the Cold* (1965). Larive was highly decorated for his service, including the Knight of the Military Order of William, Knight of the Order of Orange-Nassau, the Bronze Cross, the War Commemorative Cross, and the Distinguished Service Cross.

Further Reading

Larive, Hans. *The Man Who Came in from Colditz.* London: Hale, 1975.

"Lieutenant-Commander E. H. Larive." Netherlands Navy. www.netherlandsnavy.nl/Men_larive.htm.

Libby Prison Escape

Conflict: Civil War
Captured: Various
Escapes: Various

One of the largest successful prison breaks in the American Civil War occurred in February 1864 at the Libby Prison in Richmond, Virginia. Over 100 Northern prisoners of war managed to escape from the Libby Prison complex, which was a former tobacco factory and grocery store. Shortly after the Civil War began, the Libby building became a Confederate prison in March 1862. The Libby Building covered an entire city block, and one side was fenced in by the James River. For a time, it was a facility only for officers. Even so, the conditions were not good, and the limited furnishings in the large rooms were not enough for the crowded conditions, and men were exposed to the weather. Food supplies were also insufficient, and the prisoners rebelled against their conditions by tunneling to get out of the prison. There were a number of small escapes, one or two men at a time, and some were successful while many were not.

Major Thomas Turner, a West Point student at one point, was the Confederate commandant of Libby Prison. Because there were no established rules for treatment of prisoners of war during this time, like at other prisons, guards did not treat prisoners particularly well, and some were cruel. Prisoners learned not to stand too closely to the windows, as some guards would shoot at them if they did.

By the start of 1864, the prison conditions had worsened and those incarcerated there struggled to keep warm and out of the elements. The three-story buildings, the East, Middle, and West Buildings, had upwards of 75 windows, and half of them

Prisoners escaping Libby Prison in February 1864, illustration from the cover of *Harper's Weekly*, March 5, 1864. (Library of Congress)

did not have glass. Bars on the windows did nothing to keep the elements out of the room. There was little wood, but with 400 men in a room that had only two stoves, getting close enough to the heat source to stay warm was difficult at best. The second and third floors had six large rooms, two in each building, and these were approximately 105 by 45 feet. In the winter, because the kitchens were on the first floor, some heat came up through the floors. Because of limited rations, disease and illness also increased. Scurvy, diarrhea, dysentery, and typhoid were common, much like in other Civil War–era prisons. Vermin and lice were also problematic. In the basement of Libby, dead bodies were piled up in the west cellar until enough for a full wagon had accumulated, and then the deceased were taken to Oakwood Cemetery. A few cells in the Middle Building cellar were also used to contain the most dangerous of the prisoners. At its height, Libby Prison had about 1,000 prisoners of war housed in the three warehouse buildings.

Those in the North were aware of the conditions at Libby Prison, and in November 1863, a *New York Times* article was published that outlined the conditions at prisons in Richmond, including Libby. The article spoke of the disease, the lack of decent shelter and food, as well as the poor morale of prisoners being held there. Those opposed to President Lincoln's efforts actually used this propaganda to blame him for the conditions and treatment of Northern soldiers. The U.S. War Department sent aid to Libby, but the Confederate guards took most of the rations intended for prisoners of war and sent them on to Lee's soldiers. Southern newspapers disputed these claims, writing stories that directly contrasted the treatment of inmates and describing feasts within Libby.

By February 1864, food rations had dwindled over the winter, and the prisoners had been banding together to work for months on a tunnel, or to act as sentries. Because of the location and the erroneous belief that the Libby Prison was not one from which prisoners could escape, the guards were not as skeptical of the inmates' activities. The prisoners worked in poor conditions in a rat-infested area in the basement of the warehouse, and they tunneled underneath the walls, over to a vacant lot next to the prison, with the exit of the tunnel opening beneath a tobacco shed on that property. Working in the straw in the basement, the workers removed a stove in the abandoned kitchen, excavating dirt and hiding it in an area most avoided in the prison due to the rat problem. The men worked on three teams for over 17 days. Once the 53-foot tunnel was complete on February 9, under the direction of Colonel Thomas Rose of the 77th Pennsylvania Infantry, men literally walked out for over 12 hours, spacing themselves in small groups of twos and threes so as not to raise the alarm. The guards were not expecting prisoners to be on the streets of Richmond. Fifty-nine of the 106 who escaped made it back to Northern lines. Colonel Rose was captured and later exchanged. The men who left Libby Prison were not unfamiliar with the landscape of Virginia, and they had knowledge of the terrain and fighting going on in the region. They used this information, along with the tried-and-true navigation scheme of following the North Star, much like the slaves who had headed north to freedom. Avoiding rebel camps was one of the biggest issues for those who escaped Libby, as the escapees traveled at night and could easily stumble into a Confederate camp if they were not careful.

When daylight dawned on February 10, 1864, they stopped the escape, and during roll call later that morning, the guards realized that some prisoners, over 100, had escaped. The Confederate guards reportedly counted inmates several times to ensure that the prisoners weren't just pulling a trick on the guards as they had done before to frustrate the guards. Once the remaining prisoners realized that their escape would be stopped, they rushed the tunnels. Those who had left during the night had a 12-hour lead on the guards, and even though there was an effort to recapture the prisoners, only 48 were recaptured. Two men were reported to have drowned in the nearby James River.

Soon after the escape, officials at Libby Prison began shipping prisoners to Georgia. Enlisted soldiers were sent to Andersonville, which would make Libby Prison look like a country club in comparison. Officers were later transferred to a newer prison in Macon, Georgia. Richmond fell on April 2, 1865, and as the city went under the control of Union troops, those leaving the prison burned as many records as they could. About 700 Confederate officials became the newest occupants of the prison in which they had been guards. Although most of the buildings in Richmond burned, Libby Prison survived. In 1880, the facility was dismantled and moved to Chicago, where it was an attraction as the Libby Prison War Memorial until 1895. The actual site in Richmond now houses part of a flood wall. There is a plaque and historical marker on the site. Stories of Libby Prison have been retold on Broadway (*A Fair Rebel*, 1891), and in silent film of the same title in 1914 (starring Dorothy Gish).

Further Reading

Bartleson, Frederick A. *Letters from Libby Prison*. Edited by Margaret W. Peelle. New York: Greenwich Book Publishers, 1956.

Beszedits, Stephen, ed. *The Libby Prison Diary of Colonel Emeric Szabad*. Toronto: B & L Information Services, 1999.

Cavada, F. F. *Libby Life: Experiences of a Prisoner of War In Richmond, VA, 1863–1864.* Foreword by Joseph John Jova. New York: University Press of America, 1985.

Sanders, Charles W. *While in the Hands of the Enemy: Military Prisons of the Civil War.* Baton Rouge: Louisiana State University Press, 2005.

Locher, Roger

Conflict: Vietnam
Shot Down: May 10, 1972
Rescued: June 1, 1972

Roger Locher was born on September 13, 1946, and was raised in Sabetha, Kansas. He went to college at Kansas State University, just 90 miles southwest. He was involved in ROTC at Kansas State, and he joined the air force in 1969. Locher trained as a navigator, and his first mission was based in Udorn, Thailand. Locher completed three combat tours and had over 400 missions under his belt in his time as a navigator and weapon systems officer on the F-4 Phantom II. He was shot down while participating in Operation Linebacker on May 10, 1972, north of Hanoi and within a few miles of a North Vietnamese air base. His rescue was the farthest north of any completed during the Vietnam conflict.

Major Robert Lodge and Captain Roger Locher had scored three kills of enemy aircraft when the radar-equipped USS *Chicago* requested assistance for a flight of four American F-4s under attack from enemy aircraft. Lodge and Locher responded to the call, and in the dogfight that ensued, the Americans shot down a number of enemy aircraft. Unfortunately for Lodge and Locher, a flight of enemy fighters maneuvered underneath them and shot a burst of 30-mm cannon into their aircraft. They immediately lost the right engine; the left engine began losing power, and soon the hydraulic system had failed. The plane was on fire, and Lodge had lost all flight control. Locher called out that it was getting too hot and they needed to get out, but Lodge would not eject. Lodge had told fellow pilots that he would never allow himself to be captured due to the sensitive nature of the information he knew. He rode the aircraft into the ground; his body was returned from Vietnam in 1977.

Locher ejected at 8,000 feet and ended up in a tree. It was impossible to hide his parachute, but he figured that a search party would be along shortly. Unfortunately, others in his squadron hadn't seen him or seen his parachute, and help was not as close by as he thought. Locher hid his tracks, then hiked up a mountain and down the other side before hiding in a pile of brush for three days to evade capture. At night, he made his way to the top of the mountain to try and contact American aircraft. Several times he heard his fellow soldiers, but they were too far to the south to hear his transmissions. He knew he needed to move farther south, toward friendly lines and American aircraft that might hear him. Locher began moving in that direction, avoiding human contact and living off the land.

On the 10th day on the ground, he was nearly discovered while using a well-traveled path, but hid himself under leaves as local children played in the area. After they left, he climbed his way to the top of a hill, where he stayed for 13 more days. He waited for an American aircraft to travel close enough to hear his radio transmission. Locher was only 5 miles from a North Vietnamese airfield and 60 miles northwest of Hanoi, which was a terrible place for a search and rescue mission. One June 1, 1972, 21 days after he'd been shot down, he was finally able to contact a flight of F-4s overhead. Captain Steve Ritchie had been with Locher the day he was shot down and recognized the call sign, and he responded to the distress call. Locher calmly asked the pilots if there was any chance they could pick him up, and of course Ritchie responded in the affirmative.

Air force officials tried to rescue him immediately the following day, but enemy air defense wouldn't let them get close enough. The following day, General John Vogt, commander of the 7th Air Force in Vietnam, consulted with his army counterpart, and they canceled the planned raid on Hanoi. Vogt committed all 150 aircraft at his disposal to rescuing Roger Locher. The nearby enemy air base was a major problem, and the American fliers had to neutralize it to proceed with the rescue. Bombers and attack aircraft attacked the Vietnamese air base for two hours, which was long enough for the rescue helicopters to get in. Antiaircraft fire erupted around Locher, and the friendly forces worked hard to hold them back. The rescue was carried out under horrendous conditions, but the rescue helicopter, a Jolly Green Giant, made it to Locher's location after some maneuvering. The helicopter crew lowered a jungle penetrator to Locher's hiding place and pulled him out.

The helicopter flew back to Udorn, and General Vogt flew to the airfield to meet Locher and welcome him home. Many remembered this day for the many records achieved. Locher had evaded capture for 23 days on the ground, a record for the Vietnam War. Additionally, the distance traveled by the rescue helicopter to get him out of North Vietnam was also a record. Finally, during the rescue, F-4 pilot Major Phil Handley shot down a MiG-19 while traveling over 900 miles an hour using only his guns—the only supersonic gun kill on record. On the evening of his return, Locher walked into the officer's club and was greeted by a standing ovation lasting over 20 minutes. What he had achieved was truly remarkable.

Locher went home on schedule and transitioned to piloting aircraft instead of sitting in the back as the navigator and weapons officer. He flew the F-4 for a number of years, then transitioned to flying the F-16. Later, he played a role in the development of the F-117 Nighthawk stealth fighter. He retired to his hometown of Sabetha, Kansas.

Further Reading
Frisbee, John L. "Valor: A Good Thought to Sleep On." *Air Force Magazine,* February 1992. www.airforcemag.com/MagazineArchive/Pages/1992/March%201992/0392valor.aspx.
Lodge, Robert Alfred (biography). P.O.W. Network. www.pownetwork.org/bios/l/l068.htm.
Ritchie, Steve. "The Rescue of Roger Locher." www.youtube.com/watch?v=QvRcP4go-eg.

Long-Range Reconnaissance Patrols

Conflict: Vietnam
Captured: Multiple
Rescued: Multiple, June 1970

Warfare has long seen the use of scouts to find out what an enemy was doing. Most countries with a military have used some form of scouting, and in the last century, these groups have become more formalized. In Vietnam, a Long-range reconnaissance patrol (LRRP or Lurp) was a five- or six-man U.S. Army Ranger patrol that went after enemy camps and missing in action (MIA) soldiers after 1966. The Lurps infiltrated behind enemy lines to gather intelligence. As long as the team went undetected, things went very well. However, when things went wrong, they usually went very wrong. The small number in the team and relatively small amount of firepower they carried limited their abilities. In these situations, the team would usually call in a helicopter rescue rather than try to fight their way out of the situation.

The political landscape in Vietnam was anything but simple. The North Vietnamese and Cambodians were aligned with China, and China and Vietnam had had thousands of years of animosity. The Lurp specialized forces, also known as Talon units, worked in the military zones in Vietnam, dealing with terrain that was as diverse as the cultures and people. The mountains, swamps, and jungles were home to Vietnamese, Chams, Cambodian Khmers, Nung Chinese, and mountain people. Although most were Communists, there were also religious groups, including Buddhists, and alliances and agreements shifted often and were unpredictable at best. Because the land and the people posed such challenges, the use of indigenous soldiers in Lurp teams was also common.

The Lurp units went through a few transformations from 1966 to 1970. Their job, to get behind enemy lines, get information, and disrupt the enemy, remained much the same during these transitions. Those in the unit had extensive training, were cross-trained as medics and as radio operators, and more than half of the trainees quit. When out in the field, the soldiers carried large rucksacks of equipment and food, with these often weighing 60 to 100 pounds. The Lurps practiced escape and evasion drills, and out in the field, worked hard to avoid contact with the enemy. Although the units were generally about reconnaissance and not attack, they would on occasion engage the enemy. The small units were successful overall, and the documents obtained from the enemy were invaluable, as was intelligence about where the enemy was or was not located. About 40 percent of the Lurp soldiers were wounded in action. Most of the men in the unit were 19 and 20 years old. In 1969 alone, the Lurp teams had a kill ratio of 44 to 1.

One remarkable rescue mission was in the Mondol Kiri Province in Cambodia on June 17, 1970. Staff Sergeant Deverton Cochrane led the five-man Lurp team, and Specialist 4 Ron Andrus was the radio/telephone operator (RTO). The other members of this team were Specialist 4 Carl Laker, Specialist 4 Royce Clark, and Staff Sergeant Dwight Hancock. Even though Cambodia was considered neutral, the team was out gathering information behind enemy lines when they were attacked by the North Vietnamese. Two of the team were immediately killed, and the radio was decommissioned. All of the surviving team members had also been hit. Without a radio, they had no way to call in help and worked to stay alive. They knew that they would be killed if captured, as the North Vietnamese Army and Vietcong had a bounty on Rangers and rarely took prisoners.

Teams were supposed to reestablish radio contact every night, and this team, Talon 52, was not responding to radio calls. Finally, the base sent out a search and rescue team. Troops from the 1st Cavalry went out, but bad weather and fog caused issues and complicated the search and rescue. The rescuers were not sure where exactly to look for the missing team. Staff Sergeant Dwight Hancock was the least injured of the three survivors, and he evaded the enemy and got back to the base. He had to be cautious coming back in so he wouldn't be shot. He led the search and rescue teams back out into the jungle to search for the location of the two survivors. They found their way back to the ambush site, and Ron Andrus waved to the helicopter team. They got the wounded out, but more North Vietnamese Army enemy fire caused additional casualties, and some of the rescuers were hit by the snipers as they attempted to find bodies of team members who had been killed. The team went back in four times before they could recover all of the bodies. The three survivors who were rescued were treated for their injuries. The bullet that struck Ron Andrus was an eighth inch from an artery.

Hundreds of Lurp stories are available in written and video form. Movies such as *84C MoPic* (1989) are specifically about these units, while many other movies include their exploits as part of the story.

Further Reading

Gebhardt, Major James F. *Eyes behind the Lines: US Army Long-Range Reconnaissance and Surveillance Units.* Fort Leavenworth, Kansas: Combat Studies Institute Press, 2005.

Jorgensen, Kregg P. J. *MIA Rescue: LRRP Manhunt in the Jungle.* Boulder, Colorado: Paladin Press, 1995.

Lanning, Michael Lee. *Inside the LRRPs: Ranger in Vietnam.* New York: Presidio Press, 1988.

Rottman, Gordon L. *US Army Long-Range Patrol Scout in Vietnam 1965–1971.* Oxford: Osprey Publishing, 2008.

Los Baños Prison Camp Rescue

Conflict: World War II
Captured: Various
Rescued: February 23, 1945

Two rescue operations took place at roughly the same time in the Philippines in the last months of World War II. In both cases, American authorities feared reprisals against prisoners of war as the Japanese military leaders realized they were going to lose the war. The Japanese military leaders had primarily two choices as the war came to an end. They could move the prisoners or they could execute them, rather than face the humiliation of losing them as the Allied forces advanced farther into Japanese-held territory. American officials had received reports that as the Japanese retreated, they were killing civilians and prisoners of war. Several rescue operations were then put into place. One of the raids, the Great Raid or Cabanatuan prison rescue, is more widely known because it involved the rescue of 500 military personnel. The Los Baños rescue operation is less well known, even though more prisoners were liberated in this event. Perhaps one of the reasons for this obscurity is that almost all of those rescued were civilian. The Los Baños rescue operation may also have received fewer headlines because on the same day of the Los Baños event, the marines raised the picturesque flag over Iwo Jima, signaling the end of fighting there.

During World War II, almost 10,000 corporate or government works were caught in the war zone. After the war began, most of them ended up in Japanese POW camps in the Philippines. The Japanese set up dozens of prisoner of war camps, most of them hastily and not well built. Conditions varied in the camps, but none were exemplary. In many camps, such as Los Baños, executive committees of prisoners helped run the day-to-day operations of the camp. Interned prisoners purchased their own food, and especially at the beginning of the internments, Red Cross packages were withheld.

The prisoner of war camp in Los Baños was located at the then University of the Philippines College of Agriculture and College of Forestry, which is now the University of the Philippines Los Baños. The 60-acre site had both civilians and prisoners of war, though far more civilians were located there. Those interned inside the barbed-wire fences at Los Baños lived in thatched huts. Americans, British, Dutch, Norwegians, Poles, Italians, and Canadians were present, and aside from 11 navy nurses and a few servicemen, the rest of those incarcerated there were businessmen, teachers, bankers, and missionaries. Even though the inhabitants at Los Baños were civilians, conditions were not good in the camp, especially at the end of the war. Rations were thin, clothing was limited, and sanitation was nonexistent. Additionally, the Japanese guards were not any less strict or cruel because their prisoners were not soldiers.

Prior to the rescue at Los Baños, the Allied forces had liberated prisoners at the Cabanatuan prison camp on January 30, 1945, where over 500 prisoners were freed. After that, the Allied forces went to the Santo Tomas Prison on February 5, 1945, releasing more than 3,700 prisoners of war. Just a few days later, the American forces in the region found the Old Bilibid Prison complex, where 1,200 prisoners had been abandoned by their Japanese captors. Culturally, this was humiliating for the Japanese, and concern for prisoners who remained in Japanese internment camps rose. Los Baños held over 2,000 prisoners, and military leaders began planning to liberate those prisoners quickly so they would not be killed. American officials estimated that about half of the 2,130 prisoners in Los Baños were in a seriously weakened condition, either due to disease or starvation, including about 250 who were bedridden. A large number of the remaining population was elderly civilians, women, and small children. Freeing the group and walking out of the jungle, as had been done in Cabanatuan, was not a possibility.

Because the conditions at Los Baños had been difficult, some of the inmates had taken to escaping out of the camp at night to find food among the generous Philippine farmers who lived near the prison. The inmates would then sneak back into camp to share their bounty among the less fortunate. While out securing supplies one night, the inmates encountered a guerilla organization that told the prisoners of war that a rescue mission was planned for those who were living in the Los Baños camp. The guerillas helped even further, taking some of the internees to the headquarters of the 11th Airborne Division, who were tasked with leading the assault on the camp. The information provided by those who best knew Los Baños was critical intelligence data, including information on the camp routine and guard capabilities. When the American military learned that many of the Japanese guards locked up their weapons in the arms room and conducted physical training wearing only loincloths each morning, they recognized the best time of day to attack. The element of surprise by attacking at that critical time could give the Americans a decisive advantage over the Japanese guards. Additionally, the guerilla force took two lieutenants, one from the reconnaissance platoon and one an engineer, close to the Los Baños camp to gather necessary information for completing the attack plan.

The evening of February 23, 1945, was selected for the rescue mission. The 11th Airborne Division was in charge, and two battalions would be used in the assault: one would parachute onto a drop zone adjacent to the camp and lead the initial charge, while the second battalion crossed a nearby lake in Amtraks, an amphibious vehicle with tanklike tracks, and reinforced the parachute infantry. The topography of the camp was about 600 by 800 yards and was of generally level terrain, and the Los Baños camp had two rings of barbed-wire fencing that surrounded 26 prisoner barracks. After the Americans and Philippine guerilas eliminated the enemy force from the camp, which was estimated at 150 to 200 Japanese soldiers, the prisoners would be loaded aboard the Amtraks for transportation back to friendly lines, a distance of about 20 miles. The reconnaissance platoon would go in first to secure the drop zone prior to the parachute drop. Additionally, another battalion would launch an attack a few miles away to create a diversion and keep any enemy forces from responding to the attack on the camp. Of greatest concern were the 8,000 to 10,000 Japanese soldiers only a few miles away from the Los Baños location. The intelligence section of the 11th Airborne Division estimated that a significant force of enemy soldiers could arrive at the camp within an hour and a half. The division would need about three hours for the operation. The timing was tight.

At 4 a.m. in the morning on February 23, 1945, the soldiers assigned to the Amtraks began their last-minute preparations, and by 5:15 a.m., the first 54 vehicles left the base to go to the lake they would cross. Overhead, nine C-47 aircraft carrying the paratroopers were in flight as well, and the first paratroopers would jump, starting at 7:00 a.m. The first jumpers would jump at 400 feet, the second group at 450 feet, and the last group at 500 feet. The reconnaissance platoon was in place by the time the paratroopers landed, ensuring that the area at the drop zone was safe for their arrival. Everything went as planned until a dog attacked one of the soldiers, who had to shoot the animal. The soldiers waited to see if the noise would alert any of the Japanese guards, but it did not.

Once everyone was in place, the attack on the Los Baños camp began. The four reconnaissance platoons began firing on the guards, and at the same time, the transport aircraft flew over the zone and began dropping paratroopers. The Japanese soldiers were caught completely off guard. A small number of guards were immediately taken out, and as suspected, a large number of the Japanese soldiers were doing their physical training in their loincloths. While they went back to their barracks to get clothes and arms, the reconnaissance platoon and the friendly guerilla soldiers attacked further and secured the weapons rooms. Japanese soldiers who came to the arms room were engaged and many killed. Without weapons, many of the Japanese soldiers fled, running into the woods or hiding within the camp. The Philippine guerrillas and American soldiers dispatched these forces fairly quickly.

Because of the confusion in the camp, those interred tried to stay out of the way. Even so, it did not take long for them to realize they were being rescued. Some of the prisoners were overcome with emotion, and many were very weak. The male prisoners' average weight was a mere 110 pounds. The prisoners gathered their belongings and prepared to leave. The Amtrak vehicles arrived as the bulk of the fighting subsided. A caravan to and from the American base began, with the soldiers loading the Amtraks with civilians and their belongs, the Amtraks trekking back to base, dropping off the rescued prisoners, and then heading back to the Los Baños camp for more prisoners. During this process, American forces were concerned with a Japanese counterattack, but there was not another option for evacuation. The majority of the prisoners could not walk even a few miles and required transportation. The American forces set up a defensive perimeter around the camp and roadblocks on the main roadways.

By 1:00 in the afternoon, the last of the prisoners were loaded onto Amtraks and on their way to the American base and safety. The U.S. forces set fire to the prison camp so the Japanese forces still in the area could not use the facility any longer. At completion, the American military and Philippine guerilla forces rescued over 2,100 internees, with five soldiers killed and six wounded. Japanese losses were estimated at between 70 and 80 soldiers killed.

A number of books have been written about this raid, including Bruce Henderson's *Rescue at Los Baños: The Most Daring Prison Camp Raid of World War II* (2015) and G. L. Rottman's *The Los Baños Prison Camp Raid* (2010). Additionally, the History Channel produced a documentary on Los Baños in 2008, *Rescue at Dawn: The Los Baños Raid*.

Further Reading

Arthur, Anthony. *Deliverance at Los Baños*. New York: St. Martin's Press, 1985.

Flanagan, Edward M. *The Los Baños Raid: The 11th Airborne Jumps at Dawn*. New York: Presidio Press, 1986.

Henderson, Bruce. *Rescue at Los Baños: The Most Daring Prison Camp Raid of World War II*. New York: William Morrow and Company, 2015.

Rottman, G. L. *The Los Baños Prison Camp Raid*. Oxford: Osprey Publishing, 2010.

Lynch, Jessica

Conflict: Iraq War
Captured: March 23, 2003
Rescued: April 1, 2003

Jessica Lynch was born on April 26, 1983, and grew up in rural West Virginia, an area that was fairly isolated. Like many who are raised in rural areas, leaving home held an appeal, a chance to see the world, and Lynch had similar ideas about leaving West Virginia. After she graduated from high school in 2001, she joined the army. She went to South Carolina for basic training just two weeks after the September 11 attacks. Even so, Lynch did not think she would see combat. Her dream to see the world and earn money for college in the process certainly did not involve a front-row seat to combat in the deserts of Iraq. Lynch had signed up to serve before 9/11, and although the recruiter had been honest about the possibility of being sent to war, at the time before 9/11, that possibility had seemed remote.

Eighteen months later, on March 23, 2003, Jessica Lynch, then a supply clerk, was part of a convoy of the United States Army's 507th Maintenance Company and the 3rd Combat Support Battalion. The convoy had been mired down in the sand and mud, and eventually took a wrong turn and was ambushed near Nasiriyah, northwest of Basra. The convoy was supposed to avoid the town, but instead, ended up in the middle of town where they were ambushed by Iraqi soldiers. The convoy took heavy fire, and there was little to no room to maneuver or attempt to outrun the ambush. Lynch was a passenger in a Humvee that was hit by a rocket-propelled grenade. She was severely injured in the accident. Her best friend in the unit was also severely injured, and she later died at an Iraqi hospital.

Lynch was initially considered missing in action, and it was known that six others were captured or injured. Eleven soldiers died in the ambush. After spending time with captors, much of which she had difficulty remembering, Lynch was taken to a hospital in Nasiriyah, where her injuries were treated. Her treatment in the hospital has been reported in various ways, and she has disputed some of the accounts. Lynch had suffered multiple broken bones in the crash, and at one point, Iraqi doctors had planned on amputating her leg. Lynch fought against them, not allowing them to put the oxygen mask on her for surgery, arguing successfully to keep her limb. On April 1, 2003, a joint special operations task force, made up of Green Berets, Pararescuemen, Army Rangers, and Delta Force completed a nighttime rescue, retrieving Lynch and the bodies of 11 other soldiers from shallow graves and the morgue.

Lynch went first to Ramstein Air Base in Germany for initial treatment, and then to Washington, D.C., and Walter Reed Army Medical Center on April 12, 2003, just 12 days after her rescue for more treatment and rehabilitation. Approximately three months later, she was released from the hospital. In August 2003, Lynch was given an honorable discharge. She has had over 20 surgeries for the injuries sustained in the ambush and resulting accident.

The story of her rescue was distorted at first. Lynch was reported to have fought back in the initial ambush, but this was not true due to the extent of her injuries. She did not speak publicly for months, and she was critical of the reporting done about her capture and rescue. Lynch has never seen herself as a hero. She has become a motivational speaker and gave testimony to Congress in August 2007 about her ordeal. Lynch has also earned a degree in education and lives in West Virginia.

Further Reading
Bragg, R. *I Am a Soldier, Too: The Jessica Lynch Story.* New York: Vintage Books, 2003.
Fantz, A. "For Years, Former POW Jessica Lynch Kept the Hurt Inside." *CNN,* July 20, 2015. www.cnn.com/2015/07/20/us/jessica-lynch-where-is-she-now/index.html.

Mary, Queen of Scots

Conflict: England/Scotland/France
Captured: June 15, 1567
Escaped: May 2, 1568

Mary Stuart, also known as Mary, Queen of Scots, or Queen Mary I, earned her crown in infancy. Mary was queen of Scotland for 25 years, though 18 years of that reign occurred before she was an adult. She was born on December 8, 1542, at Linlithgow Palace in West Lothian, Scotland. Her father was King James V, and her mother was his second wife, Mary of Guise. When her father died, Mary was only six days old, and she became queen. Henry VIII, her great-uncle, tried to take over her country, but her mother, Mary of Guise, acted as regent and held the crown for her daughter. Mary was sent to France and was engaged to the son of the king and queen of France when she was just six years old. They married in their teens. Mary also had a claim to the throne in England; Queen Elizabeth I of England was Mary's first cousin. To state that there was court intrigue during Mary's lifetime would be an understatement. Although Mary's life is well documented, one of the most notable episodes involves an escape after she'd been imprisoned by her cousin, Queen Elizabeth I.

In 1558, at the age of 16, Mary had married the Dauphin of France. He soon became the king of France, but he died a year after their marriage. When Mary returned to her homeland, she was unprepared for the political situation at hand. Mary was Roman Catholic, and there were extensive conflicts with her Protestant subjects. In 1565, Mary remarried, this time to Henry Stuart, Lord Darnley. Mary's family, including the Earl of Moray and Queen Elizabeth I, both of whom were Protestant, worked against her, fomenting rebellion.

Mary's new husband was not helpful in terms of ruling Scotland, and he abused his position and demanded that he be made a co-sovereign. Mary would not or could not grant his request. The marriage was not a happy one, and a jealous Darnley murdered Mary's private secretary in front of her when she was six months pregnant. Even the birth of their son, James, did not help their situation. Darnley was murdered on February 10, 1567, and some suspected that Mary or her advisers had been behind his death. One of her advisers, specifically, James Hepburn, Earl of Bothwell, was rumored to be in on the plot as well. Shortly after Darnley's death, Bothwell took her and Mary's child, James, to Dunbar Castle. Mary married Bothwell on May 15 at Holyrood. Bothwell abandoned her and left the country. On June 15, 1567, the Protestant nobles rebelled against her and she surrendered her crown at Carberry Hill. She was imprisoned at Loch Leven Castle. Accusations against her included adultery and murder. Mary never again saw her infant son, James, who was appointed king of Scotland.

Loch Leven Castle was built on an island around 1300, and the castle had long been the home of the Douglas family. Mary had been to the castle in 1565, a guest of William Douglas, and while there, met John Knox, the Calvinist. While imprisoned in the Glassin Tower at Loch Leven, the former queen miscarried twins. After she recovered, she disguised herself as a servant and tried to escape the castle, but someone noticed her very white hands and her attempt was thwarted. Within 11 months of her imprisonment, she attempted a second escape, and this one was more successful.

The Douglas family, including Sir William, and his mother, Lady Margaret Douglas, were in residence at Lock Leven, and they were not unsympathetic to the young woman they held captive in their home. Margaret Douglas was the mother of Mary's half brother, the Earl of Moray, and George Douglas. As Mary convalesced after the miscarriage, she became closer to the family, especially George Douglas. After her failed escape attempt under disguise, the family helped her escape, with Willie Douglas, an orphaned relative, stealing the keys and letting Mary out of the castle on May 2, 1568. The family had drugged the revelers who were celebrating May Day, and young Willie Douglas had snagged the keys to Mary's tower while dancing as part of the festivities in the great hall. Mary went to the docks and had help navigating the lake in a rowboat, and once on shore, George Douglas and 200 supporters on horseback waited to escort her to Niddry Castle, about 22 miles away.

Mary's half brother, the Earl of Moray, ended her two weeks of freedom, though Mary had tried to raise an army to regain her throne. At a battle near Glasgow, Mary watched as the men who supported her were killed, and she retreated to Dundrennan Abbey, located near the Solway Firth. Mary decided to request assistance from her cousin, Queen Elizabeth, hoping that her cousin would show mercy. Mary was concerned that Elizabeth might betray her, but she went to England anyway. Unfortunately, Mary's intuition was correct, and Queen Elizabeth also imprisoned Mary. She would be held captive in England for 18 years. Because Mary had a line to the throne, and because of her Catholic background, English Catholics engaged her help to overthrow Queen Elizabeth. The plot was uncovered, and in 1586, Mary was found guilty of treason and sentenced to death. Mary, Queen of Scots, was 44 years old when she was executed at Fotheringhay Castle, Northamptonshire, on February 8, 1587. She was originally buried at Peterborough Cathedral, but her son King James I, moved her remains to Westminster Abbey.

Mary, Queen of Scots, as well as her cousin, Queen Elizabeth I, have been the subjects of multiple books and films. Films entitled *Mary Queen of Scots* were produced in 1936, 1971, 2013, and 2018, and the fictionalized TV series that details the young Mary, *Reign,* ran from 2013 to 2017. Hundreds of books have been written about the queen and her reign. Mary, Queen of Scots, is also one of the most notorious spirits in the region, said to be haunting places in Scotland, England, and France. Some of the places rumored to have her spirit in resident are Stirling Castle, Borthwick Castle, Loch Leven Castle, Craignethan Castle, Niddry Castle, and Bolton Castle, among others.

> ### Early POW Treatment—Middle Ages
>
> There were few prisoners of war during the medieval period, as at that time, only nobles were taken prisoner. The victor would ransom the noble back to his family for a hefty sum. A noble might also release his captive after he gave his word of honor to fulfill certain promises. Commoners had no honor, the nobles believed, and therefore they had no value in medieval society. Commoners were either driven away after a battle, enslaved for a period of time, or massacred.
>
> The numerous French wars of the 14th century and the changes in tactics, weaponry, and army composition led to more concrete definitions of the laws of warfare. Armies became much larger during this period and were filled with common soldiers who fought with pikes, longbows, and eventually, firearms. Under this scenario, a commoner could kill or capture a noble, a situation that was not conceivable in the days of chivalric combat in the early medieval period.
>
> Nobles refined the rules even further between the 16th and 17th centuries, when the aristocratic officer corps commanded large armies and the number of prisoners could number into the thousands. Ransom was no longer feasible because the large numbers of commoners filling out the ranks had no family who could afford the expense. Prisoner exchanges became more common, and states often paid for the release of prisoners. Nations negotiated binding treaties, called cartels, which outlined how prisoners would be exchanged or ransomed. States did not desire to feed or guard prisoners, so it was in the best interest of each side to trade prisoners as quickly as possible, or to entice the prisoners to switch sides and serve in the opposing army.

Further Reading
Fraser, Antonia. *Mary Queen of Scots.* New York: Delta, 1969.
Guy, John. *Queen of Scots: The True Story of Mary Stuart.* Boston: Mariner Press, 2017.

Mayaguez Incident

Conflict: Post-Vietnam
Captured: May 12, 1975
Rescued: May 15, 1975

Though official hostilities ceased between United States military forces and the government of North Vietnam in February 1973, there continued to be a period of confusion and adjustment in Southeast Asia. The government of Cambodia initially supported the Americans in their endeavor to keep South Vietnam free of Communist influence, but the North Vietnamese and the Chinese Communists exerted great influence within the region. In April 1975, the Khmer Rouge and Pol Pot consolidated power in Cambodia, turning that nation into a Communist regime. At that point, the governments in the region were still weak and vulnerable, constantly on guard against nations that sought to benefit from the disorder. In particular, Cambodia had a number of islands just off their mainland that its government feared the Vietnamese would attack and occupy. The Cambodians diligently defended their territory from invasion by sovereign nations or hired insurgents to create chaos within neighboring borders. As evidence of their determination to hold contested territory, Cambodian forces also routinely seized ships throughout the Gulf of Thailand.

The SS *Mayaguez* was a 10,485-ton American cargo ship, planning to cruise from Hong Kong to Singapore, with an intermediate stop in Thailand. The ship carried supply goods, repair parts, and commissary items, but no weapons or ammunition were aboard. At 2:18 p.m. on May 12, 1975, two Cambodian patrol boats fired on the *Mayaguez*. As soon as the attack occurred, the radio operator immediately reported that the ship was taking fire. The captain ordered his ship to stop, allowing a Khmer Rouge boarding party to take control of the ship. The Communists then ordered the captain, Charles T. Miller, to proceed to Kompong Som, a port complex on the Cambodian mainland. The radar was not functioning, however, which made navigation in the shallow waters dangerous. Initially, the Cambodians tried to tow the ship into port, but they quickly abandoned the idea. Exactly why the Cambodians took the ship remains unclear. Perhaps they sought to embarrass the United States or hold the crew for ransom, or more likely, the local commander decided to take the ship, putting their national government into a tricky situation. A number of stations heard the "Mayday" message that the *Mayaguez* radio operator sent announcing that Cambodians had fired upon and boarded the ship. Within hours, the American government was working on the problem, focused on getting the ship and crew back into American hands.

One of the first tasks for military forces in the Gulf of Thailand was to find the exact location of the SS *Mayaguez,* and American aerial reconnaissance pilots found the ship near the island of Koh Tang. Confusing the issue were Air Force reports of 30 to 40 Caucasians aboard a ship bound for Kompong Som, a port on the Cambodian mainland. American military officials decided that the best course of action was to prepare to occupy the island of Koh Tang, in case the crew was there, despite reports that the crew was not there.

The overarching objective of the American government was the safe retrieval of the ship and its crew. Available to assist within the area was the destroyer escort USS *Harold E. Holt* and the guided missile destroyer USS *Henry B. Wilson*, along with the aircraft carrier USS *Coral Sea* with its complement of fighter and attack aircraft. Also, available Marine Corps units were 120 officers and men of the 1st Battalion, 4th Marines out of Cubi Point, in the Philippines, and two companies from the 2nd Battalion, 9th Marines out of Okinawa. Also in the region were various air force aircraft, including CH-53C and HH-53C helicopters. The military had plenty of firepower in the region. The plan was straightforward but complicated, and called for one marine assault force to retake the *Mayaguez* while another marine force attacked and occupied the island of Koh Tang, where the crew was possibly being held. In the meantime, American military forces would attempt to verify the location of the crew and prevent the Cambodian military from interfering with ongoing operations by bombing bases on the Cambodian mainland.

Planning continued to refine the broad objectives into a coherent scheme. First, a contingent of marines, D Company of 1st Battalion, 4th Marines, would use the USS *Holt* to transport them to and then board the *Mayaguez,* clearing it of any enemy personnel. Accompanying the marines were navy and Military Sealift

After the *Mayaguez* was seized by Cambodian forces in 1975, American forces attacked the island of Koh Tang in the Gulf of Siam in what would be a failed rescue mission. The crew were never in danger and were eventually released. (Bettmann/Getty Images)

Personnel (MSP), who could get the ship under way and safely into international waters in case the crew had not been found when the ship was retaken. The main effort of the operation, carried out by 2nd Battalion, 9th Marines, was an assault on the island of Koh Tang to rescue the crew, which was assumed to be held by 18 to 30 enemy soldiers. In actuality, Koh Tang had about a 100 dug-in and well-armed soldiers. Eight CH-53C and HH-53C Air Force helicopters would insert 175 marines onto the island in the first wave, with follow-on waves deploying about 650 marines and other personnel. The island was covered with thick trees and other vegetation, leaving only two beaches, East Beach and West Beach, as viable landing points. The marines would secure the island first, and then search for the missing crew. While the *Mayaguez* was being retaken and the island secured, air force assets from Thailand and navy aircraft from the USS *Coral Sea* would provide security for the operation, including close air support. Additionally, the U.S. military planned to hit targets on the Cambodian mainland before the actual operations began.

In the early morning of May 15, 1975, the operation began, with air force planes moving the marines to air force bases in Thailand, and then the marines were transported to staging areas closer to their target. Once they got to the *Mayaguez,* the actual assault was not even a conflict, as no enemies were aboard the ship. Navy and Military Sealift Personnel began the work of moving the ship back into neutral international waters. At the same time, air force helicopters were transporting marines to Koh Tang to prepare for further attacks. Unfortunately, word that the ship had been retaken had not been passed along yet, and no one knew that the Khmer Rouge had released the crew the previous day. They had not wanted to risk the wrath of the American military by holding the crew. However, the sailors had not yet returned to the ship, and news of their release had not been shared with the military. The captain had planned to get any attacks stopped, but they arrived back at ship just after the marines took over the *Mayaguez*. The air attack on Koh Tang could not be stopped, as it had already begun.

At just after 6:00 a.m., the first group of marines approached Koh Tang in eight helicopters. Some landed on West Beach and came under heavy machine gun fire. More helicopters landed on East Beach and were also immediately under fire. Though the mission started with eight helicopters, three were shot down and four more damaged to the point that they had to go back to base in Thailand. Two reserve helicopters and two that had been flying in the area came into the fight, which now had five helicopters and crews to take on the mission. At noon that day, six hours after the attack began, the White House found out that the crew had been released and were safe. Orders came immediately to disengage and leave Cambodian territory. However, there were marines on the ground, and a second wave of marines was put onto the island. About 225 marines were now engaged on Koh Tang. Fortunately, the Cambodians pulled back, and the marines began their evacuation, which was complete about 8:00 p.m.

Fifteen Americans were killed in the Koh Tang attack, and another 50 were wounded. Three Americans were missing and presumed dead. Additionally, an air force helicopter crashed, killing the 5 crew members and 18 Air Force Security Police. The three missing, Lance Corporal Joseph N. Hargrove, Private First Class Gary Hall, and Private Danny G. Marshall, were uncharacteristically left behind. Rescue operations were proposed and then dismissed as too dangerous. The U.S. government declared the men Missing in Action (MIA) and then Killed in Action, Body Not Recovered (KIA-BNR) on July 21, 1976. In 1999, a joint task force between Cambodia and America tried to find out what happened to the missing soldiers, but were unable to retrieve their bodies, though some Cambodian survivors of the attack provided information that was relevant to the three soldiers. Khmer Rouge forces also took extensive losses, with an estimated 13 to 25 enemy soldiers killed. In 1996, John McCain was involved in the dedication of the embassy grounds in Phnom Penh, and the *Mayaguez*-Marine Corps Memorial was dedicated, which lists the names of the 18 U.S. military members who died or were missing in the attack at Koh Tang. The *Mayaguez* rescue attempt is often referred to as the last battle of the Vietnam War; however, those who participated in that event are not eligible for the Vietnam Service Medal. Soldiers who were in Koh Tang were eligible for the Armed Forces Expeditionary Medal.

Further Reading
Chun, Clayton K. S. *The Last Boarding Party: The USMC and the SS* Mayaguez. Cambridge, UK: Osprey Publishing, 2011.
Guilmartin, John Francis. *A Very Short War: The* Mayaguez *and the Battle of Koh Tang.* College Station: Texas A&M University Press, 1995.
Wetterhahn, Ralph. *The Last Battle: The* Mayaguez *Incident and the End of the Vietnam War.* Cambridge, MA: Da Capo Press, 2001.

McBrayer, James

Conflict: World War II
Captured: December 8, 1941
Escaped: May 10, 1945

James McBrayer, born September 9, 1918, was originally from Lorena, Texas. He graduated from the United States Naval Academy in 1939, and then he went on to receive a commission in the United States Marine Corps. McBrayer was initially assigned to the American embassy in Peking, China.

Japanese soldiers had taken James McBrayer and another U.S. officer, Richard Huizenga, captive on December 8, 1941. After four years of imprisonment, McBrayer and Huizenga joined two other prisoners of war, John McAllister and John Kinney, in an escape attempt. They were all being held near Shanghai, and the conditions in the prison were poor. In planning for their escape, they had limited provisions: a hacksaw blade, pair of pliers, and little else. When they learned that the Japanese were planning to move them, the group knew they needed to act sooner rather than later. They did not have a detailed plan, but between the bleak conditions in the prisoner of war camp and thoughts of dying there or on the move to a new camp spurred their urgency to leave the camp. They focused on the hope that they could get a distance away from the prison and guards before being caught by Chinese peasants, who would likely turn them over to the Chinese military, either Communist or National, who were better bets than the Japanese. They were fully aware that the Japanese offered reward money for the return of any escaped American prisoners.

In April 1945, they decided to escape on the move to the new prisoner of war camp. McBrayer and the others found out that they would be taken by train to the coast, and then by ship to Japan. They decided that they had to escape on this journey, because once they were in Japan, they figured it would be impossible to escape from there. They learned that they would be in boxcars, about 50 prisoners in each, with 6 guards in each boxcar. With their hacksaw, they determined they could either cut a hole in the floor of the boxcar or remove the iron bars from the windows. When they actually got a glimpse of the train, they noticed that the cars had only two bars across each window, when these types of transports generally had three or four bars. The boxcars also looked to be well used and rusted, including the bars on the windows. They knew they could get through the windows, and they scrapped their second idea of cutting a hole in the floor.

Once on the train, the men determined that they would try to get out of the train on the first night. Though blankets covered the windows, they took turns slipping under the blanket and sawing through the bars. McBrayer worked first, then Huizenga. They cut through the bars as well as the barbed wire that had been added, and the guards did not notice their efforts. The four men drew straws, and McAllister and Huizenga were the first ones to go out the window, followed by McBrayer and Kinney. Though the men had intended to stay together, McBrayer was separated from the group when he leapt from the train and was momentarily dazed. When he regained his faculties, his first coherent thought was that the train was still moving away from him and had not stopped. They had not been noticed when they had jumped from the train. They were free, so far.

When McBrayer landed, he landed hard. Though he had not broken any bones, he was stiff and sore, and in the fall, he had broken his iodine bottle and crushed his canteen. He was also wet and cold. As they had planned, McBrayer got up and headed west, away from the Japanese soldiers, and into Communist China. McBrayer got as far away from the rail line as possible the first night and camped on a small hill in a farm field. Without his iodine bottle, he had no way to purify water, and though he was thirsty, he did not drink from a nearby stream. The risk of disease was too high. An older man walked near him the next day, and McBrayer took the risk of approaching him and perhaps getting something to eat. When McBrayer had first been captured, he had weighed about 180 pounds, but after years in the prisoner of war camp, he was down to 110 pounds and knew he needed food to gain strength. The old man invited him to his home, and McBrayer was fed cabbage soup and given potable water. Some of the village elders came to the home as well, and McBrayer shared that he needed to get to an area where the Chinese Communists were in charge. Though this prompted discussion among the elders, they did agree to help him get where he needed to go. Even further, they would help him by providing a guide.

The next day, the guide led McBrayer out of the village, and they avoided Japanese patrols and took shelter with friendly Chinese families. Though all were very poor, they shared hot water and a gruel for meals. The continued walking, and lack of food and disease reduced McBrayer's weight further. In four days, and after four guides, McBrayer was brought to the area where Chinese Communists were located. His last guide told him to walk down a path, and McBrayer did that, soon walking into a Communist outpost, where friendly soldiers greeted him. From there, McBrayer was taken to a regional camp, where he discovered that three other Americans were being held nearby. McBrayer also met another prisoner, a Texan named Lewis Bishop, who had singularly escaped as well, leaping from the train the same night the rest of them had done so. The five Americans soon began their journey to the headquarters of the New Fourth Army, where they could be put in touch with American forces.

They headed out of the regional camps on mules and donkeys, riding for much of their journey through Japanese-controlled territory. They stopped many times at small garrisons. McBrayer and the others were surprised at how well the Chinese Communists treated their Japanese prisoners. While the Americans had seen firsthand how harsh the Japanese were with their prisoners, the Chinese treated their prisoners with respect. The Chinese soldiers had shared that the Japanese were more willing to surrender if they knew they would be treated humanely, and they did not try to escape. After several days, the five Americans finally arrived at the New Fourth Army Headquarters in Hankou.

As the Americans waited for a decision on their next steps, they were allowed to tour the area. Finally, they received word that the Communists and Nationalists had reached a truce, and that the escaped prisoners of wars could be returned to the Americans. McBrayer and the others left the camp the following day, heading again on mule and donkey to an airstrip that the American forces controlled. Finally, they came to a river where the ferry was too small to move the horses, and they headed on foot in the general direction their Chinese escorts told them to go.

Americans met them outside a small outpost used by the Office of Strategic Services, which was 300 miles inside Japanese lines. Seven days from this outpost was an airfield where a transport plane brought in supplies every two weeks. It took McBrayer and the others a week to get to the airstrip, and when they arrived, a C-47 transport was sitting at the end of the runway. Though the pilot had planned to leave the day before, he had heard about the escaped prisoners of war and had waited for them. McBrayer and the others were soon aboard and the plane was airborne. Once they leveled off at cruising altitude, McBrayer, Huizenga, McAllister, Kinney, and Bishop asked for food. To get to their flight out of China, they had walked or ridden 800 miles in 48 days.

McBrayer returned to the United States on July 9, 1945. After his escape, McBrayer continued his service in the marines. He ended his career as a brigadier general in 1965. During his distinguished military career, he served in the United States, Korea, Panama, Great Britain, and the Middle East. He then turned his attention to academic endeavors. He earned a master's degree and a PhD in political science, and then taught in the Georgia university system between 1973 and 1983. He suffered a stroke in 1988, and passed away in 2006. His many medals and awards included two Legions of Merit, one with Combat Valor Device, and two Purple Hearts.

Further Reading
"BGen James D. McBrayer, Jr." The Military Hall of Honor. www.militaryhallofhonor.com/honoree-record.php?id=223103.
McBrayer, James D. *Escape!: Memoir of a World War II Marine Who Broke Out of a Japanese POW Camp and Linked Up with Chinese Communist Guerillas*. Jefferson, North Carolina: McFarland and Company, 1995.

Morgan, John H.

Conflict: American Civil War
Captured: July 26, 1863
Escaped: November 28, 1863

Born on June 1, 1825, in Huntsville, Alabama, Brigadier General John Hunt Morgan earned many nicknames during the Civil War, including "the Thunderbolt of the Confederacy," and "the King of Horse Thieves." Morgan was a Confederate Civil War cavalry officer who was well respected by his men and known as being so bold as to be reckless. He had at his command 2,000 Confederate soldiers, and their exploits were legendary during the height of the Civil War. His unit blew up railroad lines and warehouses, sacked villages and towns, and demanded thousands of dollars in extortion to spare certain cities from his wrath. Even so, he was popular, and his reputation bothered the other Confederate generals. Morgan was not known as being a particularly good follower. In fact, his superior officer, Braxton Bragg, had warned Morgan not to visit his pregnant wife or cross the Ohio River to invade the North. Morgan did both.

Against Bragg's direct orders, Morgan led his men on a raid through Kentucky, Indiana, and Ohio, venturing farther north than any other Confederate mission. For

25 days, Morgan raided towns, destroyed bridges and supply depots, and fled Union patrols, leading his men on one of the longest organized cavalry operations in history. Behind Morgan were no fewer than 110,000 Union soldiers, virtually all of the cavalry located in the Midwest, who were trying to catch him. The Union cavalry chased him across southern and northeastern Ohio, and they finally caught up with him near the Pennsylvania border. Knowing he was beaten, Morgan had one more grand gesture, and he gave the order to dismount, then waited for the Union cavalry to catch them. Some of his men were exhausted and they laid down and went to sleep; many of them awoke in Union custody. Morgan's notoriety was so great that three different Union officers claimed the credit for capturing him. Although most of his men ended up in the infamous Camp Douglas Prisoner of War Camp in Chicago, Morgan and a number of his officers were sent to the Ohio State Penitentiary in Columbus.

At the Ohio State Penitentiary with Morgan were three of his brothers, Charlton, Calvin, and Richard, as well as his chief scout, Captain Thomas Hines, and Morgan's second in command, Colonel Basil Duke. Morgan had a fourth brother, Thomas, on the Northern raid with him, but he had been killed on the raid about two weeks before their capture. Morgan was not a model prisoner, and he had reasons to try to escape. He found that for him, in addition to being unable to fight in the war, the worst part about being a prisoner was not knowing how his wife was doing. She was pregnant, and he had not heard from her for the several months that he was in the prison.

Another man who was determined to escape was the scout, Thomas Hines, who was also a former college professor who spoke, read, and wrote French fluently. This was a skill that served him well because the only book he could acquire from the prison library was Victor Hugo's masterpiece, *Les Miserables,* the story of Jean Valjean, who among his other talents, repeatedly escaped from prison. While reading this book, Hines began to look at his cell with a new interest. The ceiling in his cell dripped water and the walls were always wet, but the floor was always dry. Hines began to think what that could mean, and he soon deduced that the floor was not attached to the ground. Hines was sure that there was space between the ground and the floor. To verify his suspicions, he took a stick and hit the stone tiles, which returned a hollow sound and confirmed his suspicions. Later, a prison guard unknowingly confirmed that an air shaft ran the length of the prison.

Hines shared his secret with Morgan, who shared it with five other officers in cells near them. Together, they acquired knives from the kitchen and began digging through the concrete flooring under the bunk in Hines's cell. By a stroke of luck, Morgan had complained that the civilian guards were mistreating the Confederate prisoners, and he demanded that General John Mason, commander of the Union military prison in Columbus, provide actual soldiers to perform the guard duty. To his great surprise, the general agreed, and the new guards had no desire to perform daily cell checks. The prisoners were free to concentrate on their escape plans with no interference. The work was slow but constant, and the soldiers worked almost around the clock in shifts of one hour each. Because they worked slowly and for short shifts, they were easily able to get rid of the chipped concrete and mortar. The knives were not well made, and they broke often. Surprisingly, the guards did not notice the number of stolen knives from the kitchen.

John Hunt Morgan was a successful Confederate raider until he was captured and imprisoned in July 1863. Though he did escape and rejoin the Confederate army, his career as an effective raider was over. (Library of Congress)

Though the concrete floor was 26 inches thick, the digging went fairly quickly. After three days, Morgan and his cohorts had dug a hole 14 inches in diameter, and on the fourth day, the men had dug through the depth of the barrier. Morgan decided that Hines, who was small and slender, would feign an illness and stay in his cell during dinner, and then inspect the tunnel. While the others were away,

Hines lowered himself into the hole, lit a candle, and discovered the space was about 5 feet high and 20 feet long. He determined that the foundation of the building was made of granite, a particularly hard stone, but the ground was soft. Their best bet, he thought, was to dig under the foundation, but he was not sure. When the men returned from dinner, Hines suggested that Captain Lorenzo Hockersmith, who was a stonemason by trade, should inspect the tunnel and give his opinion. Hockersmith descended into the space and inspected the tunnel. Over the next several days, the men inspected the grounds outside where they figured the tunnel led and determined that a tunnel under the foundation, and then out into the prison yard, was the best route to escape. It took several days to dislodge one of the granite boulders that formed part of the foundation, and then move it, but they began to dig the tunnel into the yard soon after they were able to move the large stone.

While the men proceeded with their escape plan, Morgan received a Bible from his sister. He opened to the page where a ribbon marker was placed, and a close examination of the page revealed a mark next to the passage, "The last shall be first and the first shall be last" (Matthew 20:16). Morgan was sure it was a message, so he peeled back the front and back covers of the Bible, where he found 10 federal bank notes, each in the amount of 100 dollars. With 1,000 dollars, one of Morgan's problems was solved. However, his cell was on the second floor of the prison, not on the first floor where the tunnel was, and each man was locked into his cell at night. Of the men who had been working on the tunnel, only Hines could get out from his first floor cell. Morgan and the others had to rethink their plan, and a significant change had to be added. Each of the seven men involved in the escape plan would dig a hole from the tunnel up toward his bunk, but only 25 inches in depth. The last inch would be just under the concrete flooring beneath the bunk, and this would be the last part they would take out, waiting until the night of the escape.

The men completed the tunnel by Thanksgiving, poking a wire through the last few inches of dirt to make sure that they knew where it brought them out. The last obstacle also had to be considered, which was an outer wall that was 25 feet high. Not surprisingly, Morgan had also been working on the problem of getting over the wall. He fashioned a rope by braiding together bed sheets, and he tied loops every few feet. Morgan had also fashioned a hook by bending a discarded fireplace poker. By November 27, 1863, all of the parts of the escape plan were in place. However, one of Morgan's brothers, Richard, was too badly injured to try to escape. He volunteered to trade prison cells with his famous brother, allowing Morgan to escape with the group. When the men learned that General Mason was to be transferred to another prison the next day, and that his replacement could reasonably be expected to make an inspection of the cells, Morgan and the others knew that the escape had to be that night.

Just after midnight on November 28, the escape began. The men put on their civilian clothing, provided by their families, shortly after the last guard check of the night. Each man made a dummy under the blankets, then stomped through the thin concrete floor under their bunks with the heel of their boots. The group made their way under the prison and through the tunnel, coming out into the prison yard. One of the men threw the metal hook attached to the rope up and over the stone wall, making more noise than they had planned to, but the guards were inside out of the rain and trying to stay warm, so they did not hear the activity. The men scaled up the wall using the rope, then slid down the other side. Once they were all on the outside of the wall, they left in different directions.

Morgan and Hines decided to stick together and headed for the small railroad depot in Columbus. With the money Morgan's sister sent, Hines purchased two tickets for Cincinnati while Morgan kept out of sight. When they got aboard the train, they sat in separate spots. Morgan noticed a Union officer and sat beside him in an effort to control the situation. As the train stopped at depots throughout the night, the men waited for some sign that their escape had been discovered, but none came. Just outside of Cincinnati and not wishing to push their luck, they jumped from the train, stopping beside the campfire of two Union soldiers. Morgan and Hines told the men that they lived nearby, and it made no sense to go all the way into the city then have to come all the way back out into the countryside. By the time the guards at the prison had discovered the escape, Morgan and Hines had hired a boy with a raft to take them across the Ohio River to Kentucky. They were a long distance from the prison before their absence was even noticed.

After Morgan's escape, he rejoined the Confederate army and again made raids into Kentucky. He launched multiple raids into that state, but the men he now led were not the same caliber of those that he had led and lost the previous year. His last Kentucky raid was carried out in June 1864, and he won a minor victory against a smaller Union force on June 11. The next day he ran into a superior Union force that devastated his regiment, as much of his force was killed or captured. Morgan was able to escape on that occasion. On September 4, 1864, Morgan was killed during a raid on Greeneville, Tennessee.

Further Reading
Cahill, Lora Schmidt, and David L. Mowery. *Morgan's Raid across Ohio: The Civil War Guidebook of the John Hunt Morgan Heritage Trail.* Columbus: Ohio Historical Society, 2014.
Horwitz, Lester V., and James A. Ramage. *The Longest Raid of the Civil War: Little-Known & Untold Stories of Morgan's Raid into Kentucky, Indiana, and Ohio.* Loveland, Ohio: Farmcourt Publishing, 1999.
Mowery, David L. *Morgan's Great Raid: The Remarkable Expedition from Kentucky to Ohio (Civil War Series).* Stroud, United Kingdom: History Press, 2013.

Munich Olympics

Conflict: Terrorism
Captured: September 4, 1972
Failed Rescue: September 4, 1972

Terrorism in the Middle East was growing in the early 1970s, and unknown to the Israelis at the time, the year 1972 was pivotal. The Palestine Liberation Organization (PLO) was moving toward a more aggressive stance in their operations, including assassinating officials and hijacking aircraft. International intelligence pointed to a planned attack in Europe, but no specific information about an attack at the

Olympics in Munich that year was specifically mentioned. German and Israeli officials had no warning about the events that would unfold in front of an international audience at the 1972 Munch Olympic Games.

For their part, the Germans were mindful of the image of their past, especially of that of a militaristic nation, and they were eager to host and represent the 1972 Olympic message of peace. Unwilling to have the world see armed guards on international television, no armed personnel or police were stationed within the Olympic Village itself. Instead, 2,000 ushers in blue uniforms were employed inside. The perimeter fence was next to useless, as athletes regularly jumped over it on their way back from the Munich beer halls. This concern on the optics of the event and the perceptions of Germany in general helped the members of the PLO's Black September terrorist group, who planned to kidnap Israeli athletes with the intent to free hundreds of Palestinians held in Israeli jails. The Olympic team at Munich in 1972 had 27 Israeli athletes, which represented the largest team for that nation. The lack of security and large number of Israeli athletes provided an unprecedented opportunity for the Black September group to strike in a seemingly meaningful way and potentially free the jailed Palestinians.

From the start, the PLO operation was a bold endeavor. The leadership from the terrorist organization selected six men for a highly secret mission, but even these six did not know all of the details until they were on their way to training camps in Germany. Preceding the six members, two more members of the PLO, posing as husband and wife, smuggled in eight AK-47 assault rifles, dozens of magazines, and 10 grenades. They hide their small armory in the lockers in the Munich railway station, dropped off the keys for the lockers at the front desk of a local hotel, and then disappeared.

On September 4, 1972, the six Black September members met at the railway station and retrieved the weapons from the lockers. The men then ventured to separate hotels and changed into jogging suits, which helped them to blend in with the Olympic athletes. At around 4:00 a.m., the men reached the perimeter fence that surrounded the Olympic Village, then jumped it, joining in with American athletes who were returning from a night on the town. The men then walked with the Americans a short distance until they reached the Israeli delegation located at 31 Connollystrasse. The men waited until no others were around, then pulled their weapons from their cases and reached the front door of the first apartment.

The terrorists put a copied key into the front door of the apartment where the Israeli athletes were staying, but it would not open. The noise of trying to open the door woke one of the athletes, Yossef Gutfreund, a giant of a man at 285 pounds and an international wrestling referee. As he approached the door, it finally opened, and a Palestinian and the Israeli faced each other. Gutfreund ran at the door and threw his weight against it, yelling to his teammates to wake up and run. Tuvia Skolsky, a weight lifting trainer who had lost his entire family in the Holocaust, managed to escape from the apartment by jumping through a back window. Within a few seconds, however, the Palestinians had wedged a rifle into the gap between the door and the jamb, entered the room, and fired at the retreating athlete.

In less than 10 minutes, the terrorists had found 11 Israeli athletes. One of the coaches, Moshe Weinberg, attempted to grab for a weapon. He was shot in the chest

Police set up their positions above the apartments where Israeli Olympic team members were being held hostage by extremists at the 1972 Olympics. (Bettmann/Getty Images)

and killed. They murdered another man, Yossef Romano, a wrestler who attempted to grab a gun when Gutfreund had made his desperate attempt to keep them out of the apartment. The gunfire woke many of the athletes and officials sleeping in the surrounding buildings. The sounds of gunshots also alerted security patrols in the Olympic Village, who sent guards to investigate. Israeli officials telephoned Tel Aviv and notified them of the hostage situation.

In the early morning hours, a ringing telephone woke Manfred Schreiber, the chief of the Munich police department who was responsible for the safety of the Olympic athletes and coaches. Upon hearing about the hostage situation, he ordered his forces to surround and isolate the Israeli apartments and to block off the Olympic Village. Hundreds of reporters descended on the scene. By 5:30 a.m. that morning, the Palestinians had released their list of demands. They wanted 236 Arab prisoners released from Israeli jails and two Arab prisoners released from West German prisons. The deadline for compliance was 9:00 a.m. that same day. Once the prisoners were free, the captors were to be given transportation to an Arab country, where they would then release the Israeli hostages. If the German authorities did not comply with their demands, they stated they would execute a prisoner every hour until their demands were met.

The extremely short deadline was impossible to meet. A delegation of German and Olympic officials met with the terrorists and negotiated an extension until 12:00 p.m., but German law enforcement officials had little idea what to do. The noon deadline approached with no plan in place and no ideas for a solution. Negotiations went nowhere, and the gunmen refused to release any prisoners until their political comrades were freed. Even though this quickly became an international incident, Germany took control of the situation because the crisis occurred in that nation. However, they had little experience with international terrorism, and seemingly no unit or organization within their structure that could end the crisis.

The terrorists did agree to extend the deadline three times, possibly because the negotiators told the terrorists that they would meet their demands but were running into problems. In reality, the Germans in charge still had no real plan. Tired of the situation, the terrorists demanded a plane at a nearby airport to fly them to Cairo. They knew that they were vulnerable in the apartments in the Olympic Village and wanted to leave the country. The terrorists stated that negotiations could continue in Egypt, and the Israeli government could fly the released prisoners there. If this demand was not met, the men stated they would kill all of the hostages.

The German government had to go through with the plan the terrorists demanded, primarily because they had no other alternative, but they also had no intentions of allowing the plane to leave the airport. German officials would transport the hostages and their captors to the airport. Once at the airport, the plan was for two squads of police to ambush them. Thirteen officers, dressed as airline personnel, would take out the first group of terrorists when they came aboard to inspect the plane. A second squad of sharpshooters would take out the rest of the terrorists, who would still be with the hostages. Additionally, armored personnel carriers would strike the second group at the same time, allowing the hostages to be liberated.

Because protesters were blocking the streets, the Germans changed the plan for getting to the airport and suggested that the terrorists take a helicopter at 9:00 p.m. Suspecting a trap, the gunmen insisted on a full-sized bus to transport them between the apartment and two Bell helicopters. The hostages were bound and blindfolded, and then led to the awaiting vehicle at 10:05 p.m. Four hostages and four terrorists got on the first helicopter, and five hostages and four terrorists loaded on the second. For the first time, the German authorities realized there were eight heavily armed terrorists. They had previously thought there were only five. Unfazed by the additional information, they determined they would stay with their plan.

The two helicopters lifted off, taking the hostages and their captors to the airport. A third helicopter arrived to transport the German and Israeli officials. They boarded the aircraft and also headed to the airport, landing 10 minutes ahead of the first two helicopters, which were sent on a longer route. The officials headed directly for the control tower. When the helicopters carrying the terrorists and hostages landed, two terrorists jumped out and headed to the waiting Boeing 707, while four other terrorists stood guard outside the helicopters. Unknown to the leaders of the rescue, the German unit charged with taking out the terrorists when they boarded the plane had abandoned their posts, fearing for their lives. The first terrorists inspected the plane. They immediately noticed that it did not seem ready for flight, and they headed back to the main group. As they exited the aircraft, six of the eight terrorists were in plain sight, vulnerable to the sharpshooters, who took no action because they could not see two of the Palestinians.

At this point, Manfred Schreiber, the head of the Munich police, ordered two of the sharpshooters to engage the terrorists guarding the helicopters. They succeeded in critically injuring one man, but the other terrorists rolled under the aircraft and returned fire. The other sharpshooters engaged, wounding another one of the terrorists with a shot to the foot, and the encounter turned into an all-out firefight. In the melee, the lights illuminating the airport were destroyed, throwing the area into darkness. The Israeli officials in the control tower wanted to charge the terrorists, but the German authorities insisted that they wait for armored vehicles to arrive for more cover. Unfortunately, the armored vehicles had not yet been ordered to move from their initial locations near the Olympic Village, and they were now completely surrounded by vehicles of curious bystanders and journalists. The firefight settled into a standoff.

After nearly an hour and a half of sporadic gunfire, the armored vehicles arrived, and momentum shifted to the Germans. The Black September fighters realized this as well, and unwilling to leave the hostages alive, pulled the pins on grenades and heaved them into the helicopters, igniting fuel tanks and starting a raging fire. Another of the terrorists sprayed the hostages in the helicopter with automatic gunfire. The remaining terrorists fled from the scene. Police officers fired at the fleeing figures, hitting several and capturing three alive. When the crisis was over, all of the Israeli athletes and coaches were dead, five of the terrorists were killed, and three of the terrorists had been captured. Initial news reports published worldwide stated that the hostages had been saved and that the terrorists had been killed. ABC broadcaster Jim McKay received the correction live while on air at 3:24 a.m. the next day.

In the years that followed the Munich massacre, Palestinian authorities charged the Israeli government with covertly assassinating each of the men who participated in the plan carried out against the Israeli athletes. The Israelis denied this accusation, but the terrorist plot and the retribution carried out against the Palestinians has been relived many times in Hollywood movies, including *Munich* (2005), *21 Hours at Munich* (1976), and several documentaries such as *One Day in September* (1999) and *Munich '72 and Beyond* (2016).

Further Reading
Klein, Arron J. *Striking Back: The 1972 Munich Massacre and Israel's Deadly Response.* New York: Random House Publishing, 2007.

Reeve, Simon. *One Day in September: The Full Story of the 1972 Munich Olympics Massacre and the Israeli Revenge Operation Wrath of God.* New York: Arcade Publishing, 2011.

Mussolini, Benito

Conflict: World War II
Captured: July 25, 1943
Rescued: September 12, 1944

Benito Mussolini, born on July 29, 1883, in Predappio, Italy, was the ruler of Italy in 1922, and over the years, changed a democracy into a dictatorship. Head of the National Fascist Party, Mussolini steered policies and practices toward a one-party dictatorship by 1925. He ruled for more than 20 years, but a series of military disasters in North Africa and Greece, and then the Allied invasion of the Mediterranean, had proven his undoing. King Victor Emmanuel ousted Mussolini on July 25, 1943. Mussolini was arrested and confined to a series of prisons throughout the country. German Nazi leader Adolf Hitler knew that without Mussolini in command, Italy would fall under the control of the Allies, and that was not a setback Germany could afford. Hitler needed someone to mount a rescue operation, free Mussolini, and put him back in charge of Italy. Hitler chose Otto Skorzeny for the mission.

Skorzeny came to the attention of German high command while assigned in Austria. He demonstrated bravery while putting down a confrontation there, and Skorzeny was charismatic and a hard worker. When Hitler demanded the creation of a new combat unit, one of his mentors, Ernst Kaltenbrunner, recommended Skorzeny to lead the unit. Skorzeny was in Berlin training his men when he found out that Hitler wanted to see him at the Wolf's Lair in Rastenburg, East Prussia. A plane took him to the vicinity of the headquarters, and a car took him to meet the Fuhrer. Skorzeny was one of six men interviewed for the job of rescuing Mussolini, but he soon won the confidence of Hitler. Hitler told him the mission must be absolutely kept quiet, and that he would report directly to General Kurt Student. Hitler dismissed him, and Skorzeny walked out of the office to another room where he met with Student and head of the Gestapo and Waffen SS, Reichsfuhrer Heinrich Himmler, both of whom reiterated the importance of the mission. When Himmler left, Student and Skorzeny began planning the operation.

The first problem was to find Mussolini, whose location was not known. It took four weeks, but they eventually found where he was being held through intercepted radio messages. Mussolini was being held at Gran Sasso, a hotel near the village of Assergi. The rescuers conducted a series of reconnaissance flights to acquire information without alerting the guards, and the high altitude made gathering usable intelligence more difficult. The hotel was high on a mountaintop, but there was a small field near the hotel. There was also a small railway system that connected the local village to the hotel. Skorzeny proposed to land gliders in the field near the hotel with his commandos, while sending a battalion of German infantry on the tram to the hotel.

The day of the rescue was set for September 12, and things began to go wrong immediately. The operation was set to begin at 7:00 a.m., but the gliders did not show up until 11:00 a.m. The operation finally launched at 1:00 p.m. Of the 12 gliders, the first two hit potholes in the runway and could not take off due to fog and clouds, but Skorzeny did not know this. Next, the field he thought he had seen from 20,000 feet was actually a steep incline with rocks and boulders. It was a terrible place to land gliders, but the team had no choice; they crash-landed their aircraft onto the field.

The commandos initiated the operation so quickly that the Italian soldiers guarding the dictator had no chance to react. The communications room was destroyed and the guard force was overwhelmed. Skorzeny found Mussolini and demanded the immediate surrender of the Italian force. The Italian commander left the room and returned with two glasses of wine. He toasted the victor, ending the confrontation. No shots had been fired.

Benito Mussolini, prime minister of Italy from 1922 to 1943, was aligned with Adolf Hitler, which led to Italy's defeat and his downfall. (The Illustrated London News Picture Library)

By this point, the infantry had also arrived on the railway system. Getting Mussolini out of the alpine prison was now the primary concern. The only option was to bring a small plane into the rock-strewn field and evacuate the dictator. A Fieseler Fi 156 Stork landed, but it had only two seats and Skorzeny insisted on leaving with Mussolini and the pilot. After several minutes of protest, the pilot finally relented, and the three of them climbed into the plane. Although the plane's load was over limit, the pilot was able to take off and take the dictator and Skorzeny to Rome and then Berlin.

Hitler put Mussolini in charge of a puppet regime in Italy, but his return to power was short-lived. In late April 1945, Mussolini attempted to leave Italy for Switzerland, but he was captured and executed on April 28, 1945, by his own countrymen.

After the rescue of Mussolini, Skorzeny had a long military career. He was tried for war crimes in 1945, was acquitted, and left for Argentina, where he advised Egypt's President Nassar and Argentina's president, Juan Perón. Skorzeny also served as a bodyguard for Eva Perón. He died of cancer in Argentina on July 5, 1975.

Books and movies about Mussolini's life are prevalent, including *The Last Days of Mussolini* (1977) and *Mussolini: The Churchill Conspiracies* (2011). Several documentaries have also been made.

Further Reading

Bosworth, R. J. B. *Mussolini's Italy: Life under the Fascist Dictatorship, 1915–1945.* New York: Penguin, 2002.

Hibbert, Christopher. *Mussolini: The Rise and Fall of Il Duce.* New York: Little, Brown, 1962.

McRaven, William H. "Operation Oak: The Rescue of Benito Mussolini, 12 September 1943." In *Spec Ops: Case Studies in Special Operations Warfare: Theory and Practice.* Novato, CA: Presidio Press, 1996.

O'Grady, Scott

War: Bosnian War
Shot Down: June 2, 1995
Rescued: June 8, 1995

Scott O'Grady was born on October 12, 1965, in Brooklyn, New York, and graduated from high school across the country in Spokane, Washington. He knew from a young age that he wanted to fly airplanes, and he attended Embry-Riddle Aeronautical University in Prescott, Arizona. He did well enough in his course work to be selected for Air Force pilot training, where he qualified for assignment in the F-16. His first deployment was in Korea, and from there he rotated to a unit in Germany, and when that squadron deactivated, went on to Aviano, Italy. Part of the mission in Italy was to back up the United Nations Peacekeeping force on the ground and to enforce a no-fly zone during the Bosnian War.

When O'Grady and another pilot took off in two F-16s on June 2, 1995, he had already flown 46 missions over Bosnia with no particularly interesting stories to tell. Only one aircraft had been lost before that mission, a Harrier from the British Royal Air Force, and the pilot had returned to base the same day. Leading the flight of F-16s that day was Robert "Wilbur" Wright, call sign Basher Five-One. O'Grady's call sign was Basher Five-Two. They took off at 1:15 p.m., and the mission seemed to involve just another routine flight. Although a surface-to-air missile was always a possibility during combat, the pilots did not know that a Bosnian Serb unit had moved an antiaircraft artillery battery into the area they were patrolling. In fact, tensions between NATO and the Bosnian forces had increased to the point that NATO had recalled the 24th Marine Expeditionary Unit (MEU) back to the Adriatic Sea from exercises in Sardinia. The pilots were unaware of this recent development.

The first hint that something may have changed was when Wright had a threat alert that a radar may have locked on to him. Wright reported the threat to Magic, NATO's airborne early warning aircraft, but they could not verify the information. They chocked it up to a false alarm. Three minutes later, O'Grady received a threat on his warning system. Somebody on the ground had hit him with an acquisition radar, the kind used with surface-to-air missiles. After five seconds, the audible alarm turned off as programmed, but the threat was still likely to be out there. A second later, O'Grady got a new signal. Someone had locked onto his aircraft with a target-tracking radar, the kind that guided a missile to its target. O'Grady tried evasive maneuvers, but nine seconds after getting the first warning, O'Grady saw a bright flash of a missile exploding beside his aircraft. A second later he felt the impact of a second missile hitting his plane from below, cutting it in half. Two

Scott O'Grady (center) speaks at a press conference after being rescued in Bosnia in 1995. Captain Thomas Hanford (left) made the initial radio contact, and Captain Robert Wright (right) was flying lead on the day O'Grady was shot down. (U.S. Department of Defense)

separate halves of the aircraft spun toward the earth. He ejected from the aircraft and tumbled toward the ground. As gravity and the parachute fought for control, the falling aviator had time to pull out his radio and try to contact friendly forces to let them know he had ejected safely. His attempts came to nothing. Nobody knew he had survived the missile's impact. As he floated down, he could see a military truck and a car on a highway, waiting for him near his probable landing site. He did not know it, but within hours, the men and women of the 24th MEU were on full alert, even remaining fully dressed to enable a quicker response, should that prove necessary.

O'Grady did not land on the road, but he was not far from it. He knew that he had only a few minutes to get out of his parachute harness and begin evading those who would try to capture him. He took off at a sprint, trying to put as much distance between himself and his pursuers as possible, but he was out of breath and knew his sprint was making it easier for the soldiers behind to track him. He found a growth of thick trees, jumped into it, and tried to cover himself as best he could, giving himself time to plan an escape route. He saw a pair of civilian men within minutes, armed with rifles and heading down the same path he had taken, missing him by only five feet. How they did not detect him, O'Grady did not know. He stayed in that position for about six hours, until he felt it was safe to move to a better hiding place.

O'Grady had only moved a short distance that first night; his priority was to find a good hiding place away from the highway. He found one, and he was grateful when two more men walked right through the previous spot and again only missed stepping on him by five feet. He stayed there for a day, resting and trying to make contact with friendly forces, but he was unable to do so. He knew he had to move farther on the third day, putting distance between himself, the road, and his parachute. O'Grady planned to move toward a large hill that appeared more secluded and might offer his small radio a better chance of contacting a nearby aircraft. He began his trek when it was fully dark, and made it about a mile before he found a spot with good vegetation for concealment. During his fourth day on the ground, he collected rainwater with a sponge. That night, he tried the radio constantly, hoping to make contact with friendly forces. He activated the emergency beacon, audible to overhead aircraft, and monitored the first English transmission since landing on the ground. Someone had heard his beacon signal and was trying to contact him, although he could not communicate with his small radio. Though he was unable to make specific communications, he left the area sure that NATO knew he was alive.

The next day, O'Grady saw two cows and their owner, and he knew he had to move again so as not to risk a confrontation. Again, he went only a short distance—he was only two miles from his parachute harness—but the enemy forces had no idea where he was, and this was the best site he had found in his five days on the ground. There was a nearby clearing for an extraction site, should a rescue team be able to get to him.

He was determined to make contact with a patrolling aircraft that night, making numerous calls on his radio. At some point, he heard clicks, similar to the sounds made when someone tapped a microphone. Captain Thomas Hanford, Basher One-One, was orbiting the area, hoping to make contact with O'Grady, who had set his radio on "beacon" mode again, broadcasting a signal that anyone could detect. At 1:40 a.m., Hanford heard the beacon calls from O'Grady. And then Hanford heard the call: "Basher One-One, this is Basher Five-Two." As he got closer, communication improved until the two men actually spoke to each other, exchanging information on O'Grady's whereabouts. Unknown to either of them, Colonel Martin Berndt on the USS *Kearsarge* was also listening to the conversation. A half an hour later, a call from the NATO commander for southern Europe put the 24th MEU on alert status, setting in motion one of the largest and quickest rescue missions in modern history.

At 3:37 a.m., Colonel Berndt reported to NATO headquarters that his unit would be ready to depart in less than an hour. He assured his commander that he could complete the rescue operation in daylight, if NATO would include more air support, which they agreed to do. By 4:10 a.m., Basher One-One told O'Grady that the rescue mission was under way, some aircraft were airborne, and NATO was committed to getting him out that day. At 4:39 a.m., the decision was final: the Marines were closer to the extraction point and had the support of NATO. They would get O'Grady out.

Basher One-One called to say he was going to return to base at 5:00 a.m., and he handed O'Grady off to Rock Four-One, a pilot whose voice O'Grady recognized as a pilot from a sister squadron from Aviano. At 5:05 a.m., the rescue force lifted off the USS *Kearsarge,* waiting to rendezvous with NATO air support, which consisted of F-16 and F-15 fighters, FA-18s with radar-killing missiles, A-10 tank killers, and EF-111s and EA-6 Prowlers to jam enemy radar. Also on station were eight tankers to meet the fuel needs of all aircraft. By 5:41 a.m., the aircraft had assembled and were inbound to get O'Grady, and at 5:45 a.m., Rock Four-One communicated this to O'Grady, saying the force should be over his position in 10 to 15 minutes. At 5:49 a.m., the task force was over the Bosnian coast.

Just 11 minutes later, O'Grady heard the sound of two F-18 Hornets coming in low and fast over his position. They were marines, and their job was to confirm O'Grady's position and clear out any resistance. One of the Hornet pilots informed him at 6:35 a.m. that the rescue team should be there in about 2 minutes, and not long after, O'Grady heard the distinct sounds of helicopter blades making their way toward him. Two U.S. Marine Corps Cobra gunships appeared, the lead pilot telling O'Grady to pop smoke, a method to visually mark his position for the CH-53 Sea Stallion helicopters on their way to pick him up. Moments later, two huge helicopters appeared a short distance away; O'Grady ran toward the aircraft, seeing a crew chief waving him in. O'Grady boarded the helicopter and the rescue team took off, taking fire on the way out. They were back over the ocean at 7:15 a.m. and landed back aboard the USS *Kearsarge* at 7:29 a.m. Scott O'Grady was going home to a hero's welcome, thanks to hundreds of people involved in the rescue effort.

O'Grady's experience was part of a documentary shown on the National Geographic Channel, and it was also covered in *Escape! Escape from Bosnia: The Scott O'Grady Story* on the History Channel. Additionally, the 2001 film *Behind Enemy Lines* also was loosely based on his experiences. As of this writing, O'Grady lives in Texas.

Further Reading
Kelly, Mary Pat. *"Good to Go": The Rescue of Capt. Scott O'Grady, USAF, from Bosnia.* Annapolis, MD: Naval Institute Press, 1996.
O'Grady, Scott, and Jeff Coplon. *Return with Honor.* New York: Doubleday, 1998.
O'Grady, Scott, and Michael French. *Basher Five-Two: The True Story of F-16 Fighter Pilot Captain Scott O'Grady.* New York: Doubleday, 1995.

Operation Barras

Conflict: Sierra Leone
Captured: August 25, 2000
Rescued: September 10, 2000

In 2000, Sierra Leone, a former British colony in West Africa, had been the site of violent unrest for decades. The combination of wealth from diamonds, gold, and other valuable minerals coupled with an unstable government provided the formula for perpetual crisis in the region. A civil war raged in Sierra Leone between 1991 and 2000, when the Revolutionary United Front (RUF) opposed the government. The British army was stationed there to evacuate foreign nationals caught up in the fighting and to rebuild the Sierra Leone army. The 1 Royal Irish, a regiment of the British army, was performing this duty in the summer of 2000.

On August 25, 2000, a small group of 11 men from the 1 Royal Irish Regiment, plus an official from the Sierra Leone army acting as interpreter, met with Jordanian peacekeepers attached to the United Nations Mission in Sierra Leone. One of the Jordanian officials told the commander of the British patrol, Major Alan Marshall, that the West Side Boys, an armed group of men, sometimes referred to as a splinter faction of the Armed Forces Revolutionary Council, had begun to disband. This independent militia organization was heavily involved in fighting during the civil war, and Marshall decided to see for himself if rumors of their demise were true. He led his patrol to the location of the West Side Boys, where he was immediately beaten and the entire patrol taken prisoner. They were taken by canoes on the Rokel Creek to Gberi Bana, a village on the other side of the river.

Negotiations began between the British and the West Side Boys, and on August 31, the motley band released five hostages in exchange for a satellite phone and medical supplies. The spokesperson for the West Side Boys used the phone to contact the British Broadcasting Corporation (BBC) to outline their demands, which included the renegotiation of the Lomé Peace Accord and the release of their comrades held in Sierra Leone prisons. The British military used the satellite phone to trace the location of the West Side Boys and the hostages from the 1 Royal Irish.

The British were concerned about the increasingly erratic behavior of the militiamen. They knew that this militia group used drugs regularly, which contributed to their unpredictable conduct. One of the West Side Boys' leaders conducted mock executions of the hostages, confirming that the soldiers were in grave danger. Planning for a rescue began in earnest.

British intelligence had shown that the West Side Boys were in two locations, Gberi Bana and Magbeni, and they would require additional forces besides the special forces (SAS). Additional troops in England, specifically, A Coy, 1 PARA, were notified that they were to participate in the operation. The company was moved to Dakar, Senegal, to continue planning and to reduce reaction time. Meanwhile, SAS patrols were sending intelligence to the planning staffs, allowing A Coy to focus on its responsibility, the village of Magbeni, where a large contingent of militia soldiers lived. This attack would serve as a diversion to the main effort of rescuing the hostages, as well as prevent the West Side Boys from getting reinforcements from their comrades across the river. The SAS focused on the village of Gberi Bana, where the 1 Royal Irish soldiers were held. As planning progressed, it became clear that road and river approaches to the villages were heavily defended, requiring helicopter insertion for the operation.

On September 9, 2000, the SAS units that were watching the target locations reported that they had not seen the hostages in four days, and there was concern that the militia group would move to a new operations area soon, perhaps leading to the execution of the prisoners. These revelations increased the need to launch the assault without delay. The next day, the operation was ordered, code-named Operation Barras. The operation called for the rescue of the remaining British soldiers in the 1 Royal Irish, plus the interpreter from the Sierra Leone army, as well as a group of Sierra Leone civilians.

The rescue force took off from their initial positions at 6:15 a.m. and went into a holding pattern out of visual and audible range from the target locations. The delay allowed the SAS observation teams to get into position to prevent the execution of prisoners before the rescue teams were on the ground. The first helicopters to arrive at Gberi Bana were two Lynx attack helicopters that strafed the village, followed by two Chinook helicopters, carrying the SAS soldiers who fast roped into the village—a technique that required only leather gloves and a rope to get the soldier from the helicopter onto the ground. The West Side Boys immediately engaged the British, who returned fire. The British quickly took the village and either killed or captured the enemy combatants in less than 20 minutes. They liberated the soldiers and the interpreter, as well as 22 Sierra Leone civilians.

A third Chinook carried half of A Coy to the village of Magbeni, where the soldiers simply jumped to the ground from the low hovering aircraft. The Chinook returned with the other half of the unit, and took heavy machine gun fire on its return. The orbiting Lynx helicopters took the gun out of action. Once the company formed up, an explosion wounded seven men on the ground. Soldiers called back one of the Chinook helicopters and the wounded were loaded aboard. The helicopter then landed in the vicinity of Gberi Bana and took on the Royal Irish soldiers, all of whom were flown to the ship, *Sir Percivale,* for medical attention.

Meanwhile, at Magbeni, the company attacked each of the buildings in the village. The soldiers secured the ammunition store for the West Side Boys almost immediately, cleared each of the buildings, and set up blocking positions to prevent the reinforcement of the village. Once the village was secure, the men spread out into the jungle, looking for members of the West Side Boys who might be hiding there. They destroyed the weapons and vehicles that belonged to the militia group, and then recovered the vehicles belonging to the 1 Royal Irish soldiers.

One British soldier, Bradley Tinnion, was killed, and 12 were injured. The British military reported that 25 members of the militia organization were killed, but historians suspect the number may have been much higher, as many of the West Side Boys ran into the jungle and many were wounded. Within two weeks of the operation, 371 individuals surrendered to the Jordanian peacekeepers. The West Side Boys were finished as a revolutionary group, and many of their number later volunteered to serve in the Sierra Leone army. Many of the British soldiers were awarded honors for their service in the mission.

Further Reading
Butcher, Tim. *Chasing the Devil: The Search for Africa's Fighting Spirit.* London: Chatto & Windus/Penguin Random House UK, 2010.
Fowler, Will. *Certain Death in Sierra Leone: The SAS and Operation Barras.* New York: Osprey Publishing, 2010.

Operation Chavín de Huántar

Conflict: Terrorism
Captured: December 17, 1996
Rescued: April 22, 1997

For 126 days, starting on December 17, 1996, hundreds of Japanese diplomats, government officials, military officials, and business men and women were taken hostage while they were attending a party at the Japanese ambassador's residence in Lima, Peru. Fourteen members of the Tupac Amaru Revolutionary Movement (MRTA) who had planned the ambush were responsible for the hostage crisis. The MRTA had been functioning as a guerrilla group for about 15 years, and it had never attempted an operation of this scale. While all the guests were celebrating the emperor's birthday, the MRTA used explosives to blast a hole in the heavily fortified wall of the ambassador's compound at 8:20 p.m. Though the wall was 12 feet thick and all windows were covered with grates and had bulletproof glass, the MRTA was still able to get inside and take hostages. After the initial shoot-out, talks began for the release of the hostages. When news of the attack became public, the Lima Stock Exchange closed early as stocks dropped dramatically. The situation negatively impacted the economy, which had only recently recovered from terrorist activity in the 1980s.

Within a short time, the MRTA guerillas released the foreign female hostages after the initial takeover. However, a number of hostages were held for 126 days within the Japanese ambassador's residence. As the crisis continued, the president of Peru, Alberto Fujimori, addressed the situation five days after it began, going on television and condemning the MRTA and their demands. He refused assistance from foreign advisers and said publicly that he would work for a peaceful resolution. The leader of the MRTA, Nestor Cerpa Cartolini, then stated he would release any hostages outside of those who worked with the Peruvian government. True to his word, most of the foreign ers were released after five days. For the first few days, the International Red Cross brokered talks between the Peruvian government and the MRTA. Many high-profile members of Peru's security forces were involved, including Maximo Rivera, the head of Peru's antiterrorist forces, and the former chief, Carlos Dominguez. Seventy-two hostages continued to be held by the MRTA, including two members of President Fujimori's family. The members of the MRTA had specific demands that they relayed to the government.

To end the hostage situation, the insurgents demanded that any of the MRTA members imprisoned in Peru be released, that the government revise market reforms and address economic inequalities, and that conditions in Peru's prisons be improved. One of the people that the MRTA leadership demanded be released was their leader, Cartolini's, wife. Even some of the released embassy hostages, including Javier Diez Canseco, who was in one of the first groups released, carried the MRTA demands forward and encouraged the government to work toward a peaceful resolution. Another freed hostage, Alejandro Toledo, similarly asked for amnesty for the MRTA members, and feared that a forced rescue would be difficult if not catastrophic to the remaining hostages. He spoke of large weapons caches and explosive capabilities that the guerillas had within the ambassador's residence. He also told authorities that the group had antitank weapons and wore backpacks full of explosives that were, in essence, suicide bombing equipment.

Fujimori did coordinate a team to negotiate with the MRTA, including the Canadian ambassador, Anthony Vincent, another released hostage, the Red Cross, and religious leaders. Fujimori also included Cuban leader Fidel Castro, which some concluded meant that he was looking for a place to send the MRTA guerillas as

The Japanese ambassador's residence in Peru was engulfed in smoke when Peruvian special forces stormed the building to rescue 72 hostages in April 1997. (The Asahi Shimbun via Getty Images)

political exiles. For a little less than a month, until January 17, the group negotiated for the release of the remaining hostages, but they were unable to come to an agreement. By the first part of February, the Peruvian government brought in troops stationed around the area, playing loud music and aggressively taunting the MRTA, who engaged in a firefight with the troops. The Japanese government intervened at this time, with the prime minister publicly requesting that the Peruvian government not put the hostages' lives in danger and to reach a negotiated settlement. The Peruvian president, Fujimori, met with the Japanese prime minister, Ryutaro Hashimoto, in Canada, and they reported that they had come to a consensus on how to proceed with the hostage crisis. After this meeting, Fujimori flew to London, where he asked for a country to give asylum to the guerillas, which contradicted what he had said before.

Also at this time, the main Peruvian newspaper, *La Republica,* ran a story detailing secret plans for a government intervention with the help of the U.S. military. The story, which ran on February 17, seemed to be corroborated in a *New York Times* article, which also told of U.S. involvement, working in concert with the Peruvian army. Newspapers also reported that the government was digging tunnels beneath the walls and into the compound, and this caused the MRTA to stop negotiations, because they knew that the government was attempting to tunnel into the residence. Even the loud music being played from the military and the noise of the tanks did not cover the commotion of the digging beneath the residence.

Throughout the hostage crisis, supplies had been sent in to the hostages and MRTA. Within those supplies, messages and light clothing had been sent in to help prepare the hostages for the coming rescue attempt. The hostages were to wear the light-colored clothing to help the rescue teams know who was MRTA and who was not, and hostages were also told to stay away from the MRTA members if possible. Also, the military had managed to send in microphones and cameras, which were put around the house for listening in on the guerrillas and understanding their plans. The military leaders knew, from these devices, that night raids were not likely to be successful, but knew that the group liked to play soccer in the afternoons.

Four months after the initial raid on the compound, on April 22, 1997, 140 Peruvian soldiers undertook a raid on the residence. In mid-afternoon, Operation Chavín de Huántar was initiated. Military leaders coordinated three explosions at the same time. The first hit the room where the soccer game was held. The wall was destroyed and soldiers ran into the building, going after the MRTA members before they could harm the rescuers. At the same time, soldiers attacked the front door area, heading into the foyer where the main staircase was located. And in the third portion of the attack, more soldiers came from the tunnels located below the backyard.

The large number of soldiers overtook the guerillas, and by the end of the raid, all of the MRTA guerrillas, one hostage, and two soldiers were dead. The Peruvian media took video of the aftermath, including the released hostages singing the national anthem and President Fujimori walking through the residence. The bodies of the dead MRTA guerillas were photographed, and those images were shared. The freed hostages were taken from the residence by bus. The government actions were popular within the country, with about a 70 percent approval rating.

Internationally, reactions were more mixed. Some hostage reports claimed that the several guerillas had tried to surrender, but they were executed. Several criminal cases resulted after the escape. In 2002, several years after the rescue, additional trials and a review of the operation were conducted. A military tribunal cleared those involved of any wrongdoing. The hostage situation has been retold in movies and documentaries, including *Lima: Breaking the Silence* (1999) and *Endgame: The Untold Story of the Hostage Crisis in Peru* (1999). Ann Patchett's novel, *Bel Canto*, is a loose fictionalized interpretation of the events.

Further Reading

Brewer, Paul. *The Lima Embassy Siege and Latin American Terrorism: Terrorism in Today's World.* New York: Gareth Stevens Publishing, 2006.

Giampietri, Luis, Bill Salisbury, and Lorena Ausejo. *41 Seconds to Freedom.* New York: Presidio Press, 2007.

"Japanese Hostage Crisis and Operation Chavin de Huantar." *En Peru,* August 18, 2008. http://enperublog.com/2008/08/18/japanese-hostage-crisis-and-operation-chavin-de-huantar/.

Operation Dragon Rouge

Conflict: Terrorism
Captured: Various
Rescued: November 24, 1964

Operation Dragon Rouge was one of the largest hostage rescue operations ever undertaken and occurred in 1964 in the Democratic Republic of the Congo by Belgian and U.S. military forces. Hundreds of hostages, prisoners of the Communist Simba rebels, were being held in Stanleyville (now known as Kisangani). This rebel group, known as Simba or "Basimba," was named in reference to lions (Swahili), and the rebels were often young men or even teens, recruited from the eastern parts of the Congo. An uprising in the Belgian Congo began in 1964 and was influenced by the Communist bloc. On August 5, 1964, the Simbas of the Popular Liberation Army seized Stanleyville, which was the third largest city in the region. The Simbas were carrying out a rebellion against the Congolese government, and because of their beliefs, they thought they were impervious to bullets due to their powerful medicine. However, the Leopoldville government, which was backed by the U.S. and other Western nations, was working to stop the Simba rebellion. Because bullets did indeed stop the rebels, as the Simbas faced defeat, they began taking white hostages. Several hundred of these hostages were in the Victoria Hotel in Stanleyville. Needing assistance with the situation, the Leopoldville government asked the U.S. and Belgian governments for assistance. When negotiations failed, planning for a large rescue operation began.

By the fall of 1964, the Simbas had captured much of the Congo. They had killed thousands of Congolese citizens and dozens of white missionaries, priests, nuns, and other Westerners who lived in the nation. What the Simbas lacked in military training, they made up for in determination, and they were surprisingly effective against the Armee Nationale Congolaise (ANC). Although the Simbas acquired guns and supplies from Soviet and Chinese sources, most of the rebel weapons had been taken from the ANC.

The Simbas treated their hostages well at first, but when they suffered military setbacks at the hands of Major Michael "Mad Mike" Hoare and his band of Wild Geese mercenaries, the situation became ominous. The mercenaries were largely South African, Rhodesian, French, and Belgian, but the Simbas were convinced their adversaries were Americans, whom they particularly hated. The Simbas executed over 250 Congolese prisoners in Stanleyville, and executed thousands more in cities throughout the nation. As the number of killings increased, the rebels became emboldened, executing Westerners, including women and children. Unless something was done, many feared the Simbas would execute the 1,600 white hostages being held in Stanleyville. The Congolese government requested help from Western nations, including the United States.

President Lyndon Johnson, in response to the Congolese request, sent Joint Task Force Leo, which consisted of one platoon of paratroopers from the 82nd Airborne, and insisted the team get White House approval before firing their weapons. Belgian, American, and African diplomats discussed the various solutions, finally deciding on a course of action, code-named Operation Dragon Rouge. The plan was a three-phase operation involving 12 American C-130 aircraft. In Phase I, 545 Belgian paratroops would load into the aircraft in Belgium. In Phase II, they would fly to a staging area in the Democratic Republic of the Congo (DRC), and in the final phase, the Belgians would drop into Stanleyville to secure the hostages. The airborne support assault was also broken into three phases. First, five C-130 aircraft would drop 320 Belgian paratroopers onto the Stanleyville airport. Second, a half hour after the first assault, two more C-130 aircraft would land into the airport, bringing in eight armored jeeps. Finally, the final five aircraft would land with the remaining troops and supplies.

On November 24, 1964, as planned, five C-130 aircraft from the U.S. Air Force flew over the Sabena airport in Stanleyville, dropping the Belgian ParaCommando Regiment into the city. The men had a clear mission, which was to free approximately 1,600 European, Indian, Pakistani, and American hostages who were being held in the city. The soldiers seized the airport with minimal resistance and cleared the runway for the next landings. Word had gotten to the rescuers that the Simbas held some of the hostages in the Victoria Residence Hotel, and those hostages were in the most danger, because the Simbas were threatening to execute those individuals.

When the Simba rebels heard the planes flying over them and subsequently landing at the airport, they ordered all hostages into the street. Although 50 hostages had managed to hide inside the hotel, 250 men, women, and children were taken outside. When the Simba commander learned that Belgian paratroopers had indeed landed at the airport, he told his men to murder the hostages. The Belgian soldiers arrived in time to prevent much of the killing, but 2 little girls, 5 women, and 15 men were dead or dying, and 40 more hostages wounded. The Belgians took control of the area, and they began the work of rescuing hostages.

At the same time, two mercenary forces, totaling approximately 600 soldiers, had linked up and were fighting their way into Stanleyville. The soldiers of various nationalities rescued many Europeans and discovered many others who had also been murdered. The mercenary soldiers also killed thousands of Simbas as they moved into the city. While the Belgians focused on holding the airport and evacuating hostages, the mercenaries assumed the task of continuing to clear the city.

In all, Belgian and mercenary forces rescued over 2,000 foreign nationals and 300 Congolese citizens, taking those liberated to Leopoldville. Immediately after the hostage rescue in Stanleyville, Operation Dragon Noir took place in Paulis, where 255 Belgians landed in that city and prevented another massacre. Despite the presence of other Europeans throughout the country, the Belgians withdrew, their commander believing their number too small and the force too exhausted to effect more rescues. Hoare's forces remained behind, rescuing those that they could. An estimated 185 hostages were killed after Operation Dragon Rouge.

Further Reading
Wagoner, Fred E. *Dragon Rouge: The Rescue of Hostages in the Congo.* Honolulu: University Press of the Pacific, 2003.

Operation Dustoff

Conflict: Vietnam
Captured: 1962–1975
Rescued: 1962–1975

Although the Vietnam conflict was difficult on many fronts, one prominent issue was that there was no clear focus on mission. Many units were assigned to the conflict, but what they were supposed to do once they arrived in the area was not always clear. This was the case for one of the first helicopter medical support units sent to Vietnam, under the direction of Commander John Temperelli Jr.

When the unit arrived in South Vietnam, there was no place for them in Saigon, and they were ordered to report to Nha Trang. Temperelli was ordered to split up the helicopters to different locations, but given the difficulty in fueling and getting parts, after a year, he helped the unit settle in to Saigon and began to focus their mission. He nicknamed the unit "DUSTOFF," in reference to how the rotor blades of landing helicopters blow dust on everything. For wounded soldiers in Vietnam, a dustoff equaled rescue and evacuation. Dustoff and medical helicopter units in general were seen as symbols of hope. Soldiers expected that if they were wounded, that the dustoff crew would come and get them, regardless of the risks.

In 1963, the dustoff unit was relegated to the sidelines and not given a specific place on the base, so they claimed a piece of ground, painted a sign that read 57th MEDICAL DETACHMENT—HELICOPTER AMBULANCE, and stayed there. These medical helicopters were primarily HH-1Bs, more commonly known as Hueys. Pilots were aggressive and risk takers. In 1963, the unit also shifted to a two-pilot (pilot/copilot) model. This allowed for better navigation, as well as for a backup pilot, as it was not out of the realm of possibility that the pilot could be seriously wounded or killed while attempting a rescue.

In early 1964, Major Charles L. Kelly took over the dustoff unit from Temperelli. He learned that in the previous year, it had not been uncommon for flight crews

The UH-1 Huey helicopter was a welcome sight to an injured soldier in Vietnam, 1969. (PhotoQuest/Getty Images)

to fly 100 to 140 hours a month. The pilots quit tracking hours at 140 hours so they wouldn't be grounded. Also, the unit started the night flights in April of that year, flying over 110 hours at night in that month, and getting over 100 wounded soldiers out in those missions.

In July 1964, the dustoff pilots began to fight back against the vulnerability of their missions, and though a medical unit, they now requisitioned ammunition along with medicine. Their leader, Major Kelly, was killed July 1, 1964, in a dustoff mission near Vinh Long. Though repeatedly told to leave the area because of the heavy fighting, Kelly refused to do so. He was hit in the heart by gunfire. His copilot, Captain Dick Anderson, couldn't stop the helicopter from crashing. Another helicopter crew came in and rescued the survivors of that crash.

Captain Patrick Brady took over the unit at that point, and though he was told to take fewer risks, Brady pushed on in the aggressive style set by Kelly. In 1965, a tradition called "scarfing" was begun among the dustoff units, where they competed with each other to see who could get to the wounded first. They often went to known battle areas before they were called, so that they could be the unit to pick up wounded soldiers. This was not an official practice, but it contributed to the camaraderie and honor associated with these helicopter medical units. Although they were most known for picking up military injured, the dustoff crews also picked up wounded civilians and enemy soldiers. On at least one occasion, the medical personnel delivered a baby on the way to Saigon.

In September 1965, a bigger Huey, the UH-1D, was delivered. This helicopter had a much bigger weight limit and could hold 14 passengers or up to 4,000 pounds of weight. In early 1966, the hoist and other improvements also made it easier for the dustoff crews to do their work. The hoist, and in particular, the jungle penetrator basket, allowed the dustoff crews to hover over an area and retrieve wounded from very thick jungle areas.

The work of the dustoff crews cannot be overstated. They had an astounding 97.5 percent survival rate once getting the wounded out of harm's way. The value of the dustoff missions is critical to understanding the scope of the war. From 1962 until 1973, nearly 500,000 dustoff missions were flown, and over 900,000 patients were airlifted. As of this writing, about 100 pilots and medics from dustoff crews are still active in the Vietnam Dustoff Association.

Further Reading
Cook, J. L. *Rescue Under Fire: The Story of Dust Off in Vietnam.* Atglen, PA: Schiffer Military/Aviation History, 1998.
Vermillion, S., ed. Vietnam Dustoff Association. Retrieved October 10, 2017, from www.vietnamdustoff.com/home.html.
Vietnam Center and Archive. Lubbock, Texas: Texas Tech University, October 12, 2017.

Operation Halyard

Conflict: World War II
Captured: Various
Rescued: August 9–10, 1944

Operation Halyard involved getting American airmen out from behind enemy lines during World War II. In July 1944, the Office of Strategic Services (OSS) conceived a plan to rescue pilots who had been shot down over Yugoslavia. Over 400 airmen were in need of rescue, and the team, including the U.S. 15th Air Force and a team of Chetniks, part of the Yugoslavian army and led by General Draza Mihailovic, were called the Halyard team.

At the time the mission was being drafted, the 15th Air Force was the leading organization charged with destroying the oil fields in Romania, which was then under Nazi control. The petroleum was important to the Axis war effort; a third of all petroleum for the Nazi war efforts was coming from the fields in Romania, and the Nazis vigorously defended the fields. The main area, the Ploesti oil complex, was 19 square miles and contained oil wells, refineries, and enormous storage tanks. To destroy the complex would require a massive air campaign. The Allied aircrews suffered tremendous losses in pilots and equipment in their fight to destroy those oil wells. Sometimes Allied aircraft were destroyed in the air, and the crew was lost immediately. Sometimes when a plane was hit, the crews knew they had to bail out immediately, over or near the oil fields, where German soldiers on the ground were waiting to take them prisoner. Sometimes, however, pilots hoped to nurse a stricken aircraft back to Italy, but would have to abandon the airship on the way due to mechanical difficulties. In this scenario, the airmen would bail out over Yugoslavia, a nation at war with itself as much as it was at war with the Germans.

The government of Yugoslavia, which was involved in a civil war during the early 1940s, was torn between the Communists who supported Josip Broz Tito, and the royalists who supported Mihailovic. When the two sides were not fighting each other, they fought against the Nazis, who had invaded the nation in April 1941. When possible, both sides assisted the downed airmen who were forced to parachute into Yugoslavia and move them to safe havens within territory they controlled. The American pilots were greeted as liberators, and the Yugoslavs, including the poor, shared their food and shelter. Within months of the initial bombing raids on the oil fields, hundreds of American and Allied airmen were grounded in Yugoslavia, waiting for rescue.

Allied rescue attempts were difficult, however, because the British controlled the Allied forces in Yugoslavia, and they supported Tito and not Mihailovic. In fact, the British refused to rescue the airmen under Mihailovic's control, lest they inadvertently support his supporters and his forces. A Communist mole was feeding the British information that Mihailovic was a double agent, secretly working with the Germans. Any plan to rescue the Americans, this mole inferred, would be shared with the Germans, who would be waiting to curtail any rescue effort. The Communist mole was James Klugmann, a Soviet spy who worked with the infamous Cambridge Five, the group of Soviet operatives that included Kim Philby, Guy Burgess, Anthony Blunt, Donald Maclean, and John Cairncross.

While Mihailovic's forces had radio contact with the Americans in Italy, they ignored the messages reporting the accumulation of Allied fliers to keep peace with the British. Although the United States had no forces available to fight the Germans in the Balkans, they used special operations personnel to carry out small raids using partisan soldiers. The Office of Strategic Services (OSS) trained personnel to operate behind enemy lines, destroying enemy military capabilities and keeping the Germans occupied looking for partisans. George Vujnovich was the OSS head of operations for Yugoslavia, and he was determined to get the men out. George Musulin worked for Vujnovich and was an OSS operative in Yugoslavia performing his duties in the region that Mihailovic and his followers controlled. Musulin met many of the downed airmen when he traveled through the region, and he promised to get them out. The head of the OSS, William Donovan, convinced President Roosevelt to approve the rescue, despite the strenuous objections from the highest levels of the British government, including those of Prime Minister Winston Churchill. After Roosevelt's approval, the rescue mission was begun and was codenamed Operation Halyard.

With approval for the mission, the main problem the rescuers faced was the lack of an airfield suitable for landing the C-47, a plane that could carry 12 men but required a minimum of 700 yards of runway. The downed pilots and the local peasants were determined to remove this barrier. They located a relatively flat farm field that was 775 yards long, and they removed trees at one end. The group then leveled the potholes in the field, digging dirt from one end and smoothing out the surface elsewhere. When a German plane flew over the site, the workers took refuge in the woods until the plane passed overhead. Though the U.S. military initially sought to work with the British, the OSS decided that the conflict of interest with Britain was hindrance and continued alone. The reinserted George Musulin into Yugoslavia, and taxed him with getting the downed pilots ready for rescue. When Musulin returned to the area, he was surprised to find that over 500 downed airmen had been brought to the area from all over the Balkans.

Once the airstrip was completed, the mission began on August 9, 1944, and the men were put into groups of 12 for the flights out. The infirm were sent out first, followed by those who had been on the ground the longest. They planned to take out 72 men on the first pass. The mission took place at night, and those on the ground, including the locals, lit large pots and hay bales on fire to outline the runway. Four of the planes made it safely to the ground on the first pass, and the selected soldiers boarded the aircraft and then headed for Italy. Knowing that the Germans would eventually notice so many planes coming in to the region, the next morning, six additional C-47 planes landed, bringing with them an escort of P-51 and P-38 fighters to bomb German targets within 50 miles of the landing site, ensuring that the Germans would not bother them as they took out another round of downed pilots. This pattern of picking up soldiers and bombing German locations in the region continued until 272 Allied airmen had been rescued by the morning of August 10, 1944. Continued periodic rescue missions were flown as more Allied airmen showed up at the airfield, brought there by friendly partisans. In all, 512 Allied airmen eventually came out of Yugoslavia as part of Operation Halyard.

Further Reading
Freeman, Gregory A. *The Forgotten 500: The Untold Story of the Men Who Risked All for the Greatest Rescue Mission of World War II.* New York: Dutton Caliber, 2008.
Kelly, Lt. Cmdr. Richard M. "Behind the Enemy Lines Series: Halyard Mission." *Blue Book Magazine* 83, no. 4 (August 1946).

Operation Jericho

Conflict: World War II
Captured: Various
Rescued: February 18, 1944

Over the course of many months during World War II, the Germans had rounded up several hundred suspected resistance fighters, some of whom were scheduled for execution in late February. To show support for the French fighters, who the British depended upon for intelligence prior to the Normandy landings, the British agreed to carefully and precisely drop bombs on the wall that surrounded the Amiens Prison, the guardhouse where the majority of the German guards were housed, and Amiens Prison itself, allowing many prisoners to escape and avoid execution. Operation Jericho was the code name for this low-level bombing raid.

There was no single resistance organization to fight back against the Nazi occupation and brutality of the German forces that followed. However, many groups evolved on a local level, depending on the level of cruelty the Germans imposed and the opportunities to exact revenge against their occupiers. Some local resistance fighters helped to evacuate Allied fliers, others passed on intelligence information to British handlers, while others took active measures, such as blowing up rail systems or convoys. It was impossible for Nazis to infiltrate these small, local associations of resistance fighters. However, once they captured and turned a single informant, the resistance apparatus in a region might be devastated as the Nazis captured and interrogated many suspected freedom fighters. Those in the French

Resistance north of Paris that the Nazis rounded up could find themselves locked up in the prison at Amiens, where the Germans carried out interrogation, torture, and execution. The French government also controlled a portion of the prison where they also held common criminals. Just before the bombing raid on Amiens Prison, the Germans held 180 men and women suspected of resistance activities, while the French held over 650 prisoners for various criminal activities.

In early 1944, the British desperately needed to gather intelligence for planning the invasion into occupied France. A known resistance leader from Paris, Roland Farjon, came to work in Amiens Prison. Other resistance fighters vouched for him, but the Gestapo discovered his true identity and turned him to work for them, convincing him that the true danger to France were the Communist sympathizers. Farjon reported everything he knew about the resistance organization in Amiens to his new handlers. Armed with this information, Gestapo sweeps netted the suspects held in the prison in November 1943. A French Resistance leader named Dominique Ponchardier assembled the names of those associates incarcerated, handed it to his British counterparts, and demanded that something be done to rescue the men and women held in Amiens Prison. Additionally, two Allied intelligence officers had now been captured and sent to Amiens Prison, which added more urgency to the rescue request.

British intelligence processed the request up the chain of command, and the idea of a rescue was met with resistance. The British feared a large number of casualties or even reprisals against the French population. British authorities were further told that the execution of about 10 resistance fighters was imminent and there was nothing that could be done to save that group. However, many reasons surfaced to support the request of the resistance fighters, such as the need for intelligence on the V-1 rocket program, support of Operation Overlord (better known as the Battle of Normandy), continued assistance to downed Allied aircrews; in addition, a morale boost to the French was deemed more important than the other issues. Additionally, the estimates on the number of possible executions rose from 10 to over 100.

British authorities felt compelled to approve the request to assist the French, but turned over the details to their planning staff. The planners, in turn, soon admitted that a ground attack was foolish. It could never succeed due to overwhelming German numbers and would cause more problems than it solved. Then they turned to the idea of precision bombing. Almost jokingly, those planning the operation asked if the Royal Air Force (RAF) could blast a hole in the prison's outer wall, hit the guardhouse, kill a large number of German guards, and then hit the prison itself without killing the prisoners they intended to rescue. Surprisingly, the answer was in the affirmative, according to an RAF pilot on the planning staff. Planning for the operation took a decisive turn at that point.

Based on the assumption that the Germans would execute their prisoners as quickly as possible, there was little time between the planning and execution. Planners decided that noon was the best time to carry out the attack, as guards would be assembled for lunch while many of the prisoners would be out of their cells, performing other duties. For the operation, 18 Mosquito fighter bombers were designated to carry out the attack. The first wave of six planes would be flown by New

Zealanders of No. 487 Squadron. They would drop armor-piercing bombs to open a hole in the 20-foot-high northern and eastern outer walls and the guardhouse, where the German soldiers were located. It was also hoped that the concussion from the 500-pound bombs would knock the prison cell doors off their frames, allowing the prisoners to escape. The second wave of six aircraft, flown by the Australians of No. 464 Squadron, would drop bombs on southern and eastern walls, and it was also hoped the concussion in these locations would knock the doors out of their frames. The final six aircraft from the RAF's No. 21 Squadron would wait in reserve, in case the first two waves were not successful. Once the mission was under way, it proceeded as planned for the most part. In all, the two squadrons dropped 40 bombs on the target, 20 high-explosive bombs and 20 armor-piercing bombs. Of those bombs, 18 bounced off of the frozen ground and out of the prison, and 8 failed to detonate. However, enough of the bombs were on target and exploded with devastating results. The reserve force was not needed.

Although as many as 9 of the 20 German guards died in the attack, many of the prisoners were also killed. In total, 95 French citizens died and 87 more were badly wounded. After the rescue, the French insisted that they would rather have died by Allied bombs than by German bullets. The exact number of prisoners held in the prison is not known, as most of the records were destroyed in the bombing raid. However, it appears that around 200 prisoners managed to escape from Amiens Prison, although about two-thirds of them were eventually recaptured.

There were other losses associated with the operation. Three aviators were killed and one captured in the operation, one Mosquito fighter plane was shot down by a German FW-190, and one plane was brought down by antiaircraft fire. Additionally, two fliers from RAF Squadron No. 174, flying cover for the bombers, failed to return. It is assumed their plane went into the English Channel with mechanical difficulties. Allied troops discovered a mass grave in October 1944 from Amiens

---

The French Resistance

After Nazi Germany's occupation of France during World War II, small groups of resistors, men and women, pushed back against the invaders in any way they could. Shortly after the Battle of France in 1940, they began writing articles and published newspapers, provided intelligence information to the Allied forces, and created a network that helped Allied soldiers move from behind enemy lines and back to friendly territories. Just a number of small groups at first, in 1941, those groups began banding together to increase their effectiveness. Those in the French Resistance were seen as patriots serving their country, and in addition to helping the Allied forces, both those in advance and retreat, they also carried out sabotage activities on essential services, which limited the German's effectiveness. The efforts of the French Resistance also greatly helped with the Normandy invasion, setting the stage and providing effective intelligence to the Allied troops, often at great risk to themselves. The height of the resistance efforts, including helping Allied troops, was in 1944. By October 1944, the French Resistance numbered an estimated 400,000 men and woman, from a range of social classes and occupations, and some internal power struggles from the size of the organization. An estimated 10 percent of the French population was involved in the French Resistance at some point.

Prison, with bodies of many who decided not to make a run for freedom, but remained at the prison trying to rescue other prisoners covered with ruble. Others found in the grave were local townspeople killed by Germans who assumed they had tried to help the prisoners escape. The BBC ran a documentary on *Operation Jericho* in 2001.

Further Reading
Fishman, Jack. *And the Walls Came Tumbling Down*. London: MacMillan, 1983.
Lyman, Robert. *The Jail Busters: The Secret Story of MI6, the French Resistance, and Operation Jericho*. London: Quercus Publishing, 2015.

Operation Jonathan

Conflict: Terrorism
Captured: June 27, 1976
Rescued: July 4, 1976

On a Sunday afternoon, June 27, 1976, terrorists took control of Air France Flight AF 139 as it traveled from Tel Aviv, Israel, to Paris. Four hijackers—two Germans from the Baader-Meinhof Gang (German revolutionary cells), and two Palestinians from the Popular Front for the Liberation of Palestine—External Operations (PFLP-EO)—took control of the plane to demand the release of 53 militant prisoners held in various countries. The plane was diverted to Entebbe, in Uganda. Of the passengers, many were from Europe, including a number of French citizens, but a third of the 254 passengers were Israeli.

The Israeli government put the Sayeret Matkal Counterterrorist Unit—called The Unit—on alert as soon as they heard about the hijacking. Terrorists had previously returned their hijacked planes to Israel to make demands, and although the situation was fluid, those soldiers might be called upon to operate within the confines of the nation. The Unit waited to see how the situation unfolded. Few people thought the Israelis would see action when the plane touched down in Uganda at the airport just outside of Entebbe. The passengers were kept on the plane for nine hours while Ugandan dictator Idi Amin appeared to negotiate with the terrorists on behalf of the hostages. In the meantime, three more Palestinians joined the terrorists, making a total of seven hijackers.

The hijackers' warned that they would begin executing prisoners on July 1 if the 53 prisoners were not released. The Israeli cabinet ordered the military, and by extension, The Unit, to begin planning a military resolution. Military intervention was questionable for several reasons. The Israeli government still believed Idi Amin was working to free the hostages, the French government controlled the situation because it was their plane involved, and finally, the distance to the airport at Entebbe was thought too far for planning purposes. The Israeli cabinet announced the intended release of the prisoners requested by the terrorists, who replied with an extension on the execution of hostages until Sunday, July 4.

It soon became apparent to the Israelis that Amin was not the neutral negotiator he pretended to be, and over several days, some of the hostages were released, with the exception of 106 Jewish passengers, half of whom were Israeli. Although the

The safe return of an Israeli squadron leader pilot is celebrated after the freeing of Israeli hostages in July 1976. (David Rubinger/Corbis via Getty Images)

situation had turned dire, the viability of a rescue operation was uncertain, particularly given the deadline for executing hostages was only two days away. All the Israelis knew for certain was that the hostages were held in an old terminal building and that 60 to 100 Ugandan soldiers guarded the building. During this time, The Unit had been evaluating the situation and had developed a plan, which called for the requisition of four C-130 cargo planes, four Buffalo armored personnel carriers (APCs), a Mercedes, and two Land Rovers.

The plan was for the first C-130 to make a blacked-out landing and taxi to the north end of the runway. Along the way, a small team of soldiers would jump out and place landing lights along the runway for the follow-on aircraft. Once near the old terminal building where the hostages were held, the ramp would come down and 35 commandos, dressed as Ugandan soldiers, would depart in the Mercedes and Land Rover vehicles, proceeding to the terminal building with lights on. Once the first aircraft had landed, the Ugandan soldiers would recognize that something was taking place, and vehicles operating with their lights out would raise suspicions. Then, once the Israeli soldiers arrived at the old terminal building, they would split into three teams and assault the three entrances leading into the building, then wrest control of the building. Although the plan seemed straightforward, another complication arose. Two hundred yards east of the terminal building was a Ugandan military base. There were 1,000 soldiers stationed there and a squadron of MiG fighters. The second and third C-130 would discharge the Buffalo APCs to act as a blocking force between the terminal and military base, preventing the reinforcement of the terminal building. An infantry platoon would provide security for the aircraft, while the final C-130 would act as an aid station for wounded soldiers and provide transportation for the hostages.

All four aircraft arrived at Entebbe on time and with no difficulties. The first C-130 began its decent and then landed according to plan. The small detachment jumped out at the designated time and dropped the landing lights for the other planes, which had already begun their descent. The Mercedes and Land Rovers started their engines, and on command dropped out the back of the plane and approached the old terminal building. Two Ugandan soldiers appeared. The Israelis fired on them, and missed, inviting counterfire. Although the soldiers were killed, the other soldiers in the area were alerted by the gunfire. The Israelis hoped to take advantage of the confusion and headed for the old terminal building. Uncertainty reigned as the Israelis, dressed in Ugandan army uniforms, fired on the Ugandan soldiers.

The Israelis attacked through the entrances to the building and spread out. They immediately encountered enemy soldiers but quickly eliminated them. Almost immediately, the Israelis located and secured the hostages while other soldiers cleared the building. Unfortunately, three of the hostages were killed in the assault, but overall, the plan was successful. Within 3 minutes of the first C-130 hitting the ground, the remaining hostages were safe, and four of the seven terrorists were dead, as were a number of Ugandan soldiers. Within 15 minutes of the first plane landing, all of the terrorists were dead, the APCs had moved into position to block the movement of reinforcements from the enemy base, and the last plane was in position to receive the prisoners who were already on their way out of the terminal. While the hostages were loaded into the aircraft, the APCs took the opportunity to destroy eight MiG fighters lined up on the runway. Fifty-one minutes after the first plane had touched down at Entebbe, the first plane took off again, flying the hostages to freedom. Ninety-nine minutes after the first plane landed, the last of the C-130s took off with the last of the soldiers and equipment employed on the mission.

Originally called Operation Thunderbolt, the operation was renamed after the event to Operation Jonathon to honor unit leader Yonatan Netanyahu, the unit leader and only casualty of the event, and older brother of Israeli prime minister, Benjamin Netanyahu. Several books have been written about the rescue, and movies have also been released, including the *Raid on Entebbe* in 1976, *The Delta Force* in 1986, *Entebbe Hero: The Yoni Netanyahu Story* in 2014, and *7 Days in Entebbe* in 2018.

Further Reading

McRaven, William H. *Operation Jonathon: The Israeli Raid on Entebbe, 4 July 1976.* Novato, CA: Presidio Press, 1996.

Netanyahu, Iddo. *Entebbe: A Defining Moment in the War on Terrorism. The Jonathan Netanyahu Story.* London: Balfour Books, 2009.

Saul, David. *Operation Thunderbolt: Flight 139 and the Raid on Entebbe Airport, the Most Audacious Hostage Rescue Mission in History.* New York: Little, Brown, 2015.

Operation Nimrod

Conflict: Terrorism
Captured: April 30, 1980
Rescued: May 5, 1980

The province of Khuzestan in Iran had been in a state of unrest since the 1920s. Local tribal authorities had significant tensions, and with power in the region shifting hands, unrest simmered in the area for decades. Though leadership promoted centralization, conflicts between the central Iranian government and Arab separatists continued. In 1979, tensions rose again, fueled by the Iranian Revolution and desire for autonomy. The Iranian government put down the uprisings, which led to the disenfranchised moving to terrorist actions to have their voices be heard. For six days in 1980, the Iranian embassy in London was the site of a standoff between British authorities and Iranian separatists. The terrorists wanted recognition for their cause, an independent country carved out of Iranian territory, and the release of other terrorists who were being held. The group threatened to execute the 26 hostages unless authorities met their demands. When negotiations stall, the attackers carried out their threat to execute a hostage, which then unleashed the elite British Special Air Service (SAS), which launched an assault on the embassy. In the end, five out of six terrorists died in the SAS attack, and one hostage died as the crisis came to its dramatic conclusion.

The terrorists came from Khuzestan, an oil-rich area in southwestern Iran that had never fully accepted a centralized Iranian rule. The government in Tehran tolerated unrest, but it was quick to fight back against any outright rebellion. The Khuzestan area was economically critical for the Iranian nation, as three-quarters of its annual oil production came through oil fields located there. However, natives in the area longed for independence and closer ties with Iraq. And in 1978, the oil workers went on strike, which led to the shah's downfall and the Islamic Revolution of 1979, when oil production dropped to almost nothing. Clashes between the separatists and the central government escalated when Iraq supported the conflict through training, money, arms, and equipment. The Khuzestan leaders believed they needed international attention on their goal of achieving an independent nation.

To bring attention to their desire for autonomy, the separatists took extreme measures. Six men who were Khuzestani revolutionaries assembled backpacks containing two submachine guns, five pistols, and hand grenades. Their objective was to overtake the Iranian embassy in London, where the men planned to obtain control of the building and demand the release of 91 of their comrades under Iranian control. They sent one of their group ahead to scout the scene, and the site looked promising with over 25 potential hostages on the premises. The leader of the group was Oan Ali Mohammed, code-named Salim, and after their reconnaissance, gave the order to proceed with the attack on the Iranian embassy.

Ordinarily, the Metropolitan Police Diplomatic Protection Group (DPG) had a uniformed officer outside the building, but for whatever reason, no officer was seen at the station that day. Unknown to the attackers, Police Constable Trevor Lock was inside the building having a cup of coffee due to the cold weather. The terrorists drew their weapons and ran inside the building. They quickly encountered Police Constable Lock, who did not have a chance to pull his firearm, but he did activate a panic button, which broadcast an emergency signal to the central office. Over a dozen police officers responded to the alarm within minutes, but not in time to prevent the takeover of the embassy.

The worked their way through the rooms, taking 26 hostages. Some in the building were able to escape in the initial confusion. In those first disorientating moments, Police Constable Lock slipped his revolver into his pocket. Luckily for him, the terrorists must have assumed that one of their own had disarmed him, since his holster was empty. Because hostages were escorted everywhere, Lock refused to eat or drink, as he did not want the weapon discovered when he would be moved from the group and singled out in the restroom, where the terrorists might discover his weapon. Once only the terrorists and hostages were left in the embassy, the terrorists passed out leaflets to the hostages, explaining why they had been taken and the objectives of their mission. The terrorists demanded the release of 91 of their contemporaries, safe passage to the airport and out of the country, and recognition of their homeland as an autonomous entity. The group also distributed the leaflets to the police outside the embassy, and they explained that unless their demands were met within the next 24 hours, they would kill the hostages. The terrorists also warned the police that any attempted rescue operation would result in the building being blown up.

The local police soon realized that this event was political and beyond their capabilities and resources, and they quickly informed British officials. The ministers of defense, the Foreign Office, and the Cabinet Office were brought in, as were the specialists in the realm of international terrorism, the Metropolitan Police (MI5), and the Special Air Service (SAS), the British counterterrorism unit. The SAS traced its own beginnings back to the North Africa Campaign of World War II, but it had since evolved to meet the global terrorist threats. The 22 SAS regiment consisted of four squadrons that rotated responsibilities every six months, and at the time of the Iranian embassy takeover, B Squadron had assumed the antiterrorist duties and was known as the Special Projects Team. The B Squadron was split into two independent teams, the red team and the blue team, which often worked separately but were also effective together. Before orders were even issued, but knowing they would be involved, leaders of the SAS moved their teams from their barracks outside London to the barracks in Hyde Park, which was just a short distance from the site of the standoff. Members of the elite team arrived and would soon become part of the rescue operation known as Operation Nimrod.

The Metropolitan Police followed their standard operating procedures for a hostage situation. They isolated the building, cordoned it off from spectators, and contained the attackers. They also cleared out the immediate area, setting up their headquarters in a children's nursery across from the embassy. After cutting off all communication lines going into or out of the embassy, the police delivered a green field telephone to the terrorists. The plan was to open the negotiations between the terrorists and the police, come to reasonable terms, and get the terrorists to surrender without harming anyone. At 3:00 p.m. on the first day, the team involved met and began to set terms for ending the hostage situation. They agreed that no terrorists or hostages would be allowed to leave the United Kingdom, and all of the attackers would be held accountable under the law. Although the police would negotiate as long as possible to reach a peaceful solution, the leadership would consider an SAS assault on the building if any hostages were injured, and would launch a full assault if the terrorists killed any hostages.

When day two dawned, the SAS leadership had an initial plan to retake the building, which called for British soldiers to leap through as many doors and windows as possible and overpower the terrorists. As the day progressed and more information became available, the SAS leadership revised the plan. Carpenters built full-size replicas of the building to assist in the training of the assault teams. While one team stood ready to assault the building on a moment's notice, the other team practiced the attack, and then they switched roles. To gather more intelligence, the police lowered microphones down chimneys and drilled holes in the walls to insert cameras, and the SAS operatives went up on the roof and around the outside of the building. During this time, several hostages became sick and were allowed to leave the embassy. To help the leadership further refine their plans, the released individuals told the police and military leaders everything they could remember about the terrorists and the weapons they carried.

For six days, the police negotiators worked with the terrorists to resolve the crisis. As time passed, the attackers became less concerned about liberating their comrades and more concerned about saving themselves and getting out of the country. They demanded a number of ambassadors from Middle Eastern nations intervene on their behalf, but when the representatives learned they had no real power and the British were not going to let the terrorists or the hostages leave, they refused to participate in any further negotiations. Deadlines came and went with no repercussions for the hostages. In a classic case of the Stockholm syndrome, where the victims come to believe in and support their abductors, the hostages began to sympathize with their captors, even writing letters to the police, explaining that they had been well treated and to deliver what the terrorists wanted.

British officials had decided on the first day that the terrorists would not be allowed to leave the country, but the terrorists were unaware of that decision. Later in the afternoon on day six of the crisis, the leader of the hostage takers, Salim, demanded to speak with one of the ambassadors working on the situation. No ambassadors were available to speak with him, and the British authorities had to admit to this fact. They told Salim that they were working on getting an ambassador for them to talk to in order to avoid a confrontation, even though they knew that no coordination was possible. Salim then demanded to speak to an ambassador within 45 minutes or he would kill a hostage. After 40 minutes, the phone rang in the operation's headquarters, and Police Constable Lock informed the police that the terrorists were tying one of the hostages to the stairs with the obvious intent of executing him. The police tried to get Salim on the phone to talk him out of his plan to execute a hostage, but he refused to speak with them. A few minutes later, everyone on the call heard the sound of three gunshots. The terrorists had just executed a prisoner, and according to the boundaries agreed upon earlier by those in charge of the operation, the government gave the order to send in the SAS.

To keep the terrorists off balance and from suspecting an attack, the negotiators agreed to any demands the terrorists made. The SAS went into action. The sniper teams, code-named Juliet one and two, would cover the front and rear of the building, while the support team would lob grenades into the building. Thirty-two men, split between a Blue Team, code-named Bravo, and Red Team, code-named Romeo, would enter the building, and all forces had definite areas of operation that they would not cross to reduce the possibility of friendly fire. All members of the assault force would enter the building simultaneously. The Red Team would secure the second, third, and fourth floors. The Blue Team would secure the basement, ground floor, and first floor. Four men were stationed on the roof to provide security and create a distraction at the start of the assault, and an additional eight men were placed at the rear of the building to assist the hostages freed during the action.

At 6:15 p.m., the signal to begin the coordinated assault was given, and the first part, which called for two men to rappel down a rope to a balcony, was under way. The plan hit a snag when the rope tangled and one of the men dangled helplessly in the air. To make matters worse, his partner stopped his rappel and accidently broke a window with his foot. Salim, speaking with the negotiator, heard the sound and left the room to investigate the noise. The SAS had no time to further synchronize their assault. The commander simply shouted the code word to begin the operation, and all members of the team went into action. The security men blew a large charge in front of a glass window to distract the terrorists, and the rest of the operatives quickly entered the building and began the search for hostages and targets.

On the ground floor, charges were set to blow the door off its hinges, and team members threw a stun grenade inside the room before charging into the darkness. They cleared their areas of responsibility but found no terrorists or hostages. On the first floor, SAS men set a charge to blow a door, then realized that a hostage stared back through the glass. The soldiers told the hostage to take cover, then blew the door. From above, one of the terrorists dropped a grenade on the men, but he had forgotten to pull the pin. It lay on the ground, ineffective. Moving on, the SAS unit members found Police Constable Lock struggling with Salim. When the exterior assault started, Lock attacked Salim, who had lost his gun, and the two men rolled on the floor. Two SAS men came in as Lock rolled away from Salim, who had found his weapon. The SAS men fired on Salim, who was again armed, and took him out of action.

Above them, the men dangling on the rappel ropes freed themselves and then entered the second floor, where they expected to find hostages. They were surprised that no hostages were in that area. They moved out, searching the adjacent rooms, where they found some of the hostages. As the soldiers escorted the hostages out of the building, they found one of the terrorists setting a rug on fire. An SAS man pulled his weapon and fired on the man, but his weapon misfired. The terrorist heard the loud click and saw the soldier, and then ran from the room. The SAS operative pulled his pistol and gave chase. He cornered the terrorist, who grabbed a grenade and started to pull the pin before a bullet stopped his actions. In the confusion, three terrorists dropped their weapons and mingled with the hostages, trying to blend in and escape. An SAS soldier recognized one of the terrorists and ordered him to lie flat but he pulled his hands to his body quickly. Thinking the terrorist was going for a weapon, one of the SAS men quickly shot him. The soldiers compared notes and realized that two terrorists were still missing. One was recognized as he moved with the other hostages, and the SAS men quickly cornered him. Realizing the terrorist held a grenade in his hand and concerned that firing a round at him could injure someone around him, one of the soldiers clubbed the terrorist on the head with the butt of his gun. The man collapsed, rolled down the stairs, and four SAS soldiers fired on him. The grenade rolled out of the dead man's hand, but the pin was not pulled.

As the last of the hostages left the building, the SAS headquarters ordered all of the soldiers out as well. All hostages were handcuffed because there was still a terrorist missing. The SAS quickly worked to identify the hostages and found the remaining terrorist among them. He claimed he was a student, but the other hostages recognized him and stated his identity. Now that the situation was under control, authority for the scene passed from the military back to the local police. All hostages were loaded into ambulances and taken to local hospitals. Most had minor injuries, but two of them had gunshot wounds, sustained when the terrorists realized they were under assault and began shooting hostages. One of the men died almost immediately; another man who had been hit was bruised but in good shape, as the bullet miraculously bounced off of a coin. The SAS had responded quickly enough to save almost all of the hostages.

After the end of the siege, Police Constable Trevor Lock was widely considered a hero. He was awarded the George Medal for his part in the situation and for working to derail the terrorist leader during the siege. Something unique about this operation was that it was broadcast live and viewed by millions of people in the United Kingdom. The situation did cause additional strain on the United Kingdom and Iranian relations, even though the government and particularly Margaret Thatcher were praised publicly throughout Britain for their handling of the situation. The incident was portrayed in the film *6 Days* (2017) and inspiration for Tom Clancy's video game, *Rainbow Six Siege* (2016).

Further Reading

Fremont-Barnes, Gregory. *Who Dares Wins: The SAS and the Iranian Embassy Siege*. Oxford: Osprey Publishing, 1980.

Phillips, Russell. *Operation Nimrod: The Iranian Embassy Siege*. Trevissome Park, England: Shilka Publishing, 2015.

Operations Berlin, Market Garden, and Pegasus

Conflict: World War II
Captured: September 1944
Rescued: October 1944

Three operations were interwoven and closely related in the last days of World War II. Operation Market Garden was actually two operations, both an airborne assault to take out key bridges in Germany (Market) and a ground attack (Garden). The attack was considered the largest airborne operation in World War II. Though it was a very large operation, it was not completely successful, and at the Battle of Arnhem, the British forces were unable to secure the last bridge. Operation Berlin occurred when British forces rescued about 2,500 men, most of whom were located in the town of Oosterbeek. Operation Pegasus happened a month later, close to Arnhem, near the village of Renkum. On the night of October 22, 1944, the Allied forces successfully evacuated a large group of trapped soldiers who had been hiding in German territory since the Battle of Arnhem (the last part of Operation Market).

The Allied advance into Germany after D-day, June 6, 1944, was halted due to lack of supplies and not due to a shortage of determination. General George Patton and Field Marshal Sir Bernard Montgomery, the two most aggressive army commanders under General Dwight D. Eisenhower, competed for priority, and each hoped to lead their army into Germany and on to Berlin. To gain momentum, Montgomery devised a plan to seize key bridges across the Rhine that would give him a running start into Germany and the industrial heart of the nation, requiring Eisenhower to reinforce him and the British army. If all went according to plan, Montgomery promised the war would be over by Christmas 1944.

The plan was quite simple in its design but audacious in its execution. Operation Market Garden, as it was known, consisted of two parts. Operation Market consisted of an airborne drop by the 1st Allied Airborne Army to seize key bridges across certain rivers in Holland. The 101st U.S. Airborne Division was to capture the bridges near Eindhoven at Son and Veghel, the 82nd U.S. Airborne Division would take the bridges at Grave and Nijmegen, and the British 1st Airborne with the Polish 1st Independent Parachute Brigade were to seize the bridge at Arnhem. The airborne divisions would hold the bridges for two days while the British, under the command of Lieutenant General Sir Brian Horrocks, executed Operation Garden. Essentially, the armored unit would follow up with a ground assault, passing through Eindhoven, Nijmegen, and finally linking up with the British in Arnhem within 48 hours, consolidating the Allied hold on the bridges. Taking over these bridges would prevent the Germans from retaking them, or worse, destroying them. However, due to a shortage of transport aircraft, only half of the 1st British Airborne would be dropped into Holland on the first day of the attack.

Over 10,000 men in the 1st British Airborne Division parachuted into Arnhem on September 17, 1944, as part of Operation Market Garden. The British and Polish forces at Arnhem had several factors to contend with, the first of which was that the bridge was in an urban area, which required the airborne soldiers to hit drop zones nearly eight miles away. The glider force would bring in a contingent of jeeps that would allow some soldiers to go forward to the bridge to secure it until the other forces arrived on foot. Additionally, Allied intelligence had indicated that the German forces in and around Arnhem were lightly equipped and not the best soldiers in the German army.

Things began to go wrong on the first day. The British soldiers took fire almost as soon as they began their movement through each of the bridges, which slowed them down. Additionally, German SS Panzer Corps had moved into the Arnhem area. The Dutch resistance had reported the presence of tanks in the vicinity of Arnhem, but there were limited details in terms of the size and strength of the force. The 101st U. S. Airborne Division captured four out of five bridges assigned to them, but they had to stop to build a temporary bridge near Son when the Germans blew up the bridge located there. The jeeps that the 1st British Airborne were depending on for getting to the bridges never made it to Arnhem, which caused further issues for trying to get through the Arnhem streets to the bridges. Although much of the division was slowed by the efforts of German forces, but Lieutenant Colonel John Frost's 2nd Parachute Battalion reached the north end of the Arnhem Bridge the first evening, capturing the north end of the bridge. Two unsuccessful attempts to capture the south end of the bridge ended with numerous casualties.

The following day, a German unit tried to cross the bridge at Arnhem and took serious losses, but they were also able to inflict heavy punishment on Frost's

Operation Market Garden in September 1944 was the largest airborne assault of World War II. Paratroopers are shown landing in the Netherlands. (National Archives)

battalion. Only a small portion of the 1st British Airborne actually made it into Arnhem, but the force held the bridge for four days, even though the plan called for them to hold the bridge for only two days. The British soldiers who were to arrive at the bridge were delayed, and the mission failed. The British had mistakenly attacked in an area where the remnants of two Panzer divisions were in place, and the mission turned from one of holding the bridge to one of mere survival.

Although the British had managed to secure the bridge over the Rhine with a cobbled-together force, the Germans quickly closed off any avenues into the city and surrounded the British forces. Those outside the city could not reach the soldiers in Arnhem, either to reinforce the effort or to assist in their withdrawal from the area. Within a few days, the majority of the division, about 6,000 men, were taken prisoner and about 1,500 were killed in fighting. What remained of the division, about 2,500 men, were stuck in a small perimeter in the town of Oosterbeek. The majority of these men were rescued on the night of September 25 and early morning of the 26th in Operation Berlin, in which the men of the British airborne withdrew soldiers from the perimeter and escaped by boat across the Rhine River. They kept thinning the lines until the British had taken almost all of the men out. They unfortunately had to leave the wounded behind for the Germans to tend to.

In the local woods and town, about 500 soldiers were also in hiding, and these were the targets of Operation Pegasus. The Dutch resistance had helped hide many soldiers at great danger to themselves and their families. If the Germans discovered the Dutch civilians hiding American soldiers, they would have been executed on the spot or sent to a concentration camp. Operation Pegasus began almost a month after the failure of Operation Market Garden on October 20, 1944. That night was the deadline that the German had established for the residents of the local towns to evacuate their homes. Taking advantage of the masses of people and confusion, Allied forces thought that utilizing the darkness of the evening would give the operation the best chance for success. The British, with the assistance of E Company, 506 Parachute Infantry Regiment (the unit depicted in the *Band of Brothers* miniseries), launched boats to ferry the men across the Rhine. Communications had been sent to all Allied soldiers located on the far side of the river to meet at a certain time and place for evacuation. The rendezvous point was about half a kilometer away from the landing party, but soon the rescuers linked up with the stranded soldiers, and a total of 138 soldiers and Dutch civilians escaped that night. The soldiers were flown back to England.

The men involved in Operation Pegasus deemed it a success, but there were still more men from the 1st British Airborne who did not get out in the first rescue attempt. A second rescue was attempted but was unsuccessful. Germans were aware there would likely be another rescue attempt, and they increased the number of patrols in the vicinity of the Rhine River around Arnhem. The second rescue was set for November 30, 1944, with over 100 soldiers and civilians trying to cross into Allied lines on that day. Unfortunately, the group ran into a German patrol and about two dozen of their party was killed. No organized rescues took place following this attempt, but members of the British Airborne and Dutch civilians continued to cross into Allied territory by ones and twos.

The events around Arnhem are well documented in book and film, and several museums and memorials to the events can be found in the Netherlands. Additionally, the movie, *A Bridge Too Far* (1976) portrays the events of the rescues, as does the *Band of Brothers* miniseries episode focused on Operation Pegasus.

Further Reading

Badsey, Stephen. *Arnhem 1944: Operation Market* Garden. London: Osprey Publishing, 1993.

Beevor, Antony. *Arnhem: The Battle for the Bridges, 1944*. New York: Viking Press, 2018.

Heaps, Leo. *The Evaders*. New York: William Morrow, 1976.

Hibbert, Christopher. *Arnhem*. London: Phoenix, 1962, 2003.

Ryan, Cornelius. *A Bridge Too Far*. New York: Simon and Schuster, 1974.

P

Pekerney, Sasha, and Toivi Blatt, 300 Others

Conflict: World War II
Captured: 1942 and 1943
Escaped: October 14, 1943

One of the most extensive prisoner of war escapes of World War II happened on October 14, 1943, in one of three death camps in Poland. The death camp at Sobibor was near the eastern border of Poland, about five miles south of present-day Wlodawa. Not many documents from Sobibor have survived, as the Germans tried to erase the site of the mass executions that occurred at this location. As with many survivor stories, their tales are sometimes contradictory, though there are many similarities in the stories. From October 14 to 19, 1943, led by the Russian Alexander "Sasha" Pechersky, approximately 300 Jews escaped from Sobibor, including memoirist and public speaker Toivi Blatt, making this one of the largest POW escapes in recent history.

Sobibor opened in the spring of 1942 and was built expressly for the purpose of killing Jews. The area was remote and not good land, but it was along a rail line for access. The camp was not large, approximately 1,300 by 2,000 feet, surrounded by barbed wire and trees, and further protected by a minefield. A small staff of German SS officers and a Ukrainian police guard unit, about 150 men, were based there, and some of the Jews on site were spared because of their skills as sign painters, tailors, and goldsmiths. These survivors were forced to work in the camp as well.

Jews arrived by the trainload, usually about 10 boxcars at a time, carrying about 2,000 people, and every Jew sent to Sobibor was gassed within 24 hours. Those arriving were told they were at a transfer station, their valuables and clothing taken from them, and their hair cut before they were sent through to the showers, which were actually gas chambers. The Jews who worked there knew what they were involved in, and that knowledge caused them distress. These men had to clean up the remains after each trainload was gassed, and mass graves were used to dispose of the bodies. The smell of decay was strong, and the water in the area was contaminated as well. Jewish workers were expected to herd the Jews on the train through the camp to their death, clean up afterward, and not speak out. Those who were weak were shot or sent through the showers as well.

Though escape was a thought for many prisoners, the message they received from the soldiers was clear. Any prisoner caught trying to escape would be shot, and any who helped another try to escape would be shot as well. When 2 people did manage to escape, the guards shot 10 prisoners in retaliation. Although some knowledge about Sobibor reached people in London and Washington, leaders did not intervene. By the spring of 1943, most Polish Jews were dead, and the killing at Sobibor slowed, because the Nazis needed the trains for their soldiers. In the summer of 1943, Dutch Jews were brought in and killed, and by September 1943, there were few if any trains. The Jewish workers began to wonder when they would be killed. In late September, the trains of Russian Jews arrived, and among that group, Sasha Pechersky. Pechersky was kept as part of the workforce, for the moment, surviving within Sobibor.

Rumors within Sobibor expanded on the idea that the camp would be liquidated in three weeks, and Pechersky and others had to act quickly. Within 20 days, they made a plan and waited for the right timing for their escape. About 600 prisoners were still at Sobibor at the time. On the night of October 14, 1943, about 300 got out and into the forest, while another 160 were trapped in the tunnels. Pechersky and members of the Sobibor prison killed 11 German officers, overpowered the camp guards, and seized the armory. Though the plan had been to walk out after taking control, their plan was interrupted, and most ran during the chaos that ensued.

Some of the escapees were caught right away, but farmers helped many others, with some, such as Pechersky, living in a farmer's barn for months, awaiting a time to get to freedom. About 58 of those who escaped survived. Those who did not escape were shot. Within days of the escape, the SS ordered the camp taken apart, because they did not want the world to see what had happened at Sobibor. The Russians were close by, and trees were planted to help hide what had occurred at Sobibor and destroy the evidence. Even so, those who worked at Sobibor were tried for war crimes after the end of the war, and many were imprisoned for their role at the death camp.

Approximately 250,000 Jews were killed at Sobibor, which was part of Operation Reinhard, in which over 2 million Jews were killed. Many of those who escaped wrote books about their ordeal. Movies on Sobibor have also been released, including ones in *Escape from Sobibor* (1987) and *Sobibor* in 2018. Many of those who escaped, including the coleader, Sasha Pechersky, and Toivi Blatt, have spoken widely about the subject and their experiences. Both men are now deceased.

Further Reading

Rashke, Richard. *Escape from Sobibor.* Harrison, NY: Delphinium Books, 1982, 1995.

Shelvis, Jules. *Sobibor: A History of a Nazi Death Camp.* New York: Berg, 2007.

"Sobibor." *Holocaust Museum.* United States Holocaust Memorial Museum. www.ushmm .org/wlc/en/article.php?ModuleId=10005192.

"Sobibor Extermination Camp." *Jewish Virtual Library.* www.jewishvirtuallibrary.org /history-and-overview-of-sobibor.

Phillips, Richard

Captured: April 8, 2009
Escaped: April 12, 2009

Richard Phillips was born on May 16, 1955, and he was raised in Winchester, Massachusetts. Phillips graduated from high school there and began his postsecondary education at the University of Massachusetts, Amherst. In 1979, he transferred to the Massachusetts Maritime Academy. Phillips worked as a crew member and eventually as a ship captain.

In 2009, captains and crew were aware of the warning to stay at least 600 miles off the coast of Somalia when traveling through those waters. Somali pirates were known to attack in the waters offshore, and merchant ships were often the targets. In April 2009, Phillips was meeting up with his assigned cargo ship, the *Maersk Alabama,* in Salalah, Oman, after his three-month stint at his home. His journey aboard the ship was scheduled to take him from Salalah to Djibouti to Mombasa, Kenya. Although Phillips was specifically aware of warnings about pirate activities near the Horn of Africa, many shipping companies, including the one that Phillips worked for, banned weapons aboard the ships, fearing reprisals upon the crew for resisting pirate activities. The tools the crews had available to them in the case of an attack included handheld weapons and water cannons. Still, the crew carried out drills, practicing the actions they could take to make it more difficult for pirates to board the ship.

Pirates often operated out of local ports, using beat-up older vessels with a single outboard motor to capture fishing trawlers and cargo ships. Their modus operandi was simple: they held the ship and crew for ransom, and made millions of dollars when the ransoms were paid. When many ship captains simply veered farther out to sea to avoid the pirates, the Somali pirates changed the rules of the encounters. Pirating became even more lucrative when the pirates kept some of the larger ships and used them as operational bases. This allowed them to patrol as far out to sea as the cargo ships, operating with radar and modern communications. Once the pirates found a target, including unsuspecting cargo vessels, they would unload their fast boats with the single outboard motor, quickly approach the target vessel, board it, and take control. The victims often could do little except hope for the best. Because there were no friendly military forces in the area, captains could call their government and inform them that they were the victims of a pirate attack. The captains asked for ransom money.

Captain Phillips knew the risks as they maneuvered through the waters off the coast of Africa. As the *Maersk Alabama* sailed past the coast of Somalia, the number of incidents involving pirates had recently increased. Just days before pirates boarded the *Maersk Alabama,* the crew had successfully outrun an attempted boarding, and then the captain and crew listened to the pirates on the radio, threatening them. Repeatedly, they heard of attacks on ships in the area through their dedicated news channel.

As the sun rose on Wednesday, April 8, 2009, Somalia pirates attacked *Maersk Alabama* as it traveled over 300 miles off the coast of Africa. Although the crew saw nothing on radar, Phillips knew there had to be a mother ship in the area. The pirates were approaching in a skiff, the small boat with a single outboard motor, and quickly came alongside the *Maersk Alabama*. The crew fired flares at the attackers, hoping to hit the boat or a gas can. Meanwhile, Phillips zigzagged the ship, trying to make it more difficult to board, but to no avail. The four Somali pirates were on board, armed with AK-47 assault rifles.

Within five minutes, the ship was under the complete control of the pirates. Phillips hoped that the satellite phone, which had been left on after communicating their situation with American forces, was still transmitting their situation, and that someone on the other end knew what was happening. The leader of the pirates demanded that Phillips place a call on their satellite phone, but he pretended the phone was broken. This was only one in a series of pretenses that Phillips perpetrated on the pirates, refusing to give up important information or the location of the rest of his crew. Most importantly, the crew members hiding belowdecks had taken control of the ship from the engine room, frustrating the pirates who were currently being sailed in circles.

Only three *Maersk Alabama* crew members, including Captain Phillips, were under the pirates' control. Phillips had no intension of giving up the rest of his men. The pirates had other ideas, and the leader of the Somalis wanted them found. He had taken Phillips a number of times to search the ship, but there were many places to hide on a container ship, and they never found the crew. The leaders wanted to search again, and he took one of the crew members with him instead of the captain. The crewman led the pirate straight to the crew, who quickly succeeded in overpowering the pirate.

With the leader out of action, the remaining three pirates began to panic. They asked about the man overboard (MOB) boat, completed with running engine, and asked if they could use it to leave the ship. Philips told them they could, and offered them $30,000 in cash he had in his cabin as an incentive. The pirates wanted more money, but they were losing confidence in their ability to control the situation; nothing had gone according to plan. Through radio communications, the pirates on the mother ship and the crew agreed to exchange their hostages, and then the Somalis would leave the ship.

Phillips tried to get the pirates into the MOB boat and he thought he would drive them away from the *Maersk Alabama*. Unfortunately the batteries in the craft were dead and it wouldn't start. They switched to the lifeboat, which was smaller but would serve the same purpose. During the hostage exchange, the leader of the pirates came down the ladder and into the lifeboat, and then insisted Phillips show him how to operate the boat. When this task was completed, the pirates headed out to sea, taking Phillips with them. He was relieved that his ship, his crew, and his cargo were safe, but he was unsure how this would unfold for himself. If he survived, he suspected he would go to a dark prison somewhere, while his captors negotiated his ransom and release.

Before long, the U.S. Navy arrived on the scene in the form of the USS *Bainbridge*. The navy ship stayed nearby, trying to contact those on the lifeboat. The pirates were surprisingly informal with Phillips, allowing him to roam fairly freely. Taking advantage of the situation, he jumped into the ocean when the pirates were on another part of the boat, trying to swim to the navy ship. The pirates recaptured him, and after that, tied up Phillips to prevent another escape attempt. The navy employed a Somali interpreter who tried to negotiate for Phillips's release, but the pirates were not amenable. Over the course of several days, the pirates threatened Phillips repeatedly, threatening death at one time and telling him that it was all make believe at other times. At one point, they claimed to work for the navy and the kidnapping was just a drill.

The situation worsened on the lifeboat, as the pirates began to argue with one another. One of the pirates fired his weapon as a warning to the others. This action gave the SEALs aboard the *Bainbridge* a reason to deploy. They boarded the lifeboat and quickly dispatched the remaining pirates. The standoff was over and Captain Phillips rescued.

Phillips returned home to his family following his ordeal, and eventually went back to sea as the captain of a vehicle carrier. He wrote a book detailing the event, *A Captain's Duty: Somali Pirates, Navy SEALs, and Dangerous Days at Sea* in 2010, and a movie based on the events on the *Maersk Alabama* was released in 2013. Tom Hanks was cast as Captain Phillips. Some of the crew members of the *Alabama* disputed parts of Phillips's recounting. Phillips retired from the Merchant Marine in 2014.

Further Reading

Logan, Nick. "Capt. Richard Phillips Still Sailing Seas after 2009 Pirate Attack." *Global News,* October 12, 2013. globalnews.ca/news/899327/capt-richard-phillips-still-sailing-seas-after-2009-pirate-attack.

Phillips, Richard. *A Captain's Duty: Somali Pirates, Navy SEALs, and Dangerous Days at Sea.* New York: Hyperion Books, 2010.

Sanders, Edmund, and Julian E. Barnes. "Somalia Pirates Hold U.S. Captain." *Los Angeles Times,* April 9, 2009. articles.latimes.com/2009/apr/09/world/fg-somali-pirates9.

Pluschow, Gunther

Conflict: World War I
Captured: January 1915
Rescued: July 4, 1915

Gunther Pluschow, born February 8, 1886, in Bunde, Germany, was on a military path from a very young age, and he was an accomplished aviator and explorer. He was also an author and wrote about his explorations of Tierra del Fuego and Patagonia. Pluschow's adventures took more than 80 days, but his adventures of a nearly around-the-world trip and escape from a British prison camp have given him extraordinary status as the only German prisoner of war in World War I to escape and make it from Britain to Germany.

At age 10, Pluschow entered a military school at Plon, near the German naval base at Kiel, where he excelled in his studies. By age 14, he moved on to the Imperial Military Academy in Berlin to prepare for a career in the German navy. He participated in the traditional curriculum designed for a cadet entering the surface fleet, and accepted postings to various ships for the first few years of his career. The new aviation branch captured his attention, however, and he applied for a slot in the Imperial Navy's new aviation school. Once accepted, he reported for flight training on January 1, 1914, and completed the course within a few months.

Pluschow's first posting was to Tsingtao, China, where he was one of two aviators who arrived in June 1914. The two aviators had two aircraft between them, but both of them crashed shortly after their arrival in China. Pluschow's fellow aviator, Lieutenant Friedrich Mullerskowski, crashed his plane beyond repair on his first takeoff. Mullerskowski was lucky to survive the crash, and he spent the entirety of World War I in Japanese captivity. Pluschow crashed his plane within a few days of his comrade. The aircraft underwent a series of repairs to get it back in the air. Pluschow flew reconnaissance patrols, awaiting the British and Japanese invasion that was expected to follow the declarations of war against Germany in August 1914. The Japanese and British laid siege to the German garrison at Tsingtao, and by November, the Allies began the final push to take the fortification from the Germans.

On November 5, 1914, the commander at Tsingtao ordered Pluschow to fly to neutral China and deliver a bundle of documents to German officials. He took off on the morning of November 6, 1914, hoping to refuel the aircraft a number of times as he made his way to Shanghai. Running low on fuel, he crash-landed the plane in a rice paddy, damaging the propeller. Pluschow took a boat down the Haichow River to Nanking, where the Chinese planned to detain him indefinitely. He slipped away from his guard, then made his way to the railway station and on to Shanghai. There, he met up with a German who shuffled him from safe house to safe house, eventually obtaining a Canadian passport in the name of E. F. McGarvin of the Singer Sewing Machine Company. Additionally, Pluschow obtained money and a ticket on a ship bound for the United States.

Pluschow's ship, the SS *Mongolia,* docked in San Francisco on December 29, 1914. Because the United States was a neutral country in 1914, few people paid much attention to him. He spent New Year's Eve at a popular nightclub, then boarded a train for New York City on January 2, 1915. After three weeks in New York City, Pluschow had obtained a professionally forged Swiss passport in the name of Ernst Suse and boarded an Italian liner bound for Naples. His luck ran out when bad weather forced the ship to dock in Gibraltar, a city controlled by the British, who inspected non-British passengers on each ship that docked. British officials noted that Pluschow had removed all of the labels from his clothing, which made them suspicious. The British asked another Swiss passenger if Pluschow had the right accent to claim Swiss citizenship, and when he failed the language test, Pluschow was taken aboard the *Andania,* which was used as a prison ship, and then transferred to a British prison camp at Dorchester.

The camp at Dorchester was for enlisted soldiers and civilians, and once the British learned that he was a German officer, Pluschow insisted that the British transfer him to a camp for officers. The British granted this request, sending him to the Holyport prisoner of war camp west of London. Holyport was not a difficult place to be, as the beds had clean white sheets, the food was good, and prisoners were free to move about the camp. However, as the fighting in France intensified and more housing was needed for prisoners of war, in April 1915, Pluschow found himself on a train bound for a new camp at Castle Donington, located approximately 100 miles north and west of London.

Once at the new camp, Pluschow was determined to escape. Though tall, barbed-wire fences surrounded the encampment, he looked for and found weak areas in the fencing. He studied the habits of the guards, formulating a plan to escape. One of Pluschow's biggest concerns was his lack of knowledge about the terrain and area, and he found out more regarding the region by befriending guards. Because of his limited English, Pluschow also chose an accomplice whose language skills would benefit his escape attempt. Oberleutnant Oskar T. Trefftz, also of the Imperial German Navy, was a perfect match for Pluschow's plan because of his proficiency in the English language.

The two men set the date of their escape as Sunday, July 4, 1915. When it was time to report for work, they both reported sick. Their names were recorded as missing roll call, and the sergeant found each of them in their beds. They spent the day in bed, but both rose at 4:00 in the afternoon, dressed, and packed what few possessions they had. They made their way to a summer cottage on the prison grounds located near the weak point in the fence. At the 6:00 p.m. roll call, the two men were again reported as sick, and when the sergeant checked on the men, someone was lying in their beds. The ruse worked, and the two Germans continued to wait until midnight, when they crept out of the summerhouse to the fences. The first fence was 9 feet tall and covered with barbed wire, the second fence was 3 feet tall and 30 feet wide, and the final fence looked just like the first, 9 feet tall and covered with barbed wire. They made it through the obstacles without being discovered and headed out on the road to Derby. From there they hoped to catch a train to London, then sneak aboard a ship bound for the continent. The two parted company in the Derby train station, deciding that if one was caught the other might make it to Germany. Pluschow bought a ticket to Leicester, and from there on to London with no problems. He disappeared in the London crowds. Trefftz was not as fortunate, quickly being apprehended and returned to captivity.

Once in London, Pluschow ate at several restaurants, using money he had saved from within the prison. Initially planning to go to the docks and board a merchant ship, he had to abandon that plan after discovering the area was heavily guarded. After reconsidering his options for three days, he eventually waited until night to steal aboard, but his efforts were unsuccessful, and he missed getting out to sea the first night. His second attempt, the following evening, was also unsuccessful. On the third night, determined not to drown in his attempts, he procured a dinghy tied to the pier and avoided the guards and sentries, only to have that ship sink just 15 feet from the pier.

Pluschow was miserable, hungry, and ready to give up. Because the conditions he'd left were not difficult, he briefly returning to the prison camp for a clean bed and a hot meal. However, he was determined to try one more time to escape. He found another dinghy tied to the pier, and when the local fisherman were distracted, he stole the boat from under the noses of its owners. The swift tide flung him into an anchor chain from another ship, but he tied up to it and waited for the tide to subside. After 16 hours, Pluschow made his way to the Dutch ship and to the steel cable that held it to the pier. He climbed the cable and hid under the tarp of a lifeboat until the ship was well under way, then he came out to mingle, carefully, among the other passengers. His clothes were filthy from the mud and he had not bathed in over a week, so he must have made quite a sight, but he was free.

Pluschow made his way to Holland, which was neutral in the war, where he met some old friends who gave him fresh clothes and food. From there, he caught a train back to Germany. He had no papers to show the border guards, which worried him, but the worst that could happen was that he end up in prison in his home country. When he crossed into Germany, officials asked to see his papers. When he replied that he had none, a senior official arrived who just happened to be another old friend. Temporary papers were obtained, and he returned to Berlin and a hero's welcome. Pluschow was the only prisoner to escape from England and make it back to Germany during World War I.

After receiving a number of awards, including the Iron Cross, First and Second Class, Pluschow was promoted to lieutenant commander, and went on to several important assignments in the German navy. Following the Treaty of Versailles, Pluschow left the military and headed to South America where he explored areas in Chile and Argentina. He died in 1931, when the plane he was flying had mechanical problems. Pluschow bailed out of the airplane, but his parachute failed to open.

Further Reading

Pluschow, Gunther. *My Escape from Donington Hall*. Pen and Sword Military, 2015.

Rippon, Anton. *Gunther Pluschow: Airman, Escaper, Explorer*. South Yorkshire, UK: Barnsley, 2009.

Whittaker, Robert E. *Dragon Master: The Kaiser's One-Man Air Force in Tsingtau, China, 1914*. Compass Books, 1994.

Rowe, James N. (Nick)

Conflict: Vietnam War
Captured: October 29, 1963
Rescued: December 31, 1968

James (Nick) Rowe was born February 8, 1938, in McAllen, Texas, and he attended West Point, graduating in 1960. He was one of only 34 American prisoners of war to escape captivity during the Vietnam War. Colonel Rowe was also responsible for developing the U.S. Army Survival, Evasion, Resistance, and Escape training program. He also was responsible for techniques and principles to be followed by captured U.S. military personnel.

In Vietnam in 1963, Rowe was stationed at the front of the war with Vietnamese and Cambodian soldiers. Rowe's memories of his camp included the canals prevalent to the area, the coconut palms and banana trees, and the water buffalo and spirit birds of the region. He remembers the dogs and chickens in the camp, along with the seven-and-a-half-foot-long python, which he did not mind because it ate the rats. But at night, Rowe knew that mosquitos and the Vietcong came with the darkness, and though he knew he was in a dangerous region, it was not until they tried to chase the Vietcong out of Le Coeur village that he realized just how dangerous. The first company to go in to Le Coeur had been ambushed, and Rowe's company was also attacked. They had received bad intelligence, and had gone into a village, not realizing they were going to have to fight against the main force units of the Vietcong, which they never would have done without a larger group. Rowe and another soldier were captured.

At first, their treatment by captors was mild. They were given some medical supplies so they could care for each other, though they were separated for a bit. Staged photographs were taken, showing the two captives getting medical care and eating. They were interrogated by the Liberation Front (Vietcong) and told they would be released in six months, but they were not. Multiple prisoners came through the various camps, and Rowe's retelling of their illness—dysentery, beriberi, and malaria—is gripping and detailed. Many of the POWs did not survive, but Rowe managed to stay alive.

After a year in captivity, Rowe attempted his first escape, but it was unsuccessful. He was punished for his attempt. Many prisoners of war were subjected to nonstop propaganda, and they were aware that other POWs were being executed, as they heard the retelling on Radio Hanoi. Many months later, in January 1968, Rowe tried to escape again, but unknowingly walked into an enemy camp. Rowe discusses the difficulty in being questioned about politics and the ethics of your own country and government. Rowe's health deteriorated and he finally wrote an appeal as directed so that he could get the medicine and food he needed to stay alive. Guards again told him he would be going home, but that did not occur.

Rowe's captors took away his clothing and mosquito nets as a punishment, and he was severely impacted by the insect attacks at night. Rowe was taken on "tour" as propaganda and shown the wreckage of the villages. In one village, someone recognized him and asked if he was okay. This person had known him before the initial raid when he was captured, and thought that Rowe was a good person. That recognition did not garner him release, and he tried to escape again. Bombers were close by, and he managed to signal a chopper while they were trying to avoid the bombers. Rowe signaled the chopper so they would not fire on him, and ran and got on board. He spent 1,903 days in captivity and was liberated 5 years after his capture. When Rowe was debriefed, he feared court-martial from writing the statements to get medicines and food, but no such actions were taken.

Rowe continued in service to his country until he was killed in April 1989, in the Philippines by guerrillas outside the base where he worked. Rowe is buried in Arlington National Cemetery. He is memorialized by a high school and street in McAllen, Texas, by a training facility at the U.S. Army Intelligence Center and School that is named in his honor, as well as a training facility in Fort Campbell, Kentucky. His West Point classmates and fellow soldiers also dedicated a memorial to him in October 2004 in Veteran's Memorial Park in Union Beach, New Jersey.

Further Reading

Fowler, Glenn. "Col. James Rowe, 51, War Hero, Is Killed in an Ambush in Manila." *New York Times,* April 22, 1989. www.nytimes.com/1989/04/22/obituaries/col-james-rowe-51-war-hero-is-killed-in-an-ambush-in-manila.html.

Rowe, James N. *Five Years to Freedom.* Boston: Little Brown and Company, 1971.

Ruffatto, Barney

Conflict: Korean War
Captured: July 20, 1950
Escaped: October 21, 1950

Master Sergeant Barney Ruffatto, born November 25, 1906, was originally from Lead, South Dakota. Ruffatto was one of the oldest men to survive his capture by the North Korean army during the Korean War. Ruffatto had joined the U.S. Army in 1932 and decided to make the military his career. He had extensive experience, campaigning in North Africa and in the Pacific during World War II. Ruffatto was 44 years old and a 19-year veteran of the U.S. Army when his unit, the 24th Infantry Division, was sent from Japan to South Korea where the North Koreans had invaded on June 25, 1950. In the U.S. Army's rush to stabilize the front lines and to prevent the North Korean army from capturing all the southern peninsula, many units were rushed north to meet the invasion. However, the forces were too unorganized and poorly supplied to put up more than a token resistance.

Shortly after the North Korean invasion, Ruffatto and his division were near the border, working to push back the soldiers, but they were outmanned and without the supplies and arms needed to effectively turn back the North Koreans. During this confusion in the early phases of the war, when the mission was uncertain and the front lines were fluid, Ruffatto and his fellow soldiers in the 24th Infantry Division were captured on July 20, 1950. At first, the North Koreans were unsure what to do with their prisoners, who had been captured after a short battle. The first location they were taken to was in the city of Taejon, where they were kept, without medical care, in an insane asylum. A number of the prisoners had been hurt, and Ruffatto recalled the status of some of the wounds as seriously infected. Ruffatto recalled that one man had an open sore on his leg running from his knee to his hip, and it was covered with maggots.

Each night, the guards awakened and tormented the prisoners, threatening to kill them. At one point, the guards took all the boots and belts the prisoners had. Later, the captors received orders to move the prisoners farther north, and the Communist guards forced the captives to walk barefoot to Seoul. The prisoners suffered on their journey north, limping along on blistered and sore feet. From Seoul, the prisoners were marched to Pyongyang, and the journey was so brutal that it earned the nickname "death march." The prisoners helped each other as they could, but some prisoners had literally walked the flesh off the soles of their feet. Some of the soldiers suffered from tropical diseases when the march began, and they lacked the stamina to keep up with the group. Many died along the way, and others were executed if they fell behind. One soldier was older than Ruffatto when the march began; the 49-year-old died of exposure and starvation on the trip to Pyongyang. At the capital city, the men were loaded on trains and moved north again.

By this time, the Americans had landed at Inchon, cutting the North Korean army in half, and decisively ending their advantage. The North Koreans were in danger of losing their prisoners to the advancing Americans, and apparently decided they would rather kill them than release them to the advancing allies. After the prisoners had been transported on the train for several days with nothing to eat or drink, the train stopped inside the Sunchon Tunnel. The North Korean soldiers told the prisoners that they were going to a field where a kitchen was set up to cook a meal for them. The soldiers then roused the prisoners out of the train, one car at a time. About 40 prisoners at a time were taken out of the cars and moved into a ravine, where the North Korean soldiers shot the prisoners with machine guns. After most of the prisoners were believed dead, the guards inspected each soldier to be certain. If anyone groaned or gasped, the soldier ran the prisoner through with a bayonet.

When it came time for the prisoners in Ruffatto's car to go to the field, the men crouched down in a ravine when the guns opened up on them. When he realized what was happening, Ruffatto fell down and rolled away from the main group. He lay face down against a bush and did not move. Most of the men had been shot in the stomach, which caused a painful wound that few men could endure silently. The guards went through the ranks and killed those who moved or made a sound, but Ruffatto was unharmed and remained silent. When the guards moved away, Ruffatto stayed where he was until dark, playing dead. After dark, he discovered that two other men had also survived. Because it was cold, they took as many clothes as they could from the dead, and then moved away from the site of the massacre

> ### The Code of Conduct
>
> In the aftermath of the Korean War, where the enemy had used allied prisoners of war for propaganda purposes, the United States military developed the code of conduct. It consisted of six articles that were designed to both guide American conduct while a prisoner, as well as to give prisoners strength to resist torture or other influences. The code reminded prisoners that they were Americans prepared to sacrifice their life for their country, that they would never surrender of their own free will, and that they would resist their captors if taken prisoner. Further, the military members promised that if taken prisoner, they would not reveal sensitive information, only giving name, rank, and serial number. Prisoners promised to make no statement against the American government, and finally, the code reminded prisoners that they were Americans, and as such, responsible for their actions. The code was designed to instill pride and fortitude into American prisoners, but it also placed an unrealistic expectation upon the Americans who faced a determined enemy in Vietnam. Many prisoners discovered that they lacked the ability to resist an enemy who would resort to any means of torture to extract confessions or other information, leaving prisoners with a sense of shame and guilt when the punishment could not be withstood.

and into a cornfield. None of the three men could walk very well, but they helped each other move away from the carnage. The next day, they saw and then heard an American patrol. Ruffatto and the others attracted their attention, and they were evacuated to a field hospital where medics were able to care for their wounds.

In addition to Ruffatto, 21 men survived the massacre in October 1950. Ruffatto had been an athletic 180 pounds when taken prisoner in July 1950, but 3 months later, he weighed only 130 pounds due to physical exertion and starvation rations. In the subsequent years following the Korean War, the Senate and the army investigated atrocities carried out during that conflict. It was determined that about 300 prisoners had survived the death marches to reach Seoul, but only 68 men survived to incarceration to make it to the Sunchon Tunnel Massacre.

Further Reading
Helm, M. M. *Prairie Boys at War. Korea: Volume I: June—October 1950*. Fargo, ND: Prairie Boy Books. 2014.

S

Son Tay Raid: Operation Ivory Coast/Kingpin

Conflict: Vietnam
Captured: Various, 1970
Rescued: Attempt failed

Son Tay is about 35 kilometers west of Hanoi, and during the Vietnam War, the village was one of many places where prisoners of war were held. The village had many army barracks and a military academy, the Vietnamese People's Army Infantry Academy. The U.S. intelligence community knew that Son Tay was used as a POW camp, and in 1970, the agencies had enough information to plan a rescue mission.

Many POW rescues were attempted, and many if not most were unsuccessful. Son Tay was in an isolated area, and it was difficult to get information about the whereabouts of American POWs. The government did a feasibility study on a rescue attempt on Son Tay in May 1970, and in that study, determined that prisoners were trying to communicate through their laundry. It was decided that the air force would lead the raid into Son Tay. Admiral John S. McCain was the commander in chief, Pacific Command, and he approved the Son Tay raid, even though he knew his son, Senator John McCain, was in the Hanoi Hilton, the infamous prison. In addition to air force teams, the Army Special Forces would be involved in the rescue.

Colonel Arthur "Bull" Simons, Air Force Brigadier General LeRoy J. Manor, Lieutenant Colonel Elliott "Bud" Sydnor, and Captain Dick Meadows were part of the Combat Talon unit, which included 12 aircraft and the personnel needed to man them. There were former POWs on the team, including James V. "Beetle" Bailey, who had planned and trained at the Eglin Air Force Base in Florida. About 50 physically tough men, ages 20 to 42, trained for the mission. They created three-dimensional models of the Son Tay prison camp at Duke Field, created various assault plans, and conducted extensive drills and multiple scenarios for the rescue. Elite "Blueboy" groups of 11 men, 4 men on the clearing team, 4 on the assault team, 3 to free prisoners, and 3 on the helicopter team, had multiple plans and additional fighter aircraft support plans if needed. From May to November 1970, they prepared for the rescue mission.

The Son Tay mission would take precision flight plans, including drafting helicopters in on air force fixed-wing aircrafts. There was much secrecy about the plans, due to the low altitude that would be needed for the intrusion. The plan was to divert the enemy's attention with high-altitude fighter jet flyovers. They moved the team to Thailand to prepare for the mission. They knew that enemy fire could be an issue, as well as the weather. Typhoon Patsy was a problem, and the mission was moved up by 24 hours.

As planned, the enemy fell for the diversion, following the high-altitude fighter jets. Unfortunately, the weather also got worse, and it was the middle of the night when the Blueboys got to the Son Tay prison camp. They found the gates open, and only four guards in their way. The guards were dispatched quickly, and the teams searched for the POWs, but none were found. The team was on the site for 12 minutes. There was some small arms fire, but the team was able to extricate with only two casualties and two lost aircraft. The crew was understandably disappointed and angry that no prisoners of war had been rescued.

The Vietnamese were shocked by the boldness of the rescue attempt, and by some accounts, embarrassed that it had been carried out so easily. The 60-plus POWs had been moved from the camp four months earlier due to flooding issues, but the rescue attempt at Son Tay did have a positive impact on the prisoners, as rations improved and many were moved out of solitary confinement, which improved morale.

Operation Ivory Coast was the first joint military operation overseen by the Joint Chiefs of Staff in U.S. history. Although the mission technically failed because there were no prisoners at Son Tay, it was also considered a tactical success because of the size of the undertaking and the coordination of efforts. However, the mission was considered an intelligence failure because they didn't have knowledge that the POWs had been moved. The lack of success fueled major changes in the U.S. intelligence community over the coming years, as well as the formation of the special operations forces in the U.S. military.

The crew members of the unit received multiple commendations for their efforts, including 6 Distinguished Service Crosses, 5 Air Force Crosses, and approximately 85 Silver Stars, which went to both those on the mission as well as members of the ground force.

Further Reading
Garus, John. *The Son Tay Raid: American POWs in Vietnam Were Not Forgotten.* College Station, TX: Texas A&M Press, 2007.
Schemmer, Benjamin. *The Son Tay Prison Rescue Mission.* New York: Ballantine, 2002.

Stalag Luft III: Great Escape

Conflict: World War II
Captured: Various
Escaped: March 25, 1944

Stalag Luft III translates to Main Camp, Air, III, and was a Luftwaffe-run prisoner of war camp in Germany in World War II. The camp primarily held Allied air force personnel. Stalag Luft III was built in March 1942, near the town of Sagan, Poland, which was about 100 miles southeast of Berlin. The land was not particularly good, and the sandy soil on which it stood was not conducive to tunneling by prisoners, which is another reason the Germans liked the area. World War II warfare included massive bombing campaigns, and it was inevitable that a large number of pilots from Allied forces would be shot down over German-controlled territories. One of the problems, though, was that the Germans were not prepared for the thousands of prisoners they found themselves responsible for, and they eventually built a number of large prison camps throughout Germany and occupied Europe.

By 1942, a large number of POWs had tried to escape or in other ways caused problems for their German captors, prompting captors to put the worst offenders into their own escape-proof camp, where the Germans could keep a closer watch on them. Because Stalag Luft III was built near the town of Sagan in German-occupied Poland, any escapees would have to travel hundreds of miles through German-controlled territory before they could get to friendly forces. The barracks were built off the ground so that tunneling efforts could be easily seen, and fences were placed back a significant distance from the barracks, so that the tunnels would have to be extremely long, which increased the number of cave-ins. Even these precautions and setbacks did not prevent the ingenious men of Stalag Luft III from plotting their escape. The Allied forces were bound to do their best to get away from their enemy captors.

Not only did the prisoners want out of Stalag Luft III, they knew a mass breakout could tie up thousands of German troops who might otherwise prolong the war effort. In January 1943, Roger Bushell began planning this event. He envisioned the construction of three tunnels named Tom, Dick, and Harry running over 300 feet from different barracks, under the perimeter fence, and ending 20 feet into

Stalag Luft III was the inspiration for the war film *The Great Escape* (1963). Here, captured British Royal Air Force officers lay the foundation for a new hut. (Hulton Archive/Getty Images)

the woods outside the fence. The idea of the three tunnels for redundancy was to ensure that if the Germans discovered one or two of the escape routes, at least one tunnel would be left as a contingency. The plan culminated with the escape of over 200 prisoners at once.

Under Bushell's plan, the men began digging their tunnels in the spring of 1943. To disguise the tunnel entrance, the Tom tunnel was built in the dark corner of a barracks, the Harry tunnel began under a stove, and the Dick tunnel was started in a shower room under a drain cover. Each tunnel went straight down for a distance of over 40 feet, which enabled them to avoid the microphones the Germans employed as they searched for escape attempts. Additionally, the Germans had located the camp in an area where golden sand was found just a few feet below the surface of the topsoil. Not only did tunnels have a tendency to collapse, but any sand seen aboveground also would immediately alert guards of tunneling under way.

Bushell directed a game of cat and mouse as they worked to mount the escape attempt. The diggers wore the same clothes to dig each day, but changed them when they came aboveground so as not to reveal soil of the wrong color on their clothing. The tunnels required wood to shore them up, which meant the prisoners stripped their beds and barracks of any extra bracing materials, removing bed slats and using them in the tunnels below. To dispose of the sand taken out of the tunnel, specific prisoners, called penguins, filled up socks with sand and hid them in their trousers. As they strolled around the camp, they released the sand from the socks, and the gait made them look like penguins. On other occasions, the prisoners mixed the sand with garden soil. The prisoners eventually ran out of places to dump sand, while the guards grew more and more suspicious of any prisoners who were not easily seen. They eventually decided to abandon the Dick tunnel and fill it with sand from the other two tunnels. They also used the spare tunnel to store the clothing and identity papers until they were needed at the time of the escape.

The diggers used oil lamps for light at first, but then they tapped into the electrical system to provide needed light through the corridors. The prisoners bribed guards with chocolate, coffee, or other items from their Red Cross packages to obtain a camera and typewriter so teams of forgers could create identity papers for those who would eventually escape. Additional teams of tailors went to work creating civilian clothing for the prisoners. When they left the camp, they had to appear as German citizens, at least in their dress.

While the prisoners dug their tunnels and perfected their identity papers, word filtered through the camp that the Germans planned to build another prison facility just for the Americans, as the bombing campaign continued to yield thousands more prisoners and conditions were just too crowded in Stalag Luft III. Bushell was concerned, fearing the Americans would miss the opportunity to escape, and he moved up the departure date. Tunneling efforts were increased on the Tom tunnel, which the Germans soon discovered. The American transfer to the new camp was expedited, and those sent to the new camp missed the chance to participate in the escape from Stalag Luft III.

With the Dick tunnel full of supplies and the Tom tunnel discovered, the Allies began working on the Harry tunnel with renewed enthusiasm. The Germans knew the prisoners had another tunnel and were determined to find it. The prisoners finished the tunnel in mid-March but had to wait over a week for the first moonless night, and on March 24, 1944, the escape began. The first out were the ones who seemed to have the best chance of survival, while others got their place in line by lottery. In the original plan, 200 of the 600 men who had worked on the tunnels would be able to escape through the tunnel. The first 100 men were those who spoke German and had attempted escapes before or who had spent a great deal of time working on the tunnel. The second lot of 100 men drew numbers in a lottery system. These men didn't speak German as well and many had papers that would be lucky to pass, if the men were questioned.

At 10:30 p.m. on March 24, 1944, the first man made it through the tunnel and found that although the tunnel had cleared the fence, it did not open into the woods. The tunnel's exit could be seen from the guard tower and Germans patrolled near it, greatly slowing down the process of getting prisoners out quickly. The men had to crawl the last bit into the forest, and to avoid being seen, the men went out at a slower pace, about 10 men per hour, rather than the planned 60 per hour. Word reached back into the barracks that only the first 100 would be able to get out before the sun came up. To make matters worse, at around midnight, the air raid sirens went off and the guards cut the electricity to the camp. Lights in the tunnel went out, and the escape was on hold until the lights went back on. Additionally, in the middle of the night, the tunnel collapsed in one area and had to be fixed. At 5 a.m. on March 25, a guard discovered the 77th man after 76 men had made it out.

The men who got out began running and split up. Most of them were unable to find their way to the rail station, and the longer they waited to catch a train, the higher the probability they would be caught. Many of them began walking, but there was still extensive snow left on the ground, and unless they went by road, travel was difficult. Only three prisoners made it home; all the others were rounded up within two weeks, and the Germans executed 50 of them as a warning to others. Bushell was one of the men executed. The three who made it back home were Per Bergsland, a Norwegian pilot; Jens Müller, another Norwegian pilot; and Bram van der Stok, a Dutch pilot. Bergsland and Müller escaped together, and they were successful in getting back to Sweden. The French Resistance helped van der Stok. For those who did not get to the tunnel, some lived to be released at the end of the war, when they were liberated from Stalag VII-A on April 29, 1945.

After the war ended, the British investigative branch of the Royal Air Force went after the German soldiers responsible for killing those who tried to escape from Stalag Luft III. Many of the men involved were prosecuted at the Nuremberg trials. Several of the German officers were convicted and either executed or imprisoned.

The story of the mass escape at Stalag Luft III has been the subject of many books, documentaries, and movies. Paul Brickhill's *The Great Escape* (1950) may be the most widely known. The American movie, *The Great Escape* (1963), was a fictionalized account of Brickhill's retelling. The film took liberties with the facts, including the role of American personnel, which is largely untrue. The film included many of the largest movie stars of the era, including Steve McQueen, James Garner, Charles Bronson, and James Coburn.

> *Escape Planning*
>
> The decision to escape from a prisoner of war camp in World War II was not an easy one. Many soldiers who attempted to escape were shot when they were returned or suffered other brutal punishment. The hardest part, however, were the logistics involved in an escape. Prison camps in Europe and the Pacific were deep in the heart of enemy territory, and prisoners had nowhere to go that was not surrounded by enemy soldiers or civilians. Prisoners also had no money with which to purchase train tickets, and most did not speak the language well enough to blend in with the local population. Because they usually wore a different uniform from the home army and were easily distinguished from the locals, escapees had to find clothing to blend in to avoid recapture and punishment.
>
> For soldiers to have a chance at escape, they had to have the help of other prisoners. Something as simple as getting outside the prison walls often relied on the assistance of others. Even before an attempt, however, escapees might need the permission of the prison's escape committee before they can even determine the best way to attempt a break for freedom. This committee was necessary to ensure that one escape attempt did not accidently foil another escape attempt. The escape committee often acted to de-conflict escape attempts, and in some cases, the committee refused to endorse plans that were not well considered. The escape committee could help escapees by making a uniform appear to be civilian attire, while other members might work on false identity papers or maps to help with planning an escape route.

Further Reading

Ash, William, and Brendan Foley. *Under the Wire.* London: Bantam, 2006.

Bishop, Patrick. *The Cooler King: The True Story of William Ash, the Greatest Escaper of World War II.* NY: Overlook Press, 2015.

Brickhill, Paul. *The Great Escape.* New York: Norton, 1950.

Carroll, Tim. *The Great Escape from Stalag Luft III.* New York: Gallery Books, 2005.

Nichol, John, and Tony Rennell. *The Last Escape: The Untold Story of Allied Prisoners of War in Europe 1944–45.* New York: Viking, 2003.

T

Takur Ghar

Conflict: Terrorism
Captured: March 3, 2002
Rescued: March 4, 2002

Almost immediately after the terrorist attack on September 11, 2001, the U.S. government sent special operations forces into Afghanistan to go after the Taliban. The special operations forces accomplished what they did best, organizing indigenous forces to fight their own wars, and by December 2001, the Taliban had lost control of all major population centers and was no longer a combat-effective organization. Conventional forces soon followed, including the 15th Marine Expeditionary Unit, the 101st Airborne Division, and the 10th Mountain Division. The Taliban withdrew to a remote valley in the southeast portion of the country, to the Shahikot Valley. The overall commander on the ground, General Tommy Franks, believed it was time to launch conventional forces into the fight and to destroy the remainder of the Taliban forces.

The plan called for the insertion of special forces intelligence gathering teams, followed a few days later by conventional forces executing a classic hammer-and-anvil strategy. Soldiers from the 101st Airborne and 10th Mountain Division would act as the anvil, setting up blocking positions along the ridgeline of the valley, while the hammer included some 450 Afghan militia soldiers fighting with special forces elements. They were supported by attack helicopters and air force close air support.

Three special operations teams inserted on February 28, 2002, gathered information ahead of the main effort. The first team, code-named Juliet, was comprised of five Delta operators. They entered the valley from the north using all-terrain vehicles and night vision devices as they encountered devastating weather conditions of snow, rain, and high winds. The second team, India, was a three-man team of Delta operators, who walked into the valley and set up their position in the southwest corner of the valley. The final team, MAKO 31, was made up of three navy SEALs, an Air Force Combat Controller, and a Navy explosive ordnance disposal operator. All three units were to evaluate enemy strengths and equipment, particularly the emplacement of Air Defense weapons. Teams Juliet and India reached their locations with little trouble, but MAKO 31 was still a thousand meters short of its objective when daylight broke. The team hunkered down and waited for nightfall before moving into their final position. When it was dark and safe to move again, MAKO 31 proceeded the last thousand meters, only to discover that enemy soldiers had set up an observation point where the Americans had planned to go. The SEALs engaged the enemy with small arms, and an orbiting AC-130 gunship destroyed what was left of the camp.

The conventional fight began to fall apart when the Afghan soldiers lost their way in the night and turned on their headlights, alerting the enemy soldiers of their arrival. Additionally, when the six CH-47D helicopters arrived with elements of the 101st Airborne and 10th Mountain, they were immediately under fire. The infantry companies attempted to set up blocking positions, but opposition was intense, and they withdrew by the end of the day. The next day, another task force inserted into the valley, and this time they were successful in their mission, clearing the enemy from the ridgelines and the valley floor with the aid of air support.

For some reason, the special operations commander, Brigadier General Gregory Trebon, ordered the insertion of additional special operations forces. Trebon was 1,600 kilometers away, and perhaps he did not understand the situation on the ground. The ranking special operations officer on the ground, Lieutenant Colonel Pete Blaber, objected to the change. The teams on the ground were fine, needed no resupply, and were quite effective in their assignments. Two SEAL teams arrived, MAKO 21 and MAKO 30, with orders to insert as additional surveillance on the valley. Blaber objected to Trebon, with no success. Blaber's headquarters tried to bring the men up to speed as quickly as possible before inserting them that night. MAKO 21 was to link up with team Juliet at the northern end of the valley, resupply them, and then establish a position on the eastern side of the valley, above the task force's blocking position. The second team, MAKO 30, would insert near the mountain, Takur Ghar, and then proceed to the top of that summit. This was the highest elevation in the area and commanded views of the entire valley, and it was an obvious site for an observation point.

The teams were to approach their positions aboard two MH-47E Chinooks, Razor 03 and Razor 04. Delays prevented them from getting to their initial landing sites, and rather than delay the mission for another day or risk detection as they walked to their positions, headquarters ordered them to insert the teams directly onto their final positions. This was a misguided idea because the presence of helicopters not only alerted the enemy, but also told them exactly where the teams were positioned. The MAKO 30 team leader, Senior Chief Petty Officer Britt Slabinski, did not like the options, but felt he had no choice but to follow orders. The seven members of the team would insert at dawn.

As Razor 03 prepared to land on the mountainside, one of the pilots spotted heavy machine gun positions, complete with sandbags. Another crew member saw a donkey tied to a tree, and goat carcasses hanging from trees, and finally a human being raised up from behind a boulder. Soon after, machine gun fire erupted from the trees, and a rocket-propelled grenade (RPG) swept past the cockpit, and then another hit just behind the cockpit and started a fire in the cabin of the helicopter. Another RPG hit on the right side of the aircraft, knocking out the electrical system. Two more RPGs hit the helicopter, forcing the pilot to pull up and try to escape the ambush. He threw the helicopter into a turn to gain altitude quickly, accidentally knocking one of the SEALs off balance and out the back of the ramp.

Petty Officer First Class Neil C. Roberts fell 10 feet into the snow that covered the mountain. He marked his position with an infrared strobe, but there was no support aircraft in the area, and the closest one did not have the team's radio frequencies. Roberts engaged the Taliban fighters, but he was hit and passed out.

Unbeknownst to his fellow soldiers, three enemy fighters took Roberts to their headquarters and executed him with a single gunshot to the head.

The helicopter continued to take fire and only made it seven kilometers from the firefight until it had to land at 3:00 a.m. The SEALs provided security while headquarters dispatched another helicopter to pick up the soldiers. The SEAL team did not know the condition of Roberts, but Slabinski demanded that the new helicopter, Razor 04, take them to Roberts's last location, which headquarters denied. This was now a rescue mission, not an insertion, and the extra helicopter crew and much of the equipment had to return to base. By 4:45 a.m., Razor 04 was ready to take the SEALs back to Roberts's location, but the Chinook was critically short of fuel. They would have one shot at inserting the SEAL team, and chose to drop them on the mountaintop, directly over an enemy unit. After a short but intense firefight, the SEALs lost one man who was dead, one was seriously wounded, and one was slightly wounded. They broke contact and withdrew from the peak, calling in the quick reaction force (QRF).

The QRF was supposed to include a platoon of 35 Rangers from the 1st Battalion of the 75th Ranger Regiment, but half of them were on an exercise, and only 18 soldiers were available, comprising the teams Chalk 1 and Chalk 2. Also attached to the QRF were seven air force members. Once they got the word, Chalk 1 took off in a Chinook helicopter, Razor 01, and Chalk 2 departed in the second helicopter, Razor 02. During the flight, communications were intermittent and the information coming from headquarters was not effective. Chalk 1 was told to land directly on the mountaintop where Razor 03 had been chewed up. The helicopter came in to land and immediately took machine gun and RPG fire. It was shot down, losing power and falling the last 15 feet to the ground. The aircraft continued to take fire and within minutes, three Rangers were dead, one of the aircrew was dead, both pilots were wounded seriously, and several others were badly hurt. The Rangers regrouped, and the Chalk 1 commander, Captain Nate Self, organized a hasty counterattack. The ground forward air controllers called in F-15E and F-16CG aircraft to strafe the enemy, which allowed the Rangers to move forward. The Rangers ran up the ridgeline only to discover that the enemy held a fortified bunker complex, which was too well protected for the Rangers to capture. Captain Self ordered the men to withdraw and seek cover.

When Razor 01 was shot down, Razor 02, with Chalk 2 on board, was ordered to return to base until the situation was clearer. Eventually Razor 02 took off again, this time with the SEAL commander Lieutenant Commander Vic Hyder going along, looking to link up with MAKO 30. Razor 02 landed at 8:30 a.m., on March 4, 2002, three kilometers down the mountain from Chalk 1 to avoid the enemy that had already shot down two helicopters. Hyder took off and met up with MAKO 30. They moved the injured men farther down the mountain and waited for extraction. In the meantime, Self had continued to request F-15 and F-16 bombing runs against the bunker, and he even employed a Predator drone with an AGM-114 Hellfire II antitank missile to hit the bunker. It scored a direct hit. Chalk 2 moved to link up with Chalk 1 at 10:20 a.m., and Self lost no time in moving the Rangers up to clear the bunker, which they did, only to discover another bunker near the first. When they cleared the second bunker, they made a grisly discovery. They found the bodies of both Roberts and Chapman in the bunker complex, though how Chapman got inside the bunker remains a mystery. The Rangers cleared the peak at 11:14 a.m., then waited most of the day for extraction, which came after dark at 8:00 p.m.

The Battle of Takur Ghar is also called the Battle of Roberts Ridge, in honor of the first man to lose his life on the mission. The battle is also depicted in the 2010 video game, *Medal of Honor*. The mission and subsequent battles were also depicted on the *Situation Critical* series. Seven U.S. soldiers lost their lives that day: Neil Roberts, John Chapman, Jason Cunningham, Matthew Commons, Bradley Crose, Marc Anderson, and Phillip Svitak.

Further Reading
MacPherson, Malcolm. *Roberts Ridge: A Story of Courage and Sacrifice on Takur Ghar Mountain, Afghanistan.* New York: Dell, 2005.
Neville, Leigh. *Takur Ghar: The SEALs and Rangers on Roberts Ridge, Afghanistan 2002.* New York: Osprey Publishing, 2013.

Tapscott, Robert, and Wilbert Widdicombe

Conflict: World War II
Lost at Sea: August 21, 1940
Rescued: October 30, 1940

Two British soldiers, Robert Tapscott and Wilbert Widdicombe, were the only two survivors of a cargo ship, the SS *Anglo Saxon,* which was sunk by a German cruiser on August 21, 1940. Seven members of the crew were able to get into a jolly boat and survive the strafing gunfire from the Germans, but only Tapscott and Widdicombe survived the 70 days at sea, rescuing themselves when hope appeared to have been lost.

In early August 1940, the SS *Anglo Saxon* left Wales, traveling toward Argentina carrying coal. Just two weeks into the journey, the 41 members of the crew realized they were in danger about 10 p.m., when the German ship, the *Widder,* started firing at them from about a mile away. The *Anglo Saxon* was hit by large 150-mm shells, and ammunition on board was hit. Most of the crew was killed in the initial hit. The *Widder* came closer and opened fire, killing more of the crew and aiming for the lifeboats, rendering them useless for survivors. One lifeboat was not damaged, and seven of the men on board were able to hide in the small jolly boat after a torpedo struck the ship and she sank. The crew of the *Widder* did not search for survivors after the attack.

The seven men who were able to hide and eventually escape in the jolly boat were Robert Tapscott, age 19; Wilbert Widdicombe, age 24; Barry Denny, age 31; Lionel Hawks, age 23; Leslie Morgan, age 20; Francis Penny, age 21; and Roy Pilcher, age 21. Morgan, Penny, and Pilcher all had injuries from the attack. When the sun came up the next morning, the sailors reoriented and sailed west, hoping to find an island or get into shipping lanes and signal a passing ship. They knew they were off the coast of Africa, approximately 800 miles west of the Canary Islands. They had a long way to travel to be rescued. A jolly boat is small and not designed for use at sea, as it is only 18 feet long and 6.5 feet wide at its widest point. The lifeboats had minimal supplies on board, including a sail, oars, compass, anchor, flares, matches, and a medical kit. There was also a small cache of rations on board, including biscuits, condensed milk, and meat tins. The boat held four gallons of water.

Once under way, the men calculated the rations available for each person and began conserving their supplies as much as possible. A half cup of water and a half of a biscuit were the initial amounts doled out to each man. On September 1, 1940, 10 days into their rescue voyage, Pilcher died from gangrene in his foot, the original injury received in the attack on the *Anglo Saxon*. It did not take long for their rations to run out, and though surrounded by water, it was not potable. The men recorded events in a logbook, noting severe thirst and the low morale. Several of the men—Penny, Denny, and Hawks—went overboard, preferring suicide to the long, slow death of starvation. The last log of a suicide was that of Leslie Morgan, where the log states that he "goes mad dies."

By September 9, only two men were still in the boat, Tapscott and Widdicombe. They were able to gather more rain, but by September 24, five weeks into their rescue attempt, they were out of food. Though they were unaware, they had five more weeks in the jolly boat before they would be rescued. The men were able to eat seaweed, and had at least one flying fish, which precipitously landed in their boat. Sixty-nine days after their ship was sunk, they saw an island and were able to use the last of their strength to steer to the beach.

On October 30, 1940, 70 days after their ship was sunk and about 2,800 miles later, Tapscott and Widdicombe landed on the beach of a Bahamian island, Eleuthera. They were found by a local and taken to a hospital in Nassau. Both suffered from extreme burns, exhaustion, and exposure. The men had both lost significant amounts of weight. After a long recuperation, including visits from the Duke and Duchess of Windsor, Prince Edward and his wife, Wallis Simpson, both men went on to fully recover.

After Widdicombe's recovery, he went to New York, and then in February 1941, he headed for England as a passenger on the *Siamese Prince*. A German submarine sunk this boat on February 17, and all 58 of those on board, including Widdicombe, died at sea. The *Siamese Prince* was just one day short of entering the port at Liverpool.

Upon Tapscott's recovery, he moved to Canada, where he joined the Canadian army. It appears that he suffered from significant post-traumatic stress disorder from his ordeal. Tapscott moved back to Wales, and in 1963, killed himself at his home in Cardiff. In his suicide note, he detailed the depression and issues he suffered from his experience at sea in 1940.

The jolly boat, which had been on display at a museum in Connecticut, was returned to London in 1997 for display in the Imperial War Museum. The story of this rescue was detailed in *Survived,* a documentary on the events following the downing of the *Anglo Saxon*.

Further Reading
Cussans, Thomas. "The Attack on the SS *Anglo Saxon."* In *Incredible Journeys.* Collins & Brown, 2007.

"Ships Hit by German U-boats during WWII: Siamese Prince." Uboat.net, 2016. https://www.uboat.net/allies/merchants/ships/766.html.

"The Sole Survivors of the Anglo Saxon." *The Tribune,* November 13, 2013. www.tribune242.com/news/2013/nov/13/the-sole-survivors-of-the-anglo-saxon.

Task Force Smith: Battle of Osan

Conflict: Korean War
Captured: July 5, 1950
Escaped: Multiple, September 4, 1953

On June 25, 1950, the North Korean People's Army invaded South Korea, and the attack caught the South Korean and American forces by surprise. There were not enough forces in the area to push back against the invasion. In particular, the South Korean army lacked personnel, equipment, and training to repel the attack. In previous skirmishes, the South Koreans had tended to retreat in the face of battle. Because of the strategic need to protect South Korea, U.S. President Harry S. Truman ordered ground forces to the peninsula to counter the Communist offensive. To support that effort, General Douglas MacArthur ordered the 1st Battalion, 21st Infantry Regiment, 24th Infantry Division into the battle because they were the closest unit to the fighting. The divisional commander, Major General William F. Dean, ordered a single battalion, Task Force Smith, flown into Korea, and they had orders to drive as far north as possible, to engage the enemy, and to garner the rest of the division, and thus the rest of the army, time to get there and to deploy in force. Peacetime budgets had resulted in significant reductions in the army's equipment procurement, and the unit was well under strength and under-armed. These factors led to one of the greatest debacles in American military history, when North Korean forces overran the unit on July 5, 1950. Many soldiers in the unit had to escape and evade capture to return to friendly lines. Of the 400 soldiers sent north with Task Force Smith, 60 were killed, 21 wounded, and 82 captured, of which 32 died while in captivity.

On July 5, 1950, the North Korean forces first engaged the United States military in the Battle of Osan, the first official battle of the Korean War. The U.S. task force in the area, Task Force Smith, was 400 infantry soldiers and an artillery battery. The task force was moved to Osan, which was located south of Seoul, South Korea. Their mission was to protect the rear and stop the North Korean forces from advancing until more U.S. troops could arrive to strengthen the southern border. Task Force Smith was not adequately armed, lacking both enough equipment and modern equipment, and they also did not have equipment large enough to stop the North Korean's Soviet-made tanks.

The task force had a number of deficits going in first and being expected to hold the line against the North Koreans. There were B and C Company units, but no A Company unit, and the Headquarters Company was at half strength. Many of the soldiers in the unit were inexperienced new recruits, most having just come out of basic training. Only a third of the officers had previously seen combat, and only one in six noncommissioned officers had combat experience. They entered the country with 120 rounds of ammunition and rations for two days. The weapons platoon had out-of-date rocket launchers, and the artillery battalion had 6 howitzers and 1,200 high-explosive rounds, which were capable of penetrating the armor on enemy tanks, and just 6 high-explosive antitank rounds. They had very little ammunition to move into position and make a prolonged stance, and this caused the task force issues almost from the start.

Though the invasion began on June 25, the task force didn't arrive in country until July 1, and they began moving north that day. By July 4, 1950, the unit was south of Seoul and north of Osan. At this point, Task Force Smith set up their defensive position along two ridgelines and waited to engage the North Korean army as they moved south. On the morning of July 5, the members of Task Force Smith saw eight North Korean tanks two miles away and heading straight toward them. They fired high-explosive rounds at the tank, many of which hit the tanks but had no discernible impact. The tanks kept moving toward the soldiers. When the tanks were about 700 meters away, the task force team again fired on them, this time with recoilless rifle fire. Again, the arms had little to no effect on the weapons bearing down on them. When the tanks were just 15 meters from their position, the soldiers fired the M9A1 Bazookas. The tanks ignored the engagement and continued down the road. The howitzer with the high-explosive antitank rounds damaged the first two tanks and set one of them on fire, but the task force soldiers were then out of the more potent explosive rounds, and fired less high-power rounds at the tanks until the third North Korean tank fired at them, destroying the gun. The tanks then continued southward, not stopping to investigate the small group of U.S. soldiers who had tried unsuccessfully to stop them.

Less than an hour later, a second column of North Korean tanks headed toward the location of Task Force Smith, and the soldiers engaged them in a similar way, and although the weapons were still mostly ineffective, they were able to inflict some damage on these tanks. The column did not stop, though, and at 11 a.m., three more tanks were seen heading toward their position, with a column of trucks behind them carrying two full regiments of infantry soldiers. Over 5,000 North Korean troops headed straight toward the men of Task Force Smith. Of the 406 men who had started the effort to stop the North Koreans, dozens were dead or wounded. When the approaching column was 1,000 meters away, the task force commander, Lieutenant Colonel Charles Bradford Smith, ordered the men to fire with all the weapons the unit had. The mortars, artillery, machine guns, and rifles did manage to destroy several of the trucks, which caused the North Korean soldiers inside to scatter. The three tanks at the front of the column were not stopped, and they continuing firing as they approach the task force. The North Korean infantry soldiers also flanked their position.

After three hours of combat, Lieutenant Colonel Smith ordered a methodical retreat, his troops holding off the superior North Korean force as long as possible. They had very little ammunition left, and their communications were cut. Smith did not know if there was additional artillery support. First, C Company pulled back, then the headquarters group, and finally, B Company retreated. One of the units, 2nd Platoon, B Company, had not gotten the word to pull back, and by the time they realized the rest of the troops were retreating, it was too late. All of the equipment that could not be carried, as well as the wounded, had to be left behind. When the U.S. forces were eventually able to return, they discovered that the wounded had been executed, and the medic who had stayed with the wounded was never found.

As Task Force Smith retreated, the fighting and harassment by the North Korean forces turned the orderly movement into a rout. The North Korean forces punished the task force soldiers, and they fought their way to the rear, reaching the remnants of the A Battery artillery, where the arms were disabled and abandoned. The entirety of the remaining task force continued to the village of Osan, where most of the unit's vehicles were located. About 250 members of Task Force Smith were able to flee in their original vehicles; another 150 members of their unit had been killed, wounded, or were missing. For those who did not make it back to the village, they had to make their way back to friendly lines on their own. Many of the stragglers did eventually make it back to U.S. forces over the next few days, with the remainder of the 2nd Platoon, B Company, making it back to friend lines after five days, just 30 minutes ahead of the North Korean army.

The 24th Infantry Division continued to fight against the invasion. They received better ammunitions that would destroy the North Korean's Soviet-built tanks, and they also employed additional munitions, such as hand grenades, to disable the tanks. The division continued to try to establish defensive lines, but the North Korean forces were extensive and consistently pushed U.S. forces back. At the end of the day on July 20, 1950, Major General Dean ordered the division to withdraw, and every soldier who could walk was loaded onto one of the 50 available trucks. As the convoy was leaving the city, they were ambushed, and soldiers dispersed as their vehicles were destroyed. The men escaped through enemy territory once more, back to friendly lines. During the ambush, Major General Dean's vehicle took a wrong turn and was separated from the rest of the U.S. forces. Finding themselves outside the city, Dean and the others found a wrecked truck and several wounded soldiers. As they tried to escape together, the jeep was hit with machine gun fire, and the group escaped on foot. They were again ambushed, and Major General Dean was separated from the rest of the men. He fell down a slope and hit his head. When he woke, he realized he had a broken shoulder. For 36 days, he walked through the mountains, working his way back to U.S. lines. He had no food or medical treatment. He finally met two South Korean soldiers who said they would take him back to friendly forces, but they walked into a group of enemy soldiers. Dean, who weighed 200 pounds when the war had begun, weighed only 130 pounds by this time. Though he attempted to fight, he was captured. Dean tried to escape several times, but was unsuccessful. He was eventually freed with the rest of the United Nations prisoners on September 4, 1953.

The Battle of Osan had taken an extensive toll on Task Force Smith. The group suffered the losses of 60 dead, 21 wounded, and 82 captured. Thirty-two of those captured died in captivity. During the Pusan breakout offensive in mid-September 1950, U.S. troops moving northward discovered a series of shallow graves that contained the bodies of soldiers from the 24th Infantry Division. All had been executed, shot once in the back of their head, with their hands tied behind them.

Although the net impact of the Task Force Smith only delayed the North Korean advance by approximately seven hours, the mission was considered a success, as the troops had done what they were supposed to do. On September 19, Osan was the location where allied troops would push the North Koreans back, defeating them and stopping their invasion into South Korea.

In the village of Osan, a monument to the American forces who fought and died there stands to commemorate the events of those three months. There is an annual event remembering the Battle of Osan, which is led by the Eighth Army, headquartered in South Korea.

Further Reading
Appleman, Roy E. *South to the Naktong, North to the Yalu: United States Army in the Korean War.* Washington, D.C.: Department of the Army, 1998.
Fehrenbach, T. R. *This Kind of War: The Classic Korean War History.* Fiftieth Anniversary Edition. Washington, D.C.: Potomac Books, 2001.
Millett, Allan R. *The War for Korea, 1950–1951: They Came from the North.* Kansas City: University Press of Kansas, 2010.

Third Platoon, George Company

Conflict: Korean War
Captured: August 31, 1950
Rescued: September 1, 1950

After the initial surprise invasion by the North Koreans into South Korea on June 25, 1950, the situation south of the established border was chaotic. Journalists trying to report on the news in that initial wave had difficulty determining what American units were fighting and where. The initial American response to the North Korean invasion was to send quickly organized infantry divisions north, through the southern port city of Pusan, to try to slow down the North Korean attack and buy time for additional American units to get into position, with the ultimate goal of stabilizing the front lines.

In one significant but unnamed battle, the Third Platoon of George Company was cut off from other U.S. forces for over 38 hours. During this battle, all of the officers were killed, and most of the ammunition was spent fighting off the North Koreans. Even without their officers and with limited ammunitions, the remainder of the platoon held on to a hilltop as the North Korean forces tried to destroy the remaining soldiers. Though the platoon had 40 men at the beginning of the battle, just 12 soldiers remained, and the highest rank among the survivors was Corporal Junior G. Poovey of North Carolina. The area the soldiers were defending was important because it was at the confluence of the Naktong and Nam Rivers, where the North Koreans were trying to drive into the Pusan Perimeter. Getting through this area would force the Allied forces further against the natural barrier of the sea.

The North Korean offensive began on August 31, 1950, and they planned to make it through the Pusan Perimeter and drive a wedge between the 25th and 2nd Infantry Divisions, using surprise to gain further advantage. They sent an entire regiment through the center of the 25th Division forces, taking a straight-line route to

Pusan. From his forward observation post, artillery spotter Corporal Gerald Smith watched as enemy artillery fired on a company to his right, and then begin to fire on his own George Company. Overnight, the North Koreans had moved forward, pushing to overtake the hill once more, but the soldiers of the George Company held on, using heavy machine gun fire to keep the enemy from breaking through. The North Koreans moved back down the hill.

By the next morning, the Americans watched as the enemy regrouped at the bottom of the hill, adjusting as the next attack came from a different side of the hill. Again, the remaining troops of Third Platoon repelled the attack, but not without loss. The North Koreans took over their ammunition dump as well as food and water supplies. The soldiers were without a method to get more supplies, were completely surrounded, and their limited tools included radio communication with Allied forces. They called for artillery support to help retain their position, and on occasion, the friendly fire landed so close to the American soldiers that they had to take cover in the trenches as well. Shortly after 10:00 a.m., the commander requested another air strike near his own position. The F-51 Mustangs dropped the requested ordnance, and when the air force asked for verification that the target was hit, the news that the commander had been killed was sent back. A lieutenant now took command and he continued to request air support, but he was also killed a few hours later.

The battalion commander knew his unit was in trouble, and he ordered his reserve force, which consisted of four tanks and a unit of infantrymen, to break through the North Korean lines to assist the Third Platoon. When the U.S. tanks got to the hill, the enemy soldiers withdrew, and the relief force was able to get to the remnants of the Third Platoon. They immediately evacuated the most seriously wounded, but the enemy force in the area, which greatly outnumbered the U.S. forces, was of concern. Though the forces had been fighting for nine hours already, the battalion commander ordered the rescue battalion back to the hill once more to rescue the rest of the soldiers. They fought their way back to the Third Platoon, literally ramming through enemy roadblocks, killing a number of North Korean soldiers who tried to defend their position. The relief forces pushed forward through the night, taking small arms fire and mortar rounds. At about 6:30 a.m., the battalion encountered another roadblock, and this time the tanks mowed through the blockade, running over 29 enemy soldiers. By 2:00 p.m., the relief forces made it back to Corporal Poovey and the remaining soldiers. At this point, the unit all left the hill, moving back to a defensive position because the tactical situation had changed.

Although all fought heroically in this battle, one of the heroes was Hideo Hashimoto, who used his skills as a baseball player to help defend their location. Hashimoto had been a pitcher, and he threw grenades at the approaching North Korean troops. Though he had been born in the United States, he had spent the last years of World War II in a Japanese internment camp because of his nationality and because his parents had emigrated to the United States. Hashimoto worked to keep the enemy back, but often the North Korean soldiers were within 10 to 15 feet before he had a chance to engage him. To keep the enemy from throwing grenades back, troops often pulled the pin and waited a few seconds before lobbing the grenade.

A few hours later, when American planes flew over the sight of the battlefield, they found another American unit surrounded and at risk. The men had spelled out the word "Help" using men and rifles, hoping that pilots patrolling the area would see it. This group had also been cut off for over 24 hours, and they were nearly out of ammunition as well when the 2nd Infantry Division launched a rescue mission to save this group.

Shortly after the rescue of these two units, the entire situation changed when General Douglas MacArthur launched attacks at Inchon. These maneuvers allowed the American military to surround the North Korean army. The Battle of Inchon was a decisive turning point in favor of the U.S. and United Nations forces and involved 75,000 troops and 260 naval vessels. The battle began on September 15, 1950, and ended on September 19, 1950, and led to the recapture of Seoul two weeks later.

Further Reading
Appleman, Roy E. "The North Korean Great Naktong Offensive." *South to the Naktong, North to the Yalu*. Washington, D.C.: Center of Military History. history.army.mil/books/korea/20-2-1/sn24.htm.
"G.I. Unit Stranded on Hill Spells 'Help' with Guns." *New York Times,* September 3, 1950.
"Surrounded GIs Saved after Stand." *New York Times,* September 3, 1950.

Villingen Prison

Conflict: World War I
Captured: Multiple
Escaped: October 6, 1918

Villingen is located in southern Germany, not far from the Swiss border. A relatively small village until the 19th century, this area became known for its watchmaking company. The village is on the eastern edge of the Black Forest, and in World War I, a prison camp was located in an unused barracks in the town.

A significant prison escape of aviators took place at Villingen in October 1918. They were a rather unusual group, but they were united in their efforts to escape from Villingen. Sergeant Harold Willis was a Harvard graduate from Boston who went to France almost as soon as the war began. He worked as an ambulance driver, then switched to aviation in 1916. The Germans captured him on August 18, 1917, and he became the only member of the famed Lafayette Escadrille to be captured during World War I. Willis was flying an escort mission for bombers near Verdun when a German formation jumped his squadron. He shot one enemy plane before another slipped behind him, forcing him to crash-land. Willis told the Germans he was an officer, and he was sent off to the prison camp. Another American pilot who ended up in a prison camp was Blanchard Battle, a graduate of Georgia Tech. He was on a reconnaissance mission on June 12, 1918, when he test-fired his machine gun and shot off his own propeller. He crash-landed a mile from friendly lines, where German infantrymen captured him.

In addition to Willis and Battle, there were several men from one squadron, who had the dubious honor of being the only American squadron captured wholly intact. The 96th Aero Squadron, who had taken off in bad weather to bomb German rail yards on July 10, 1918, found themselves completely lost in the weather. To make matters worse, they were running out of fuel while battling thunderstorms and 90 mile per hour winds. They landed, one by one, behind enemy lines and all six pilots were taken prisoner, including Rowan Tucker. Another dubious capture happened to George Puryear on July 26, 1918, and was, perhaps, the most unusual capture because he was not shot down. He landed willfully. He had shot down a German aircraft earlier; the enemy plane headed toward the ground, but the German pilot pulled up and made a perfect landing. Puryear landed next to the plane, intending to receive the surrender of the pilot, but realized he was behind enemy lines when a squad of German infantry appeared.

Only one of the escapees was not an aviator. Edouard Izac (Isaacs) was a 1915 graduate of the U.S. Naval Academy and served aboard the *President Lincoln.* On May 31, 1918, when a torpedo hit it, the men abandoned ship. The Germans picked up officers to learn what they could about the Allied war effort. Isaacs boarded the ship and met the captain, who handed him a glass of wine. He was on the ship 11 days before it docked and Isaacs was sent to a prisoner of war camp.

Though all had been captured separately, each of these men made their way through the German prison camp system until they ended up at Villingen prison camp, which was just 18 miles from the Swiss border. A number of men thought to escape, but they kept their thoughts hidden due to the spies in their midst. Intermingled among the American prisoners were a number of Russians, who the Americans suspected of spying for the Germans. However, on October 5, 1918, a rumor spread through the Villingen camp that the Germans would move the Russians to another camp. Everyone suspected that once that happened, the Germans would focus on the Americans and conduct a thorough search of the camp, thwarting any escape plans. For the men planning to escape, they needed to move out before the prison guards could scuttle their plans.

Some of the men planning to escape held a meeting with others they knew planned to break out or suspected of planning to break out, and a unified plan emerged. They agreed to leave that night after developing two escape plans and a diversion to cover their attempt. Some of the men would leave from two windows in one of the barracks, each team maneuvering a ladder to the top of the barbed-wire fence, crawling across it, and dropping to freedom on the other side. Others decided to cut a hole in the fence separating the prisoners from the German guards. Once inside, they would blend in with the guards until they could make their way to the gate leading out of the prison. Most of the men hoped to go out in pairs, while others hoped to join up once outside the fence. Tucker and Battle chose the shorter route to Switzerland, while Puryear and another prisoner teamed up and decided on the longer route, as did Isaacs and Willis. None of the others seemed to have a plan on where they would go once outside prison walls.

The most direct route to freedom was due south to the Swiss border, a distance just under 20 miles. However, the Germans patrolled this area heavily, especially after an escape attempt. An alternative, safer route was farther to the west, but over twice the distance at 40 miles and through more rugged terrain. Additionally, the escapees would have to swim the Rhine, which was particularly cold that time of year. For exhausted and malnourished soldiers, this idea posed a formidable challenge. The advantage to the longer route was that the border was virtually unguarded.

When the time came for the escape attempt, the Russian soldiers created much noise and confusion as a diversion, while other soldiers short-circuited the camp lights, which was the signal to go. The guards responded much faster than the prisoners had counted on, and the ladder from one of the windows fell to the ground. The escape was not executed according to plan, with only 6 men out of 13 getting out: Battle, Tucker, Isaacs (Izac), Willis, and Puryear. The Germans captured one man the night of the escape, 2nd Lieutenant Caxton Tichener, of the 96th Aero Squadron.

Battle was outside the camp for three days, having avoided border guards, police, and curious civilians on his way to the border. He was cold and hungry when he found the Rhine River, and he knew that freedom lay on just the other side of the water. He had moved to a point where he prepared to enter the water when he heard a low growl behind him. He was apprehended by a border guard before he could swim to freedom.

Rowan Tucker was also lucky enough to make it out of the camp and to avoid capture, but the three days on his own had taken their toll. He no food, and was cold, hungry, and so tired that he had difficulty thinking clearly. He knew that he was taking a chance following a heavily traveled road, but he also knew he did not have much energy left. He traveled at night and slept during the day, but on his fourth night of travel, his luck ran out about two miles from the border when a German soldier stepped out of the shadows along the road and ended his escape attempt.

Isaacs (Izac) and Willis were the only ones to make it out of camp and then join up outside. They took the long route that they thought would result in fewer border guards, willing to trade time and distance for security. They were surprised at how densely populated this region of the Black Forest was, which presented a danger that someone might spot them and report them to the police. However, the additional population meant numerous gardens that offered food for the hungry men. They spotted but avoided several civilians on the way to the border, reaching the Rhine River after five days on the move. They were surprised to find a number of guards along the river, but they avoided them long enough to slip into the river. The guards heard one of the men when he stumbled into the water, but they were swept downstream and away from the guards. They met up a few hours later, on the Swiss side of the border, free men.

George Puryear, often viewed as the leader of the group, went to one of the pre-arranged spots once outside the camp, but no one came. He made his way through the Black Forest and eventually reached Switzerland, the first American to escape from the Germans and return to his post during World War I.

Further Reading
Bowman, Martin. *Lost Wings of World War I: Downed Airmen on the Western Front, 1914–1918.* Barnsley, South Yorkshire: Pen and Sword, 2014.
Messimer, Dwight R. *Escape from Villingen, 1918.* College Station: Texas A & M University Press, 2000.

Vrba, Rudolf, and Alfred Wetzler

Conflict: World War II
Captured: 1942
Escaped: April 10, 1944

Auschwitz was the largest concentration camp in Germany and was located about 50 miles from Krakow, Poland. The main camp was built in 1940, with the sole purpose of exterminating Jews and other undesirables who posed a threat, real or perceived, to the Third Reich. The following year, 1941, the Nazis built Auschwitz-Birkenau, again with the main purpose of executing Jews. At the height of its concentration camp operations in 1944, the Germans executed over 12,000 people per day in these compounds, but hardly anyone outside of the camps knew what was happening within the barbed-wire fences. The Jews who were sent to their death at Auschwitz had no way of getting word to outside nations or agencies about the horrors that were happening within the camps. Although the sign at the entrance of the camp, *Arbeit Macht Frei*, "Work Brings Freedom," made people think they would eventually leave this place, this was not the case. However, two young men, Rudolf Vrba and Alfred Wetzler, would eventually make their escape and bring word to the outside world of the horrors occurring within Auschwitz.

In 1942, 17-year-old Rudolf Vrba, the son of a sawmill owner from Slovakia, was captured when he tried to flee the country. Vrba was sent to Auschwitz, arriving on June 30, 1942. One of the lucky ones, he was not killed when he arrived at the concentration camp. The guards separated the Jews upon their arrival into two groups: those who would die shortly after arrival and those who were chosen to work to support the camp. About 400 were chosen to do the farmwork. He pretended to be a tailor, and he was given one of the few jobs at the camp. Vrba collected luggage from the Jews and others who arrived at Auschwitz, and the people arriving had usually filled their baggage with their valuables. Vrba learned how to survive in the camp by moving when told, staying silent, and being as invisible as possible. He watched as the prisoners calmly followed orders of the guards upon their arrival, knowing they had willingly boarded the trains all over Europe on their way to these camps. Vrba believed that if he could get the truth about the camps out to the public, people would stop boarding the trains or at least try to escape. Vrba was determined to find a way to tell the world what was going on at Auschwitz.

Vrba desperately wanted to escape from Auschwitz, but getting out of the camp was nearly impossible. Many had tried to escape, but the Germans captured nearly all within a few hours. The lucky ones were outside the fences for a few days at most. Anyone who assisted escapees suffered the same fate as the returned prisoners, which included extreme torture and then being hung in front of all prisoners within the camp. Despite the dangers, Vrba was determined to escape and turned to 25-year-old Alfred Wetzler for help. Wetzler had also been sent to Auschwitz from Slovakia in 1942, and he was connected with the underground in the camp. Wetzler used his connections to get Vrba a new job as a secretary for camp officials, and with these new duties came new benefits. Vrba no longer had to wear a prison uniform, and he could go anywhere in the camp unchallenged. His desire to tell the world about Auschwitz was strong. He now had access to the German records of all prisoners they had killed as well as the determination to escape, but Vrba still did not have the means or opportunity to get out of the death camp.

In 1944, the Germans had the prisoners begin work on expanding the camp to double its size, and the workers understood that this meant more people would be coming to Auschwitz to die. The new construction began at the same time that Germany was invading Hungary, and the prison workers knew that's where the next trains would be coming from. Many workers had to work outside of the prison, and Vrba's opportunity soon presented itself. He and Wetzler hid in a hollow inside of a woodpile, and they knew from experience that the guards would only look for an escaped prisoner for three days. They thought that if they could remain hidden those three days, then they could virtually walk away from the concentration camp. On April 7, 1944, they began their plan. Once in the woodpile, they covered themselves with gasoline-soaked tobacco, hoping it would keep the camp dogs from finding their scent.

As they hoped, they went unnoticed for three days, and on the third day, they emerged from the woodpile and went into the nearby woods. Though they were stiff, they were free, and they traveled at night, finding food where they could, and only minimally aware of where they were and what direction they were heading. They decided the best course was to head south toward Slovakia, and at one point near the Slovakian border, they accidently stumbled into a town. They were hungry, and took a risk by asking for help. Fortunately for them, a peasant woman fed them and gave them shelter until night. Leaving her home, they encountered a woman taking care of crops in her field, and she connected the pair to another peasant who showed them where they could best avoid guards and get across the border.

After 3 days hiding in the woodpile and 15 days walking through 85 miles of occupied Poland to the Slovakian border, Vrba and Wetzler arrived at the Jewish Council headquarters, which was an administrative organization designed to assist Jews. Those at the organization knew that the concentration camp conditions were terrible, but they had no idea about the atrocities that were really taking place. The men were so stunned at Vrba and Wetzler's stories that they claimed they could not be true. It wasn't until Vrba started reciting the names of hundreds of exterminated Jews, the names of those he had written in the records while working in the office at Auschwitz, that they finally started to believe their story. The Jewish Council members asked Vrba and Wetzler for as many details as they could recall, and when they learned of the Nazi plan to start killing the Jews of Hungary, they actually locked up Wetzler and Vrba because they considered the information they had so dangerous. The report contained detailed descriptions of the camp, the treatment of the worker prisoners, and the transports that had arrived at Auschwitz, as well as how the gassings took placed. Vrba and Wetzler had knowledge of conditions that would only be known to someone who had been at the concentration camp.

Copies of the reports Vrba and Wetzler generated went to the British and the Americans. Officials from these nations eventually released the information to the public, and called on Admiral Miklos Horthy to stop the exportations. The media also picked up the story, and in late June 1944, the *New York Times* reported on what was happening at the concentration camps, and on June 16, 1944, the *Jewish Chronicle* in London also published a story, as did the British Broadcasting Company. Soon, other papers were picking up the details of the report written by Vrba and Wetzler, and their vow to tell people what was happening was fulfilled.

On January 27, 1945, Auschwitz was liberated by the Russians. Vrba went on to receive several degrees, and he testified against those who ordered and ran the death camps in Nazi Germany. Vrba moved to Israel and then Canada, and he worked as an associate professor of pharmacology in British Columbia, studying the chemistry of the brain, diabetes, and cancer, and he published over 50 papers on these subjects. Vrba died on March 27, 2006, in Vancouver, Canada. Wetzler died February 8, 1988, in Slovakia. Their stories were written and published many times, and several films and documentaries about their lives (mostly Vrba's story) were also produced, including *Genocide* (1973), *Shoah* (1985), and *Escape from Auschwitz* (2008).

Further Reading

Bestic, Alan, and Rudolf Vrba. *Escape From Auschwitz: I Cannot Forgive.* New York: Glove Press, 1964.

Wetzler, Alfred. *Escape from Hell: The True Story of the Auschwitz Protocol.* New York: Berghahn Books, 2007.

Wattenberg, Jürgen: Camp Papago Park Escape

Conflict: World War II
Captured: September 3, 1942
Escaped: December 23 to 24, 1944

Jürgen Wattenberg was born in Lübeck, Germany, on December 28, 1900. He joined the German navy, eventually becoming an officer. When World War II began, Wattenberg served in several capacities, eventually commanding U-boats. He was a decorated commander with a highly successful record. In one year, his campaigns sank 14 ships. He was one of the oldest U-boat commanders during the war, and he ran several successful campaigns before British warships sunk his boat, the *U-162*, on September 3, 1942. Only two of the crew died in the attack. Wattenberg was one of 49 survivors who were rescued and taken prisoner.

Wattenberg was held in several places, and in late January 1944, he was sent to Camp Papago Park, which is located near Phoenix, Arizona. Camp Papago Park was built inside Papago Park in 1943 and consisted of four areas for enlisted men and one compound for officers. Though it originally held Italian prisoners, by January 1944, it was used exclusively for German prisoners. At its largest, about 3,000 prisoners were held here, guarded by 371 Americans. The camp was surrounded by barbed wire and also had the obligatory watchtowers. Camp Papago Park was not a work camp, and those held there often felt the bleakness of boredom. Wattenberg was the highest-ranking German officer in the officer's compound, and perhaps, the most dangerous, as he had caused issues in his previous locations. In a miscalculation, the camp commander put Wattenberg and other trouble-making prisoners together, allowing them to work together to plan an escape. Though the captors believed the location in the Arizona desert would preclude escape attempts, the German prisoners soon proved their thinking to be incorrect. Between sight line obstructions and an unawareness of the tunneling that was going on within the barracks, the camp commanders would soon find themselves dealing with the largest World War II prisoner of war escape on American soil. Wattenberg and the other officers, all good leaders and unwilling to wait for release, planned their escape for December 23, 1944.

The Germans began tunneling in September 1944. Working inside the barracks, they took apart a wooden wall inside the showers, and at night, the German officers took turns going into the tunnel and removing dirt. Because there was construction around the camp, they were able to place the dirt outside without notice. They placed a large coal bin in front of the opening to the tunnel, effectively hiding it from the guards. The prisoners claimed they needed tools to help with the gardening, so the American guards provided shovels to them only during the day. The prisoners did not always return their tools, and the guards didn't notice. At completion, the tunnel was 178 feet in length, coming out near the Crosscut Canal. By the time the tunnel was complete, the German officers had also stockpiled clothing, food, and fake papers, as well as had determined how to get to Mexico and then back to Germany. Wattenberg was in charge of the preparations as well as the distraction, which was a party that would be held on the night of December 23 to keep the guards occupied. Additionally, Wattenberg and the officers refused to go to roll call unless an American officer conducted the exercise. The camp commander would not agree to this, and all of the prisoners had a restricted diet until the officers complied with camp regulations. The strike lasted 16 days and ended with a compromise. All had to be present at roll call except on Sunday mornings and afternoons at 4:15. Additionally, German officers could show themselves in the doorway and not have to come out into the yard. This was done to allow the German officers more travel time away from the camp before the alarm was given.

On the evening of December 23 and early morning of December 24, 1944, between about 10 p.m. and 2:30 a.m., 25 German officers, including Wattenberg, escaped through the tunnel and into the Crosscut Canal. They had thought about using a raft to float down river, but water levels were low and there was not enough current to keep the raft moving. They split up and headed out into the desert. Because there was no roll call on Sunday morning, December 24, the guards did not realize the Germans were missing until after supper on Sunday night. At that time, hundreds of soldiers, Native American scouts, and FBI agents undertook the search for the missing prisoners. Unprepared to be in the desert for a long period of time, most of the Germans surrendered or were recaptured within a few days. A few, however, did make it quite a distance from the camp. On January 1, 1945, two prisoners were captured just 30 miles from the Mexican border. Soon after that, another trio was caught near the town of Gila Bend on January 8, 1945.

Wattenberg eluded capture for over a month, but was finally apprehended on January 28, 1945. He had gone in the opposite direction from most of the escapees, heading north, sheltering in a cave north of Phoenix with two other escapees. Wattenberg was apprehended when he headed into Phoenix for a meal, his accent giving him away. None of the prisoners were injured during the recapture, and most had not left Maricopa County.

None of the prisoners received extensive punishment for their escape, though they did receive just bread and water for as many days as they had been gone from the camp. Wattenberg was released at the end of the war and returned to Germany. At one point, he managed the Lübeck branch of the St. Pauli Brewery. He died in 1995 at the age of 94. Camp Papago Park is still in use by the Arizona National Guard, and the Arizona Military Museum on base highlights the story of Wattenberg and his fellow German prisoners of war and their escape.

Further Reading
Lloyd, Keith Warren. *The Great Desert Escape: How the Flight of 25 German Prisoners of War Sparked One of the Largest Manhunts in American History.* New York: Globe Pequot, 2019.

Lynch, Adam. "Escape into Arizona's Desert: German Prisoners in World War II." *World War II History Magazine,* January 11, 2016. warfarehistorynetwork.com/daily/wwii/escape-into-arizonas-desert-german-prisoners-in-world-war-ii.

Thomas, Jr., Robert, MCG. "Jurgen Wattenberg, 94, P.O.W. Who Escaped." *New York Times,* December 6, 1995. www.nytimes.com/1995/12/04/us/jurgen-wattenberg-94-pow-who-escaped.html.

Webb, Kate

Conflict: Vietnam War
Captured: April 7, 1971
Escaped: April 30, 1971

Kate Webb, born March 24, 1943, was from Christchurch, New Zealand. Webb was a journalist's journalist in a time when very few women ventured into the dangers of combat zones. Her work for the United Press International (UPI), as well as her later work for Agence France-Presse, was honest and straightforward. As the bureau chief for Phnom Penh, she found herself in the middle of the conflict in Cambodia. She had spent three years covering the conflict in Indochina. Rather than taking the safe route, which had never been in her nature, she forged directly into the fighting. With her field interpreter, she headed down the infamous Highway 4 on April 7, 1971, hoping to get the story on what was happening in the nearby war zone.

Kate and her interpreter stumbled into the middle of a fierce attack. They took shelter in the ditches with four other civilians, waiting for the attack to subside enough to escape. Though they managed to elude soldiers for several hours, they were captured the next morning by the Cambodia Liberation Front. The six prisoners—two Vietnamese, four Cambodians, one Japanese, and Kate Webb, originally from New Zealand—were held for 23 days, marched through the jungle for much of that time, and housed in small camps for the rest. Though they were generally treated without rancor, the prisoners endured thirst, bugs, interrogations, and isolation during their captivity.

Although Webb's foray into journalism was still fairly radical at the time, her determined will and strong personality served her well during the time spent with her captors. Unsure how they would treat a female captive, Webb used her wit and understanding of the culture, as well as her understanding of the human condition, to keep from being singled out from the group. She was interrogated, and she stated that the process was lengthy, because every question and answer had to pass through an interpreter. She found that he was more literate in French than English. Her captors could not understand the concept of a free press, and they were certain she worked for the government. She spent much of her time trying to explain how UPI worked, and that she was not a government employee or representative of any government. She had to write statements to specific questions as well.

They often walked at night, and their shoes were either gone or ill fitting. All of the prisoners suffered from sores on their feet. Additionally, infection and dehydration were significant problems. Although the soldiers were not cruel, they were also not lenient when moving the prisoners, often marching 10 to 12 hours overnight. Given the environment they were in, with the heavy, dense foliage of the jungle, Webb recounts being afraid whenever helicopters could be heard, as she never knew if they were friend or foe, or if they would open fire, as they often did, into the dense foliage, knowing that enemy soldiers could be below. They often slept on the ground, or in bunkers, so exhausted that even the poor conditions did not matter.

In the trek through the jungle, they met up with soldiers, civilians, and even elephant patrols. Webb's attention to detail and memory for the unusual circumstances, such as the elephant brigade, earned her accolades when she recounted the experience. Her ability to inject humor in a situation that was anything but humorous makes her account of the experience engaging and intriguing.

When the group finally arrived at their destination, Webb named the small hut where she would stay until her release: *Phum Kasset*. Press village. One of the other captives told her she spelled it incorrectly, but that detail did not matter. Webb described the utter boredom being a prisoner of war, and although this is known not to be the case for soldiers who were captured, her experiences as a civilian POW were different. Even the arrival of new clothes punctuated the boredom, as did the attendance of the quasi-doctor who treated their feet and infections.

After two weeks in captivity, Webb was told to answer, in writing, a detailed questionnaire about her feelings on the war. She worried over telling the truth versus telling her captors what they wanted to hear. In the end, she followed her moral compass, writing what she perceived to be the truth about the conflict, the participants, and the overall situation. She was surprised when the soldiers took her answers verbatim. She knew that they would be broadcasting them as propaganda.

Twenty-two days after capture, they began to hope that they would be released. New clothes came in for them. They had to sign papers for their belongings. Webb's camera, of course, was not returned. When the time came for them to be released, they shook hands with the soldiers, some of whom could almost be called friends. As they traveled to the release point, they again feared that they might be killed in cross fire or stumble into a conflict. Suffering with double malaria, Webb found the journey difficult and arduous. After their release, they traveled back toward Phnom Penh. They were met by military personnel who picked them up and immediately took them back to the city where they could receive military care.

Kate Webb never knew exactly why they were released, and she didn't know until she returned that there had been extensive efforts to find her. At least one enemy source had said she was dead, and the *New York Times* and other media outlets ran her obituary. Her family even held a funeral. Webb's decision to go after that story on April 7, to venture out on Highway 4, had changed her life.

Webb continued to work as a journalist and foreign correspondent for UPI and Agence France-Presse (AFP), working in Iraq during the Gulf War, and in Indonesia in their war for independence. She was also in Afghanistan after the collapse of Najibullah's regime, and again captured. She was brutally beaten and escaped with the help of two other journalists. She retired in 2001 and died of cancer in 2007. She was memorialized on an Australian postage stamp in 2017.

Further Reading

"Kate Webb: UPI's Woman in Vietnam." National Public Radio (Weekend Edition Saturday), May 19, 2007. www.npr.org/templates/story/story.php?storyId=10275881.

Martin, D. "Kate Webb, War Correspondent, Dies at 64." *New York Times,* May 15, 2007. www.nytimes.com/2007/05/15/world/asia/15webb.html.

"War Correspondent: The Story of Kate Webb." Vietnam War, June 30, 2009. www.vietnamwar.govt.nz/memory/war-correspondent-kate-webb.

Webb, Kate. *On the Other Side: 23 Days with the Viet Cong.* New York: Quadrangle Books, 1972.

Werra, Franz von

Conflict: World War II
Captured: September 5, 1940
Escaped: January 21, 1941

Franz von Werra was born July 13, 1914, in Leuk, Switzerland. Werra was a lieutenant in the German air force, and on September 5, 1940, he was escorting German bombers over England. During the Battle of Britain, Werra was one of 30 fighter pilots on that mission that were surprised as three British Spitfires rose to meet them. As the British planes flew through the formation of German fighters, one of the planes sprayed the German formation with bullets. A one-in-a-million hit to Werra's plane caused the engine start to overheat and then seize. He was forced to crash-land the plane in a farmer's field, and he was taken prisoner almost immediately. Some accounts of Werra's capture indicate that his first escape attempt occurred as soon as he hit the ground, but these reports are not confirmed. Ironically, the man who shot Werra down, Flight Lieutenant John Webster, went back into action later that day to meet another German raid, and he was killed in the attempt.

Werra was interrogated for weeks in a London facility known as Cockfosters, and then British authorities transferred him to Officer's POW Camp No. 1, Grizedale Hall, near the end of September. Only a few days after his arrival, Werra worked out a plan for an escape. As with all escapes, he briefed to the escape committee, as it was imperative that all escapes be approved and that no prisoner work unilaterally on a plan. Most commonly, the escape committee disapproved of plans that had limited opportunity for success. However, Werra's plan was well conceived, and it worked, although he was recaptured later.

On October 7, 1940, Werra made his first major escape attempt. The plan revolved around the practice of taking prisoners for a long walk outside the fence at the prison camp. British guards escorted approximately 25 prisoners several times a week on a hike of about two miles. If the party headed north, there was little chance of escape. If the party marched south, however, there was a thick wood near the spot where the soldiers rested before returning to the prison camp. Werra convinced his comrades to stage a distraction while he leapt over a bridge and into the woods. The plan worked; he was not seen making his escape and the soldiers moving about in formation during the walk back to camp prevented the guards from getting an accurate count. In addition, two women working in farm fields had seen Werra escape into the woods and tried to alert the guards by waving and shouting, but the prisoners all waved and shouted back greetings.

Eventually, the guard force stopped the march and made everyone stand still. They discovered one prisoner was missing. Soldiers from camp and police officials began a concerted effort to find the escapee, but Werra seemed to have disappeared. The Home Guard, made up of small patrols of civilian volunteers, took part in the search as well, checking remote locations when Werra was not found quickly. A pair of guardsmen were checking *hoggarths,* small stone huts used to store sheep feed high in the remotest parts of the district, when they found one with a broken lock on the door. When the men opened the door, they found Werra. At first he pretended to be a lonely shepherd, but the guards knew his real identity. Once the game was up, Werra took off running and quickly lost his pursuers. His location was now known, and the ring around Werra tightened as the Home Guard, the police, and the British Army concentrated on capturing the escaped prisoner. A shepherd reported seeing a strange man traveling across a sheep field. Forces converged on the location, but the man seemed to have evaporated. Eventually, Werra was discovered, hiding in a deep mud puddle within a few yards of the search party. Cold and shivering, Werra was transferred back to the POW camp after six days on the run. For his escape attempt, Werra received 21 days in solitary confinement.

Werra was not finished with his attempts to escape, especially when his transfer to another camp presented an inviting opportunity. Swanwick Camp was used in both World War I and II as a POW camp, and contained a long, three-story building with 180 rooms that housed German officers. The unique thing about this building, known as the Garden House, was that it was only a few feet from the double barbed-wire fences that separated the prisoners from freedom. Werra and four other men dug a tunnel under the fences, under the road next to the fences, and broke out in a small patch of woods, which was perfect for concealing their movements. While the other prisoners broke off into pairs, Werra went forward alone. He pretended to be a Dutch flier from Coastal Command who had nursed his Wellington bomber back to England, crash-landed, and needed transportation to the nearest Royal Air Force base. He then planned to bluff his way into a plane and fly back to Germany.

Once out of the tunnel, Werra walked down the road away from the prison. After walking most of the night, Werra heard a train whistle, and he made his way to a small railroad station. He walked inside and explained his predicament to the clerk inside. Suspicious, the clerk called the local police and asked them to interview the man. In the meantime, Werra continued to talk to the clerk, and eventually convinced him that his cover story was real. He desperately needed a ride to the nearest RAF base to report the working of a new, top-secret bomb site he had seen on the bombing raid the night before. Eventually, the clerk picked up the phone and placed a call to the RAF base at Hucknall, a small training facility nearby. The adjutant promised to send a car for the pilot. Werra waited to see who would get there first, the RAF or the police.

Three police officers arrived at the railway station, suspicious about the man, especially given the fact that three German prisoners had escaped the night before.

Werra was nothing if not charming and so dedicated to his story that it never changed. Before long, the police were convinced of his story, and they waited with him until the RAF car appeared. When it arrived, the police bid Werra good luck as he got into the car with the driver. He was soon heading to the airfield at Hucknall. However, the officer there was already suspicious of Werra. The duty officer had spoken at length with the pilot, whose story was just a little too good, and he seemed to talk too much, going into details of the flight and the crash that no ordinary pilot would see as helpful. The duty officer placed a call to the airfield where Werra had supposedly flown out of the previous night. The connection was bad, and the duty officer had trouble communicating with the officer on the other end of the line. Werra took advantage of the distraction and left the building in search of an airplane. The longer that people looked into his story, the sooner someone would realize that his story was not true. Werra knew he should get out of England as soon as possible.

Werra wandered around the base, searching for the airfield where operational planes were kept. He walked past a guard point by taking advantage of confusion and construction projects going on in the area. Werra made his way to the nearest plane, which was also the newest in the Royal Air Force, the Hawker Hurricane. Unfortunately, he had no idea how to fly it. The controls and dials were completely different from the FW-109 he had flown in the Luftwaffe. Werra approached a mechanic working on one of the Hurricanes and introduced himself. He asked the mechanic to help him learn how to fly the plane, since it was new. The mechanic assumed the pilot was just another foreign ally who made up the team of ferry pilots who came and went quite regularly. However, the mechanic couldn't help Werra until he signed the visitor's book, as was protocol. Werra tried everything to talk the young man out of the requirements, to no avail. Because they were short ferry pilots, the manager did everything to expedite the required paperwork. Within a few minutes, Werra was sitting inside the Hawker Hurricane as the mechanic explained the basics of the aircraft. Werra was ready to take off once he got an auxiliary power supply, and he convinced the mechanic to go find one. As Werra sat at the controls and familiarized himself with them, he heard a voice behind him say simply, "Get out." It was the duty officer, who had gotten through to the base where Werra said he had flown out of the night before. They had never heard of Captain van Lott, the name Werra was using. Werra quickly confessed to being an escaped prisoner, before the British shot him as a spy. Werra's audacious plan had nearly worked; instead, he was transferred back to the POW camp at Swanwick.

The camp commander sentenced Werra and the other escapees, all of whom had been caught, to 14 days in solitary confinement, but they did not serve out the whole sentence because the prisoners at the camp were transferred to a POW camp in Canada. The prisoners boarded buses at the camp, railcars at Butterly, and boarded the liner *Duchess of York* for the transatlantic crossing. The ship was part of a convoy and bound for Halifax, Nova Scotia, where the prisoners would be taken by railcar to another prison camp. Werra volunteered to work in the kitchen, and he soon found he could get almost anywhere, and hatched another plan for escape. He devised a plan where the prisoners took over the ship and sailed it back to Germany. The success of such a plan depended upon the liner breaking away from the

Franz von Werra, a German pilot whose escape attempts were legendary. (ullstein bild via Getty Images)

convoy with no other escort ships. The destroyers accompanying the convoy would never let a hijacked prison ship make it back to Germany without a battle. One the last day of the crossing, all ships but one destroyer broke away from the convoy, scuttling any chance of success for their idea. The prisoners abandoned the escape plan.

When the ship docked, the prisoners were counted, then moved to trains for the final leg of the journey to the next prison camp. Guards considered the train escape-proof, as guards were at the front and rear of each car, and the windows were frozen shut. But Werra hatched another plan. The heat inside the railcar slightly melted the ice in and around the double-pane windows each time the car stopped. When the train was in motion, the ice froze solid again. Werra managed to open the first window crack, allowing the ice to melt much faster, and continue to melt even with the train moving. The ice did not melt fast enough though, so Werra opened the inside window as high as it would go. Before long, the window was ice free. He planned to wait until the train was going slow enough to jump out so he did not kill himself in the process. His plan was aided when the diet of apples made many of the prisoners sick, and the guards assumed that nobody could escape if they were that ill.

Werra was ready to make his escape, as the window was completely ice free. The train slowed, then stopped at a small rail station, and the guards exited the train to stretch their legs. He forgot that his window might attract attention, being the only window on the train without ice covering it, making the inside opaque. Werra's window was completely clear and allowed light from the inside of the train to be seen clearly from the platform. However, none of the guards seemed to notice. When the train began to roll out of the station, Werra made his move. He had his comrades make a fuss out of opening a blanket, and behind it, he opened the window and jumped out. Incredibly, nobody noticed a thing. The date was January 21, 1941.

Werra was stunned when he hit the ground, his fall broken only slightly by the snow piled next to the track. When he had recovered from the fall, he took a bearing on the North Star. He moved south and headed for the border with the United States, a nation still neutral until the end of 1941. He had left the train near the town of Smith Falls, only a few miles from the international border, where the St. Lawrence River separated the two nations. Werra was close to the border, but walking through the woods and the deep snow took hours. He was exhausted and suffering from frostbite when he reached the river. He knew that freedom awaited him on the other side. Assuming the river was frozen, he attempted to walk across it, but found that the last few meters were an ice-free channel. If he tried to swim that length, he would freeze to death. The only thing to do was go back to the Canadian side and look for a boat. After about two miles, he came upon a summer camp, boarded up for the winter. He found a usable boat there and pushed it down to the river and across the frozen part of it. Once to the channel, he jumped aboard the small craft, allowing the current to take him to the American side of the river.

Once ashore, he was afraid to celebrate, for fear that something may have gone wrong and he was still in Canada. He walked down the road until he found someone who could help him understand where he was. The man shared that he was in

America, in Ogdensburg, New York. Werra walked away, looking for the local police station to turn himself in. He was taken into custody and the German consul in New York City was notified. While in jail, he gave an interview to the press, and told a wildly exaggerated story of his escape, which complicated his legal case. Werra was charged with entering the United States illegally, but those charges were eventually dropped while Canada and the United States discussed their common problem. Canada wanted their prisoner back, and the United States wanted him gone. During this time, Werra made frequent trips between New York City and Washington, and he wrote many reports on his interrogation at the hands of the British.

Convinced that American officials were about to return him to Canadian authorities, Werra left for Mexico with the help of German intelligence operatives. He reached South America, where he caught a ship bound for Spain, and then headed to Italy. Upon his return to Germany in April 1941, Adolf Hitler awarded him the Knight's Cross of the Iron Cross. Werra spent much time explaining the British interrogation techniques he had experienced. When he finally returned to duty with the Luftwaffe in July 1941, he went to the Russian front where he scored 13 aerial victories, which brought his total to 21. He soon returned to Germany, and then on to the Netherlands where he transitioned to a new fighter, the BF 109F-4. On October 25, 1941, Werra took off in his new aircraft. This was to be his last flight, as the engine shut down and the plane crashed into the sea. Werra's body was never found. The book about his life, *The One That Got Away,* was also the basis for a 1957 film of the same name. Additionally, parts of that movie were used in a documentary about his life, titled *Von Werra,* was released in 2002.

Further Reading
Burt, Kendal, and James Leasor. *The One That Got Away.* London: Collins Clear-Type Press, 1956.

Bibliography

Aharoni, Zvi, and Wilhelm Dietl. *Operation Eichmann: The Inside Story of History's Most Notorious Manhunt Told by Its Chief Investigator.* New York: John Wiley & Sons, 1996.

Aharoni, Zvi, and Wilhelm Dietl. *Operation Eichmann: The Truth about the Pursuit, Capture and Trial.* London: Arms and Armour, 1997.

Anderson, William C. *Bat 21.* New York: Bantam, 1980.

Appleman, Roy E. "The North Korean Great Naktong Offensive." *South to the Naktong, North to the Yalu.* Washington, D.C.: Center of Military History. https://history.army.mil/books/korea/20-2-1/sn24.htm.

Appleman, Roy E. *South to the Naktong, North to the Yalu: United States Army in the Korean War.* Washington, D.C.: Department of the Army, 1998.

Arthur, Anthony. *Deliverance at Los Baños.* New York: St. Martin's Press, 1985.

Asada, Teruhiko. *The Night of a Thousand Suicides.* Sydney, Australia: Angus & Robertson, 1970.

Ash, William. *Under the Wire.* London: Bantam, 2006.

Badsey, Stephen. *Arnhem 1944: Operation Market Garden.* London: Osprey Publishing, 1993.

Bartleson, Frederick A. *Letters from Libby Prison.* Edited by Margaret W. Peelle. New York: Greenwich Book Publishers, 1956.

Bascomb, Neal. *The Grand Escape: The Greatest Prison Breakout of the 20th Century.* New York: Arthur A. Levine Books, 2018.

Bascomb, Neal. *Hunting Eichmann: How a Band of Survivors and a Young Spy Agency Chased Down the World's Most Notorious Nazi.* Boston: Houghton Mifflin Harcourt, 2009.

Beevor, Antony. *Arnhem: The Battle for the Bridges, 1944.* New York: Viking Press, 2018.

Benuzzi, Felice. *No Picnic on Mount Kenya: A Dangerous Escape, A Perilous Climb.* London: William Kimber, 1952.

Benuzzi, Silvia. *No Picnic on Mount Kenya: Felice Benuzzi's Daughter Reflects on her Father's Adventure.* Waterstones (blog), September 30, 2016. www.waterstones.com/blog/no-picnic-on-mount-kenya-felice-benuzzis-daughter-reflects-on-her-fathers-adventure.

Bestic, Alan, and Rudolf Vrba. *Escape from Auschwitz: I Cannot Forgive.* New York: Glove Press, 1964.

Beszedits, Stephen, ed. *The Libby Prison Diary of Colonel Emeric Szabad*. Toronto: B & L Information Services, 1999.

"BGen James D. McBrayer, Jr." The Military Hall of Honor. www.militaryhallofhonor.com/honoree-record.php?id=223103.

Bishop, Patrick. *The Cooler King: The True Story of William Ash, the Greatest Escaper of World War II*. New York: Overlook Press, 2015.

Bosworth, R. J. B. *Mussolini's Italy: Life under the Fascist Dictatorship, 1915–1945*. New York: Penguin, 2002.

Bowden, Mark. *Black Hawk Down: A Story of Modern War*. New York: Grove Press, 1999.

Bowden, Mark. *Guests of the Ayatollah: The Iran Hostage Crisis: The First Battle in America's War with Militant Islam*. New York: Grove Press, 2007.

Bowman, Martin. *Lost Wings of World War I: Downed Airmen on the Western Front, 1914–1918*. Barnsley, South Yorkshire: Pen and Sword, 2014.

Boyle, David. *Dunkirk: A Miracle of Deliverance*. CreateSpace Independent Publishing Platform, May 30, 2017.

Bragg, R. *I Am a Soldier, Too: The Jessica Lynch Story*. New York: Vintage Books, 2003.

Braude, Mark. *The Invisible Emperor: Napoleon on Elba From Exile to Escape*. New York: Penguin Press, 2018.

Braun, Jutta, and René Wiese. "'Tracksuit Traitors': Eastern German Top Athletes on the Run." *The International Journal of the History of Sport* 31, no. 12 (2014): 1519–34. doi:10.1080/09523367.2014.922549.

Brickhill, Paul. *Escape to Danger* (with Conrad Norton). London: Faber and Faber, 1946.

Brickhill, Paul. *The Great Escape*. New York: Norton, 1950.

Brooks, Richelle. Veteran's History Project. Library of Congress. Personal interview, April 27, 2017. memory.loc.gov/diglib/vhp/story/loc.natlib.afc2001001.72186/transcript?ID=sr0001.

Breuer, William B. *The Great Raid on Cabanatuan: Rescuing the Doomed Ghosts of Bataan and Corregidor*. New York: John Wiley & Sons, 2002.

Brewer, Paul. *The Lima Embassy Siege and Latin American Terrorism: Terrorism in Today's World*. New York: Gareth Stevens Publishing, 2006.

Brown, Curt. "In the Foot Steps of Little Crow." *Star Tribune*, 2012. www.startribune.com/historical-narrative-of-a-dakota-chief-in-the-footsteps-of-little-crow/425712324.

Buchanan, Jessica. *Impossible Odds: The Kidnapping of Jessica Buchanan and Her Dramatic Rescue by SEAL Team Six*. New York: Atria Books, 2013.

Burns, Joe Lee. "A Ridge Too Far: Shot Down by AAA and Rescued Off Haiphong." www.keytlaw.com/f-4/a-ridge-too-far.

Burrows, Edwin G. *Forgotten Patriots: The Untold Story of American Prisoners during the Revolutionary War*. New York: Basic Books, 2008.

Burt, Kendal, and James Leasor. *The One That Got Away*. London: Collins Clear-Type Press, 1956.

Butcher, Tim. *Chasing the Devil: The Search for Africa's Fighting Spirit*. London: Chatto & Windus/Penguin Random House UK, 2010.

Cahill, Lora Schmidt, and David L. Mowery, *Morgan's Raid across Ohio: The Civil War Guidebook of the John Hunt Morgan Heritage Trail*. Columbus, Ohio: Ohio Historical Society, 2014.

Carley, Kenneth. *The Dakota War of 1862: Minnesota's Other Civil War*. St. Paul, MN: Minnesota Historical Society Press, 1976. First published 1961.

Carroll, B. "Streetcar 304" Returns to Combat. USS America Museum Foundation, February 23, 2011. http://ussamerica-museumfoundation.org/library/fields.html.

Carroll, Tim. *The Great Escape from Stalag Luft III*. New York: Gallery Books, 2005.

Cavada, F. F. *Libby Life: Experiences of a Prisoner of War In Richmond, VA, 1863–1864*. Foreword by Joseph John Jova. New York: University Press of America, 1985.

Chun, Clayton K. S. *The Last Boarding Party: The USMC and the SS Mayaguez*. Cambridge, UK: Osprey Publishing, 2011.

Clowes, Peter. "Edith Cavell: World War I Nurse and Heroine." HistoryNet, June 12, 2006. http://www.historynet.com/edith-cavell-world-war-i-nurse-and-heroine.htm.

Collins, Bob. "Bob Hoover, One of History's Greatest Pilots, dead at 94." Minnesota Public Radio News, October 25, 2016. blogs.mprnews.org/newscut/2016/10/bob-hoover-one-of-nations-greatest-pilots-dead-at-94.

Cook, Jacqueline. *The Real Great Escape: The Story of the First World War's Most Daring Mass Breakout*. Random House Australia, 2013.

Cook, J. L. *Rescue Under Fire: The Story of Dust Off in Vietnam*. Atglen, PA: Schiffer Military/Aviation History, 1998.

Cornelius, Elias. *Journal of Dr. Elias Cornelius: A Revolutionary Surgeon: Graphic Description of His Suffering while a Prisoner in Provost Jail, New York, 1777 and 1778*. Washington, D.C.: Tomkins and Sherman, 1903.

Cussans, Thomas. "The Attack on the SS *Anglo Saxon*." In *Incredible Journeys*. Collins & Brown, 2007.

Dakss, Brian. *Thomas Hamill on his Iraq Escape*. CBS, October 10, 2004. www.cbsnews.com/news/thomas-hamill-on-his-iraq-escape.

Dando-Collins, Stephen. *The Hero Maker: A Biography of Paul Brickhill: The Australian behind the Legendary Stories: The Dam Busters, The Great Escape and Reach for the Sky*. Sydney: Random House Australia, 2016.

Davis, Barry. *Fire Magic—Hijack at Mogadishu*. London: Bloomsbury Publishing, 1994.

Dengler, D. "I Escaped from a Red Prison." *Saturday Evening Post*, December 3, 1966, pp. 27–33.

Dengler, D. *Escape from Laos*. San Rafael, CA: Presidio Press, 1979.

Dengler, Dieter (interview). July 5, 2007. www.youtube.com/watch?v=IvhYWN3nW2E.

Döbler, Peter. "The Lone Swim." In *Great Escapes*. Pleasantville, NY: The Reader's Digest Association, 1977.

Dockery, Kevin. *Operation Thunderhead: The True Story of Vietnam's Final POW Rescue Mission—and the Last Navy SEAL Killed in Country*. New York: Berkeley Caliber, 2008.

Dramesi, John A. *Code of Honor.* New York: Norton, 1975.
Driggs, Laurence La Tourette. *Heroes of Aviation.* Little, Brown, 1918.
Durant, Michael. *In the Company of Heroes.* New York: New American Library, 2003.
Durnford, H. G. *The Tunnellers of Holzminden.* London: Cambridge University Press, 1920.
Echternkamp, Jorg, ed. *Germany and the Second World War.* Oxford: Clarendon Press, 2014.
"Escape into East Germany Not Blocked by Wire, Mines." Associated Press, July 7, 1963.
Fantz, A. "For Years, Former POW Jessica Lynch Kept the Hurt Inside." CNN, July 20, 2015. www.cnn.com/2015/07/20/us/jessica-lynch-where-is-she-now/index.html.
Fehrenbach, T. R. *This Kind of War: The Classic Korean War History.* Fiftieth Anniversary Edition. Washington, D.C.: Potomac Books Inc., 2001.
Fields, Kenny. *The Rescue of Streetcar 304: A Navy Pilot's Forty Hours on the Run in Laos.* Annapolis, Maryland: Naval Institute Press, 2007.
Fischer, Marc. "'Let There Be Light': The Fall of the Berlin Wall and How Fear Dies." *Washington Post,* February 5, 2018. www.washingtonpost.com/news/retropolis/wp/2018/02/05/and-let-there-be-light-the-fall-of-the-berlin-wall-and-how-fear-dies/?utm_term=.8d0965e460ce.
Fishman, Jack. *And the Walls Came Tumbling Down.* London: MacMillan, 1983.
Flanagan, Edward M. *The Los Baños Raid: The 11th Airborne Jumps at Dawn.* New York: Presidio Press, 1986.
Fowler, Glenn. "Col. James Rowe, 51, War Hero, Is Killed in an Ambush in Manila." *New York Times,* April 22, 1989. www.nytimes.com/1989/04/22/obituaries/col-james-rowe-51-war-hero-is-killed-in-an-ambush-in-manila.html.
Fowler, Will. *Certain Death in Sierra Leone: The SAS and Operation Barras.* New York: Osprey Publishing, 2010.
Fraser, Antonia. *Mary Queen of Scots.* New York: Delta, 1969.
Freeman, Gregory A. *The Forgotten 500: The Untold Story of the Men Who Risked All for the Greatest Rescue Mission of World War II.* New York: Dutton Caliber, 2008.
Fremont-Barnes, Gregory. *Who Dares Wins: The SAS and the Iranian Embassy Siege.* Oxford; Osprey Publishing, 1980.
Fried, J. "Dieter Dengler Identified as the First American Pilot to Escape from North Vietnam in 1966." *Daily News,* July 28, 1966.
Frisbee, John L. "Valor: A Good Thought to Sleep On." *Air Force Magazine,* February 1992. www.airforcemag.com/MagazineArchive/Pages/1992/March%201992/0392valor.aspx.
Garus, John. *The Son Tay Raid: American POWs in Vietnam Were Not Forgotten.* College Station: Texas A&M Press, 2007.
Gebhardt, Major James F. *Eyes behind the Lines: US Army Long-Range Reconnaissance and Surveillance Units.* Fort Leavenworth, Kansas: Combat Studies Institute Press, 2005.

Gershkovich, Evan. "Who Was Roland Garros? The Fighter Pilot behind the French Open." *New York Times,* June 10, 2017. www.nytimes.com/2017/06/10/briefing/roland-garros-facts-french-open.html.

"G.I. Unit Stranded on Hill Spells 'Help' with Guns." *New York Times,* September 3, 1950.

Giampietri, Luis, Bill Salisbury, and Lorena Ausejo. *41 Seconds to Freedom.* New York: Presidio Press, 2007.

Glazier, Willard W. *The Capture, the Prison Pen, and the Escape: Giving a Complete History of Prison Life in the South.* New York: United States Publishing Company, 1868.

Glazier, Willard W., and Hudson Brother. *Heroes of Three Wars: Comprising a Series of Biographical Sketches of the Most Distinguished Soldier.* Charleston, SC: Bibliolife, 2010.

Guilmartin, John Francis. *A Very Short War: The Mayaguez and the Battle of Koh Tang.* College Station: Texas A&M University Press, 1995.

Guy, John. *Queen of Scots: The True Story of Mary Stuart.* Boston: Mariner Press, 2017.

Hamill, Thomas, Paul T. Brown, and Jay Langston. *Escape in Iraq: The Thomas Hamill Story.* Accokeek, MD: Stoeger Publishing, 2004.

Harrer, Heinrich. *Seven Years in Tibet.* London: Hart-Davis and the Book Society, 1953.

Harrer, Heinrich. *The White Spider: The story of the North Face of the Eiger.* New York: Harper Perennial, 2005.

Heaps, Leo. *The Evaders.* New York: William Morrow, 1976.

Helm, M. M. *Prairie Boys at War. Korea: Volume I: June—October 1950.* Fargo, ND: Prairie Boy Books, 2014.

Henderson, B. *Hero Found: The Greatest POW Escape of the Vietnam War.* New York: Harper Collins, 2010.

Henderson, Bruce. *Rescue at Los Baños: The Most Daring Prison Camp Raid of World War II.* New York: William Morrow, 2015.

Hibbert, Christopher. *Arnhem.* London: Phoenix, 2003. First published 1962.

Hibbert, Christopher. *Mussolini: The Rise and Fall of Il Duce.* New York: Little, Brown, 1962.

Hill, William Thomson. *The Martyrdom of Nurse Cavell: The Life Story of the Victim of Germany's Most Barbarous Crime.* London: Hutchinson, 1915.

Hoehling, A. "The Story of Edith Cavell." *The American Journal of Nursing* 57, no. 10 (1957): 1320–22. doi:10.2307/3461516.

Hoover, Robert. *Forever Flying: Fifty Years of High-Flying Adventures, from Barnstorming in Prop Planes to Dogfighting Germans to Testing Supersonic Jets.* New York: Pocket Books, 1997.

Horwitz, Lester V., and James A. Ramage. *The Longest Raid of the Civil War: Little-Known & Untold Stories of Morgan's Raid into Kentucky, Indiana, and Ohio.* Loveland, Ohio: Farmcourt Publishing, 1999.

Isaacs (Izac), Edouard V. *Prisoner of the U-90.* New York: Houghton Mifflin, 1919.

Izac, Edouard Victor Michel. *The Holy Land—Then and Now.* Springfield, Massachusetts: Vantage Press, 1965.

Jacobs, Timothy M. *The 1864 Diary of Union Civil War Soldier Sergeant Samuel E. Grosvenor: A First-hand Account of the Horrors at Andersonville Prison.* New York: Two If By Sea Publishing, 2011.

"Japanese Hostage Crisis and Operation Chavin de Huantar." *En Peru,* August 18, 2008. http://enperublog.com/2008/08/18/japanese-hostage-crisis-and-operation-chavin-de-huantar/.

Jorgensen, Kregg P. J. *MIA Rescue: LRRP Manhunt in the Jungle.* Boulder, Colorado: Paladin Press, 1995.

Joseph, Dilip, and Jim Lund. *Kidnapped by the Taliban.* Nashville, Tennessee: Thomas Nelson, 2014.

Kate Webb: UPI's Woman in Vietnam. National Public Radio (Weekend Edition Saturday), May 19, 2007. www.npr.org/templates/story/story.php?storyId=10275881.

Keith, Philip. *Blackhorse Riders: A Desperate Last Stand, an Extraordinary Rescue Mission, and the Vietnam Battle America Forgot.* New York: St. Martin's Press, 2012.

Kelly, Mary Pat. *"Good to Go": The Rescue of Capt. Scott O'Grady, USAF, from Bosnia.* Annapolis, MD: Naval Institute Press. 1996.

Kelly, Lt. Cmdr. Richard M. "Behind the Enemy Lines Series: Halyard Mission." *Blue Book Magazine* 83, no. 4 (August 1946).

"The Killing Machine." *Mayday.* Season 2, Episode 3. Discovery Channel Canada / National Geographic Channel, 2004.

Kiper, Richard L. "Delta Force at Desert One." In *Great Raids in History: From Drake to Desert One*, edited by Samuel A. Southworth. New York: Sarpedon Publishers, 1997.

Klein, Aaron J. *Striking Back: The 1972 Munich Olympics Massacre and Israel's Deadly Response.* New York: Random House, 2007.

Korda, Michael. *Alone.* Liveright, September 19, 2017.

Krebs, Daniel. *A Generous and Merciful Enemy: Life for German Prisoners of War during the American Revolution.* Norman: University of Oklahoma Press, 2013.

Lanning, Michael Lee. *Inside the LRRPs: Ranger in Vietnam.* New York: Presidio Press, 1988.

Larive, Hans. *The Man Who Came in from Colditz.* London: Hale, 1975.

Levy, Reginald. *From Night Flak to Hijack: It's a Small World.* Gloucestershire: History Press, 2015.

Lieutenant-Commander E. H. Larive. Netherlands Navy. www.netherlandsnavy.nl/Men_larive.htm.

Lloyd, Keith Warren. *The Great Desert Escape: How the Flight of 25 German Prisoners of War Sparked One of the Largest Manhunts in American History.* New York: Globe Pequot, 2019.

Lodge, Robert Alfred (biography). P.O.W. Network. www.pownetwork.org/bios/l/l068.htm.

Logan, Nick. "Capt. Richard Phillips Still Sailing Seas after 2009 Pirate Attack." Global News, October 12, 2013. globalnews.ca/news/899327/capt-richard-phillips-still-sailing-seas-after-2009-pirate-attack.

Lord, Walter. *The Miracle of Dunkirk: the True Story of Operation Dynamo.* New York: Open Road Media, 1982.

Lyman, Robert. *The Jail Busters: The Secret Story of MI6, the French Resistance, and Operation Jericho.* London: Quercus Publishing, 2015.

Lynch, Adam. "Escape into Arizona's Desert: German Prisoners in World War II." Warfare History Network, WWII, January 11, 2016. warfarehistorynetwork.com/daily/wwii/escape-into-arizonas-desert-german-prisoners-in-world-war-ii.

MacKenzie, Norman. *The Escape from Elba: The Fall and Flight of Napoleon, 1814–1815.* New York: Oxford University Press, 1982.

MacPherson, Malcolm. *Roberts Ridge: A Story of Courage and Sacrifice on Takur Ghar Mountain, Afghanistan.* New York: Dell, 2005.

Manchester, William, and Paul Reid. *The Last Lion: Winston Spencer Churchill: Defender of the Realm, 1940–1965.* New York: Bantam, 2013.

Mangerich, Agnes Jensen. *Albanian Escape: The True Story of the U.S. Army Nurses behind Enemy Lines.* Lexington: University of Kentucky Press, 1999.

Martin, D. "Kate Webb, War Correspondent, Dies at 64." *New York Times,* May 15, 2007. www.nytimes.com/2007/05/15/world/asia/15webb.html.

McBrayer, James D. *Escape!: Memoir of a World War II Marine Who Broke Out of a Japanese POW Camp and Linked Up With Chinese Communist Guerillas.* Jefferson, North Carolina: McFarland, 1995.

McBride, James J. *Interned: Internment of the SS* Columbus *Crew at Fort Stanton, New Mexico 1941–1945.* Santa Fe, NM: Paper Tiger, 2003.

McCarten, Anthony. *Darkest Hour: How Churchill Brought England Back from the Brink.* Harper Perennial: Media Tie, November 7, 2017.

McElroy, John. *This Was Andersonville: The True Story of Andersonville Military Prison as Told in the Personal Recollections of John McElroy, Sometime Private, Co. L, 16th Illinois Cavalry.* New York: McDowell, Obolensky, 1957.

McKay, Sinclair. *Dunkirk: From Disaster to Deliverance—Testimonies of the Last Survivors.* ReadHowYouWant, March 27, 2015.

McKenzie, Kenneth Seaforth. *Dead Men Rising.* Sydney, Australia: Angus & Robertson, 1975.

McNab, Chris. *Storming Flight 181: GSG 9 and the Mogadishu Hijack 1977.* New York: Osprey Publishing, 2011.

McRaven, William H. *Operation Jonathon: The Israeli Raid on Entebbe, 4 July 1976.* Novato, CA: Presidio Press, 1996.

McRaven, William H. "Operation Oak: The Rescue of Benito Mussolini, 12 September 1943." In *Spec Ops: Case Studies in Special Operations Warfare: Theory and Practice.* Novato, CA: Presidio Press, 1996.

Mendez, Antonio, and Matt Baglio. *ARGO: How the CIA and Hollywood Pulled Off the Most Audacious Rescue in History.* New York: Penguin Books, 2012.

Messimer, Dwight R. *Escape from Villingen, 1918.* College Station: Texas A & M University Press, 2000.

Miles, D. "*Rescue Dawn* Tells True Story of Vietnam POW Rescue." American Forces Press Service, June 20, 2007. Retrieved October 15, 2017, from www.af.mil/News/Article-Display/Article/126501/rescue-dawn-tells-true-story-of-vietnam-pow-rescue.

Millard, Candice. *Hero of the Empire: The Boer War, a Daring Escape and the Making of Winston Churchill.* New York: Doubleday, 2016.

Millett, Allan R. *The War for Korea, 1950–1951: They Came from the North.* Kansas City: University Press of Kansas, 2010.

"Mount Kenya: Simon Calder Tackles Africa's Other Summit; With a Guide, a Map and Lots of Tea Breaks, Simon Calder Retraces the Steps of Felice Benuzzi, a POW Who Escaped to Climb Mount Kenya—Then Snuck Back into Camp." *Belfast Telegraph,* October 29, 2007.

Mowery, David L. *Morgan's Great Raid: The Remarkable Expedition from Kentucky to Ohio (Civil War Series).* Stroud, UK: The History Press, 2013.

"Navy SEALs Who Killed Osama bin Laden in Rescue of 2 Hostages in Somalia: Report." Associated Press/*New York Daily News,* January 25, 2012. www.nydailynews.com/news/world/u-s-military-raid-somalia-frees-american-dane-held-hostage-article-1.1011524.

Neave, Airey. *Little Cyclone.* 2nd ed. London: Biteback Publishing, 2016.

Netanyahu, Iddo. *Entebbe: A Defining Moment in the War on Terrorism. The Jonathan Netanyahu Story.* London: Balfour Books, 2009.

Neville, Leigh. *Takur Ghar: The SEALs and Rangers on Roberts Ridge, Afghanistan 2002.* New York: Osprey Publishing, 2013.

Nichol, John, and Tony Rennell. *The Last Escape: The Untold Story of Allied Prisoners of War in Europe 1944–45.* New York: Viking, 2003.

O'Grady, Scott, and Jeff Coplon. *Return with Honor.* New York: Doubleday, 1998.

O'Grady, Scott, and Michael French. *Basher Five-Two: The True Story of F-16 Fighter Pilot Captain Scott O'Grady.* New York: Doubleday, 1995.

Olterman, Phillip. "Surfboards and Submarines: The Secret Escape of East Germans to Copenhagen." *The Guardian,* October 17, 2014. www.theguardian.com/cities/2014/oct/17/surfboards-and-submarines-the-secret-escape-of-east-germans-to-copenhagen.

Ottis, Sherri Green. *Silent Heroes: Downed Airmen and the French Underground.* Lexington, KY: University of Kentucky Press, 2001.

Painton, Frederick C. "The Elusive French General." *Great Escapes.* Pleasantville, NY: The Reader's Digest Association, 1977.

Phillips, Richard. *A Captain's Duty: Somali Pirates, Navy SEALs, and Dangerous Days at Sea.* New York: Hyperion Books, 2010.

Phillips, Russell. *Operation Nimrod: The Iranian Embassy Siege.* Trevissome Park, England: Shilka Publishing, 2015.

Pluschow, Gunther. *My Escape from Donington Hall.* Pen and Sword Military, 2015.

Ramsey, B. H. "The Evacuation of the Allied Armies from Dunkirk and Neighbouring Beaches." *London Gazette,* July 17, 1947. London: His Majesty's Stationery Office: 3295–3318. www.ibiblio.org/hyperwar/UN/UK/LondonGazette/38017.pdf.

Ransom, John L. *John Ransom's Andersonville Diary.* London: Douglass Brothers, 1883.

Rashke, Richard. *Escape from Sobibor*. Harrison, NY: Delphinium Books, 1995. First published 1982.
Reeve, Simon. *One Day in September: The Full Story of the 1972 Munich Olympics Massacre and the Israeli Revenge Operation Wrath of God*. New York: Arcade Publishing, 2011.
Rippon, Anton. *Gunther Pluschow: Airman, Escaper, Explorer*. Barnsley, England: Pen and Sword, 2009.
Ritchie, Steve. "The Rescue of Roger Locher" (video). www.youtube.com/watch?v=QvRcP4go-eg.
Rochester, Stuart, and Frederick Kiley. *Honor Bound: American Prisoners of War in Southeast Asia 1961–1973*. University Park, Illinois: Naval Institute Press, 2007.
Rottman, G. L. *The Los Baños Prison Camp Raid*. Oxford: Osprey Publishing, 2010.
Rottman, Gordon L. *The Cabanatuan Prison Raid: The Philippines 1945*. Oxford, UK: Osprey Publishing, 2009.
Rottman, Gordon L. *US Army Long-Range Patrol Scout in Vietnam 1965–1971*. Oxford: Osprey Publishing, 2008.
Roussel, Meg. "Escape Artist: General Giraud." The National WWII Museum, April 17, 2012. www.nww2m.com/2012/04/escape-artist-general-giraud.
Rowe, James N. *Five Years to Freedom*. Boston: Little, Brown, 1971.
Ryan, Cornelius. *A Bridge Too Far*. New York: Simon and Schuster, 1974.
Ryan, John P. *Fort Stanton and Its Community: 1855–1896*. Yucca Tree Press, 1998.
Sancton, Thomas. "Anatomy of a Hijack." *Time*, June 24, 2001.
Sanders, Charles W. *While in the Hands of the Enemy: Military Prisons of the Civil War*. Baton Rouge: Louisiana State University Press, 2005.
Sanders, Edmund, and Julian E. Barnes. "Somalia Pirates Hold U.S. Captain." *Los Angeles Times*, April 9, 2009. articles.latimes.com/2009/apr/09/world/fg-somali-pirates9.
Saul, David. *Operation Thunderbolt: Flight 139 and the Raid on Entebbe Airport, the Most Audacious Hostage Rescue Mission in History*. New York: Little, Brown, 2015.
Schemmer, Benjamin. *The Son Tay Prison Rescue Mission*. New York: Ballantine, 2002.
"77 Days Behind Enemy Lines: Sergeant Returns to the Land of the Living." *Corpus Christi Times*, October 2, 1950.
Shelvis, Jules. *Sobibor: A History of a Nazi Death Camp*. New York: Berg, 2007.
"Ships Hit by German U-boats during WWII: *Siamese Prince*." Uboat.net, 2016. www.uboat.net/allies/merchants/ships/766.html.
Sides, Hampton. *Ghost Soldiers: The Forgotten Epic Story of World War II's Most Dramatic Mission*. New York: Doubleday, 2001.
"Sobibor." United States Holocaust Memorial Museum. www.ushmm.org/wlc/en/article.php?ModuleId=10005192.
"Sobibor Extermination Camp." Jewish Virtual Library. www.jewishvirtuallibrary.org/history-and-overview-of-sobibor.

Sof, Eric. "The Hijacking of Air France Flight 8969." *Special Ops* (magazine), October 25, 2012.

"The Sole Survivors of the Anglo Saxon." *The Tribune,* November 13, 2013. www.tribune242.com/news/2013/nov/13/the-sole-survivors-of-the-anglo-saxon.

Souhami, Diana. *Edith Cavell.* London: Quercus, 2010.

South, John. "You Can't Hold Me: General Henri Giraud Escapes the Germans in Both World Wars." War History Online, January 15, 2016. www.warhistoryonline.com/guest-bloggers/henri-giraud-escapes.html.

Steele, Rory. *The Heart and the Abyss: The Life of Felice Benuzzi.* Brisbane, Queensland: Connor Court Publishing, 2016.

"Surrounded GIs Saved after Stand." *New York Times,* September 3, 1950.

Sweeting, Adam. "Dunkirk: The Soldiers Left Behind." *The Daily Telegraph,* May 21, 2010. www.telegraph.co.uk/culture/tvandradio/7750005/Dunkirk-the-soldiers-left-behind.html.

"Taken by the Taliban: A Doctor's Story of Captivity, Rescue." NPR, *All Things Considered.* October 12, 2013. www.npr.org/2013/10/12/232759605/taken-by-the-taliban-a-doctors-story-of-captivity-rescue.

Taylor, Judith. "Odyssey to Freedom: Remembering a Daring Escape from Behind Enemy Lines." Air Force Medical Service. November 8, 2013. www.airforcemedicine.af.mil/News/Article/582964/odyssey-to-freedom-remembering-a-daring-escape-from-behind-enemy-lines.

Thomas, Jr., Robert MCG. "Jurgen Wattenberg, 94, P.O.W. Who Escaped." *New York Times,* December 6, 1995. www.nytimes.com/1995/12/04/us/jurgen-wattenberg-94-pow-who-escaped.html.

Tolzmann, Don Heinrich. *German Pioneer Accounts of the Great Sioux Uprising of 1862.* 2nd ed. Little Miami Publishing, 2002.

"US-Dakota War of 1862." Minnesota Historical Society. usdakotawar.org.

Veith, George J. *Code Name Bright Light: The Untold Story of US POW Rescue Efforts during the Vietnam War.* New York: The Free Press, 1988.

Vermillion, S., ed. Vietnam Dustoff Association. Retrieved October 10, 2017, from www.vietnamdustoff.com/home.html.

Vietnam Center and Archive. Lubbock, TX: Texas Tech University, October 12, 2017.

Vietnam War, Memories of New Zealand and the Vietnam War, www.vietnamwar.govt.nz/memory/war-correspondent-kate-webb.

Wagoner, Fred E. *Dragon Rouge: The Rescue of Hostages in the Congo.* Honolulu: University Press of the Pacific, 2003.

Watt, George. *The Comet Connection: Escape from Hitler's Europe.* Lexington: University of Kentucky Press, 1990.

Webb, Kate. *On the Other Side: 23 Days with the Viet Cong.* New York: Quadrangle Books, 1972.

West, Andrew. *The Boys of '67: Charlie Company's War in Vietnam.* Oxford, UK: Osprey Publishing, 2012.

Wetterhahn, Ralph. *The Last Battle: The* Mayaguez *Incident and the End of the Vietnam War.* Cambridge, MA: Da Capo Press, 2001.

Wetzler, Alfred. *Escape from Hell: The True Story of the Auschwitz Protocol*. New York: Berghahn Books, 2007.
Whitcomb, Darrel D. *The Rescue of Bat 21*. Annapolis, Maryland: Naval Institute Press, 1998.
Whittaker, Robert E. *Dragon Master: The Kaiser's One-Man Air Force in Tsingtau, China, 1914*. Compass Books, 1994.
Wright, Robert. *Our Man in Tehran: The True Story behind the Secret Mission to Save Six Americans during the Iran Hostage Crisis & the Foreign Ambassador Who Worked w/the CIA to Bring Them Home*. New York: Other Press, 2010.

Index

Page numbers in **bold** indicate the location of main entries.

A-1 Skyraiders airplane, 48
A-1E airplane, 79
A-7 Corsair airplane, 61
Abu Ghraib, 82
AC-130 airplane, 92, 187
Age of Terror, 4
Aidid, Mohamed Farrah, 14–15
Air Algerie, 1
Air France Flight 8969, **1–4**
Air France Flight AF 139, 157
Airplanes
   A-1 Skyraiders, 48
     A-1E, 79
     A-7 Corsair, 61
     AC-130, 92, 187
     B-25, 88
     B-52, 79
     BF 109F-4, 214
     Boeing 707, 66, 134
     Boeing 737, 63
     C-47, 99, 115, 127, 153–154
     C-53, Skytrooper, 97
     C-130, 21, 92–93, 149, 158–159
     EA-6, Prowler, 142
     EB-66, 79
     EC-130, 92
     EF-111, 142
     F-4, Phantom, 80, 109
     F-15, 142, 189
     F-16, 90, 111, 139, 142, 189
     F-18, Hornet, 142
     F-51, Mustang, 196
     F-105D Thunderchief (Thud), 47
     F-117 Nighthawk, 111
     Fieseler 156 Stork, 138
     Focke-Wulf, 190
     FW-109, 211
     FW-190, 88, 156
     Harrier, 139
     Hawker Hurricane, 211
     MC-130, 92–93
     Mosquito, 155–156
     OV-10 Bronco, 79
     P-38, 154
     P-51, 154
     P-61 Black Widow, 27
     SPAD, 45
     Spitfire, 9–10, 19, 88
     SR-71 Blackbird, 49
     T-39, 24
     Wellington, 210
Akache, Zohair, 63–65
Alamo Scouts, 26–27
Algiers, 1–4
Allen, Ethan, 39
Allied Expeditionary Force (AEF), 86
Allied forces, 25, 41, 51, 59, 98, 113, 153, 156, 164, 167, 182–183, 195–196
Allied prisoners of war, 11, 25, 29, 37, 59, 86, 89, 180, 182–183
American Civil War, 4–7, 19, 45, 73, 68, 73–76, 106–109, 127–131
American Red Cross, 15, 28, 35, 86, 113, 145, 184
American Revolutionary War, 38–40
Amiens Prison, 154–156
Amin, Idi, 157
ANC. *See* Armee Nationale Congolaise
Andania, 174
Anders, Bob, 8–9
Anderson, Dick, 151
Anderson, Marc, 190
Anderson, Miriam, 67

Andersonville, **4–7**, 74–75, 108
  Andersonville National Cemetery, 7
  National Prisoner of War Museum, 7
  Raiders, 7
  Regulators, 7
Andrus, Ron, 112
Argo, **7–10**
  film, 10
Arlington National Cemetery, 96, 100, 178
Armed Forces Revolutionary Council, 143
Armed Islamic Group of Algeria (GIA), 1–4
  Yahia, Abdul Abdullah, 1, 3
Armee Nationale Congolaise (ANC), 148–149
Army Air Corps, 87
Army Rangers, 15, 25–27, 92, 112
Arnhem, Battle of, 164–166
Ascent, 14
Ash, William, **10–12**
Atterberry, Ed, 49
Atwater, Dorence, 6
Aufschnaiter, Peter, 83–84
Auschwitz, 201–204

B-25 airplane, 88
B-52 airplane, 79
Baader-Meinhof Gang, 157
Back to Bataan, 27
Bader, Conrad, 19
Baghdad International Airport, 81
Bailey, James V. "Beetle," 181
Balletto, Giovanni, 13
Band of Brothers, 167
Barak, Ehud, 67
Barsotti, Vincenzo, 13
Bat 21, 81
Bataan, 25–27
Batian, 13
Battle, Blanchard, 199–200
battles
  of Arnhem, 164–166
  of Britain, 209
  of Inchon, 179, 197
  of Kum River, 103
  of Leipzig, 16
  of Normandy, 155 (*see also* Normandy)
  of Osan (*see* Task Force Smith: Battle of Osan)
  of Roberts Ridge, 187–190 (*see also* Takur Ghar)
  of St. Quentin, 72

Beauharnais, Josephine de, 16
BEF. *See* British Expeditionary Force
Behind Enemy Lines, 142
Belgian ParaCommando Regiment, 149
Belgian Sabena Flight 571. *See* Flight 571: Tel Aviv Hijack 1972
Ben Gurion International Airport, 66
Benuzzi, Felice, **13–14**
Berat, Albania, 97–98, 100
Bergsland, Per, 185
Berlin Wall, 55–56
Berndt, Martin, 141
BF 109F-4 airplane, 214
Billotte, Gaston, 51
Bishop, Lewis, 126
Blaber, Pete, 188
Black Hawk Down, **14–16**
  Black Hawk Dawn: A Story of Modern War, 16
  No Man Left Behind: "The Real Black Hawk Down," 16
  True Story of Black Hawk Down, 16
Black Panthers of the 35th Tactical Squadron, 22
Black September Organization, 66, 68, 132, 135
Blackhorse Regiment, 30–31. *See also* Charlie Company
Blatt, Toivi, 169–170
Blunt, Anthony, 153. *See also* Cambridge Five
Boger, Dudley, 28
Bohan, Walt, 23
Boink, Louis, 36
Bonaparte, Napoleon, **16–18**
Bosnian War, 139–142
Brady, Patrick, 151
Bragg, Braxton, 127
Brickhill, Paul, **18–20**, 185
Bridge Too Far, 167
Bright Light. *See* Code name Bright Light
Briley, Donovan, 14
Britain, Battle of, 209
British Expeditionary Force (BEF), 51–52
British Military Intelligence Section 9 (MI9), 37–38
British Royal Air Force (RAF), 52–53, 76, 139, 155, 183, 185, 210–211
British Special Air Service (SAS), 64, 143–144, 160–164
Brockie, Adam, 33
Bronson, Charles, 185

Brown, Matt, 81
Brown, Joseph R., 43
Brussels, 27–28, 37–38, 66
Buchanan, Jessica, and Poul Hagen Thisted, **20–22**
Buller, Redvers, 31, 33–34
Burch, Newell, 6
Bureau of Land Management (BLM), 68
Burgess, Guy, 153. *See also* Cambridge Five
Burnham, Charles, 34
Burns, Joe Lee, **22–24**
Busch, Daniel, 14
Bushell, Roger, 19, 183–184

C-47 airplane, 99, 115, 127, 153–154
C-53 Skytrooper airplane, 97
C-130 aircraft, 21, 92–93, 149, 158–159
Cabanatuan prison rescue, **25–27**, 113–114
Cairncross, John, 153. *See also* Cambridge Five
Calais, France, 10, 51
Cambodia Liberation Front, 207
Cambridge Five, 153. *See also* Blunt, Anthony; Burgess, Guy; Cairncross, John; Maclean, Donald; Philby, Kim
Camp Douglas prisoner of war camp, 128
Camp Papago Park escape, 205–207. *See also* Wattenberg, Jürgen: Camp Papago Park escape
Camp Sumter. *See* Andersonville
Campbell, Neil, 17
Canseco, Javier Diez, 145
Capiau, Herman, 28
Captain Phillips, 172
Carter, Jimmy, 8
Cartolini, Nestor Cerpa, 145
Castro, Fidel, 145
Cavell, Edith, **27–30**, 37–38, 72
Central Intelligence Agency (CIA), 8–9, 47, 94
CH-47D helicopter, 188
CH-53 Sea Stallion helicopter, 142
Chapman, John, 190
Charlie Company, **30–31**
Checkpoint Charlie, 55
Checque, Nicolas, 101
Chinook helicopter, 144, 189
Churchill, Winston, **31–35**, 50–51, 53–54, 73, 138, 153
   Churchill, 34
CIA. *See* Central Intelligence Agency

Civil War. *See* American Civil War
Clark, Mark, 80
Clark, Royce, 112
Clinton, Bill, 15
Coburn, James, 185
Cochrane, Deverton, 112
Code name Bright Light, **35–37**
Code of Conduct, 7, 35, 48, 180
Cohen, Victor, 66–67
Cold War, 55
Colditz, 105–106
Comet line, **37–38**
Commons, Matthew, 190
Communists, 121, 125–126, 148, 153, 155, 179, 192
Confederate Army, 6, 68, 108–109, 127–131
Congress of Vienna, 17
Cornelius, Elias, **38–40**
Corsica, 16
Cowra, Australia, **41–42**
Cowra POW camp, 41–42
   Cowra Breakout, 42
Crose, Bradley, 190
Cunningham, Jason, 190

Da Nang, 81
Dakota, 38, 44
Dakota War of 1862, **43–45**
Dalai Lama, 84
Dam Busters, 19
Danish Refugee Council, 20, 22
Darkest Hour, 34, 54
Dathe, Bruno, 69
Dayan, Moshe, 66–67
D-day, 164
De Jongh, Andrée, 37–38
Dean, William F., 192, 194
Death Game, 65
Delhemme, Bernard, 1–4
Delta Force, 14–15, 91–92, 116, 159
   Delta Force, 159
Democratic Republic of the Congo (DRC), 148–149
Dengler, Dieter, **45–47**
Denny, Barry, 190–191
Desert One, 92–94
Deutschland Battalion, 57
Djibouti, 21–22, 171
Dominguez, Carlos, 145
Donovan, William, 153
Doolittle, Jimmy, 90
Dorchester prison camp, 174

Dover Castle, 51
DPG. *See* Metropolitan Police Diplomatic Protection Group
Dramesi, John A., **47–50**
DRC. *See* Democratic Republic of the Congo
Dry, Melvin "Spence," 50
Duchess of York, 211
Duffy, Gavin, 99
Duke and Duchess of Windsor, 191
Dunkirk: Operation Dynamo, 19, **50–54**
Dunkirk, 54
Durant, Mike, 15–16

East German escapes, **55–56**
East Germany, 55–56
EB-66 airplane, 79
EC-130 airplane, 92
Eckmann, Otto. *See* Eichmann, Adolf
Edward, Prince, 191
EF-111 airplane, 142
Eichmann, Adolf, **56–60**
Eichmann, 60
Eiffel Tower, 1, 3
84 MoPic, 112
82nd Airborne, 149, 165
Eisenhower, Dwight, 73, 165
Elba, 16–17
11th Airborne Division, 114
11th Armored Cavalry Regiment, 30–31. *See also* Blackhorse Regiment
Elizabeth, Queen (Windsor), 38
Elizabeth I, Queen (Tudor), 119–120
Endgame: The Untold Story of the Hostage Crisis in Peru, 148
Ennis, Jerry, 89
Entebbe, 157–159
Entebbe Hero: The Yoni Netanyahu Story, 159
Escape! Escape from Bosnia: The Scott O'Grady Story, 142
Escape from Auschwitz, 204
Escape from Iran: The Canadian Caper, 10
Escape from Sobibor, 170
Escape to Danger, 19

F-4 Phantom airplane, 80, 109
F-15 airplane, 142, 189
F-16 airplane, 90, 111, 139, 142, 189
F-18 Hornet airplane, 142
F-51 Mustang airplane, 196
F-105D Thunderchief (Thud) airplane, 47
F-117 Nighthawk airplane, 111
Fair Rebel, 109
Farjon, Roland, 155
Featherson POW camp. *See* Cowra, Australia
Federal Bureau of Investigation (FBI), 21, 206
Feuerzauber. See Fire Magic
Fields, Kenny Wayne, **61–62**
Fieseler 156 Stork airplane, 138
15th Air Force, 152
15th Marine Expeditionary Unit (MEU), 187
52nd Fighter Group, 88
57th Medical Detachment—Helicopter Ambulance, 150
Fire Magic, 65
1st Allied Airborne Army, 165–167
1st Battalion, 4th Marines, 122
1st Battalion, 75th Ranger Regiment, 189
1st British Airborne, 166
First Great Escape, 87
1st Independent Parachute Brigade (Polish), 165
507th Maintenance Company, 116
506th Parachute Infantry Regiment, 167
Flanders, 50, 71
Flight 181: Mogadishu Hijack 1977, **63–65**
Flight 571: Tel Aviv Hijack 1972 (aka Operation Isotope), **66–68**
Flying the Feathered Edge: The Bob Hoover Project, 90
Focke-Wulf 190 airplane, 89
Fokker, Anthony, 71
Fool Soldiers, 44
Fort Snelling, 44
Fort Stanton, **68–69**
487 Squadron New Zealand, 156
Frankfort Proposals, 16
Franks, Tommy, 187
French Resistance, 10, 155–156, 185
French Revolution, 16–18
French special forces. *See* GIGN
Frost, John, 165
Fujimori, Alberto, 145, 147
FW-109 airplane, 211
FW-190 airplane, 88, 156

Garner, James, 185
Garros, Eugene Adrien Roland Georges, **71–72**

Index

GDR. *See* German Democratic Republic
Geneva Peace Convention, 7, 18, 41
Genocide, 204
German Air Force, 11, 209
German Army, 11, 165
German Democratic Republic (GDR), 55
George Company. *See* Third Platoon, George Company
Gestapo, 10, 38, 73, 77, 105, 136, 155
GIA. *See* Armed Islamic Group of Algeria
GIGN (French special forces), 3–4
Giraud, Henri Honoré, **72–73**
Glazier, Willard W., **73–76**
Gordon, Gary, 15
Gort, John, 51
Grantz, Johannes, 69
Great Escape, 10, 12, 19, 78, 182–185. *See also* Stalag Luft, III: great escape
Great Raid, 27, 131. *See also* Cabanatuan prison rescue
Green Line, 20, 22
Griendl, Jean, 38
Grimson, George, **76–78**
Grizedale Hall, 209
GSG 9 German police unit, 63–65
Gulf of Tonkin, 23–24
Gutfreund, Yosef, 132–133

Hague Peace Convention, 18
Haldane, Aylmer, 33
Hall, Gary, 124
Hambleton, Iceal "Gene," **79–81**
Hamill, Thomas—civilian contractor, **81–83**
Hancock, Dwight, 112
Handley, Phil, 110
Hanford, Thomas, 140–141
Hanks, Tom, 173
Hanoi Hilton, 35, 48–49, 62, 181
Hargrove, Joseph N., 124
Harrer, Heinrich, **83–84**
Harrier airplane, 139
Harris Cavalry. *See* 2nd New York
Hashimoto, Hideo, 196
Hashimoto, Ryutaro, 147
Hawker Hurricane airplane, 211
Hawks, Lionel, 190–191
Heckmair, Anderl, 83
Helicopters
    CH-47D, 188
    CH-53 Sea Stallion, 142
    Chinook, 144, 189
    HH-53 Jolly Green Giant, 23, 80, 110
    Lynx, 144
    MH-47E Chinook, 188
    RH-53D, 92
    Sea Dragon, 23
    Super Six One, 14–15
    Super Six Two, 15
    Super Six Four, 15
    UH-1B Cobra, 79, 142
    UH-1D, 151
    UH-1H Huey, 47, 79, 151
Henderson, William, 80
Heninger, Otto. *See* Eichmann, Adolf
Henry VIII, 119
Heuvel, Machiel van den, 105
Heydekrug prisoner of war camp, 77
HH-53 Jolly Green Giant helicopter, 23, 80, 110, 122
Hijackers/hijacking, 1–4, 63–68, 131, 157, 213
Himmler, Heinrich, 136
Hines, Thomas, 128–131
Hitler, Adolph, 51, 57, 69, 77, 83, 136–138, 214
Hoa Lo Prison. *See* Hanoi Hilton
Hoare, Michael, 149
Hockersmith, Lorenzo, 130
Holloway, James L., 93
Holocaust, 57, 132
Holzminden: the first great escape, **84–87**
Holzminden internment camp, 87
Hoover, Robert, **87–90**
Horrocks, Brian, 165
Horthy, Miklos, 203
Howe, Jonathan, 15
Howe, William, 40
Huizenga, Richard, 125
Hundred Days, 17
Hussein, Saddam, 81

Inchon, Battle of, 179, 197
Iran Conflict, 91–94
Iran hostage crisis, 10
Iran hostage rescue attempt: Operation Eagle Claw, **91–94**
Iraq War, 116–117
Iron Curtain, 55
Islamic Revolution of 1979, 7, 160
Italian Colonial Service, 13
Izac (Isaacs), Edouard, **94–96**, 199–201

Jensen, Agnes, **97–100**
Jewish Department, 57
Johnson, Lyndon, 149
Joint Task Force Leo, 149
Joseph, Dilip, **100–101**

Kaltenbrunner, Ernst, 57, 136
Karlsruhe prisoner of war camp, 95
Kasparek, Fritz, 83
Kellogg, Robert H., 6
Kelly, Charles L., 150–151
Kempton, Jimmie D., 79
Kennard, Second Lieutenant, 85
Kenya, Mount, 13–14
Khmer Rouge, 121–122, 124
Khomeini, Ayatollah, 8
Kilpatrick, Ralph, **103–104**
Kinney, John, 125
Klugmann, James, 153
Königstein prisoner of war camp, 72–73
Korat, Thailand, 22–24
Korean War, 79, 103–104, 178–180, 192–197
Kum River, Battle of, 103
Kunsan Air Base, 22

Lafayette Escadrille, 199
Laker, Carl, 112
Laos, 45–47, 61–62
Larive, Etienne Henri "Hans," **105–106**
L'Assaut, 4
Last Days of Mussolini, 138
Leipzig, Battle of, 16
Lenana Peak, 13
Leopold III of Belgium, 53, 84
Les Internationaux de France de Roland-Garros, 72
Les Invalides, 18
Levy, Reginald, 66–67
Libby Prison escape, 6, 74–75, **106–109**
Liberation Front. *See* Vietcong
Lijek, Cora, 8–9
Lijek, Mark, 8–9
Lima: Breaking the Silence, 148
Lincoln, Abraham, 7, 44, 108
Lincoln National Forest, 69
Lithuania, 12
Little Crow, Chief, 43–44
Locher, Roger, **109–111**
Lock, Trevor, 160–164

Lodge, Robert, 109
Long-range reconnaissance patrols, **111–112**
Los Baños prison camp rescue, **113–116**
Louis XVIII, 17
LRRP. *See* Long-range reconnaissance patrols
Luftwaffe, 10, 54, 77, 89, 182, 211, 214
Luthansa Flight 181. *See* Flight 181: Mogadishu Hijack 1977
Lynch, Jessica, **116–117**
Lynx helicopter, 144

MacArthur, Douglas, 192, 197
Maclean, Donald, 153. *See also* Cambridge Five
Maersk Alabama, 171–173
Majorca, 2–3, 63
Man Who Captured Eichmann, 60
Manor, LeRoy, 181
Marchal, Anselme, 71–72
Marie Louise, 16
Marseille, France, 1–3
Marshall, Alan, 143
Marshall, Danny G., 124
Martin, Duane, 46
Mary, Queen of Scots, **119–121**
Mary Queen of Scots, 120
Mayaguez Incident, 91, **121–124**
MC-130 airplane, 92–93
McAllister, John, 125
McBrayer, James, **125–127**
McCain, John, 35, 124, 181
McCain, John S., 181
McGarvin, E. F., 174
McKay, Jim, 135
McQueen, Steve, 185
Meachin, Fred, 28
Meadows, Dick, 181
Medal of Honor, 190
Mendez, Antonio, 9
Merchant Marine, 68–69
Metropolitan Police Diplomatic Protection Group (DPG), 160
MEU. *See* 15th Marine Expeditionary Unit; 24th Marine Expeditionary Unit
MH-47E Chinook helicopter, 188
MH-53 Sea Dragon helicopter, 23
MI 9. *See* British Military Intelligence Section 9
Michel, Willy, 69

Mihailovic, Draza, 152–153
Military Sealift Personnel, 122–123
Miracle at Dunkirk. *See* Dunkirk: Operation Dynamo
Mogadishu, 14, 16, 63–65
Mogadishu, 65
Mohammed, Oan Ali, 160, 162–163
Mondol Kiri Province, 112
Montgomery, Bernard, 164–165
Morgan, John H., **127–131**
Morgan, Leslie, 190–191
Mosquito airplane, 155–156
Mount Kenya, 13–14
MRTA. *See* Tupac Amaru Revolutionary Movement
MSP. *See* Military Sealift Personnel
Mucci, Henry, 26
Müller, Jens, 185
Mullerskowski, Friedrich, 174
Munich Olympics, 1972, 63, 68, **131–135**
Munich, 135
Munich Police, 133–134
Mussolini, Benito, **135–138**
Mussolini: The Churchill Conspiracies, 138
Musulin, George, 153

Napoleon II, 16
Nassar, Gamal Adbel, 138
National Fascist Party, 135
National Park Service, 7
National Prisoner of War Museum. *See* Andersonville
NATO, 139, 141
Navy SEALS, 21–22, 36–37, 49–50, 80, 101, 173, 187–89. *See also* SEAL Team Six; SEAL Team Two
Nazi party, 10, 57–59, 83–84, 136, 152, 154, 156, 203
Netanyahu, Benjamin, 67, 159
Netanyahu, Yonathan, 159
New Fourth Army, 126
New York National Guard, 82
Nguyen, Van Kiet, 80
Niemeyer, Karl, 86
19th Regiment, 24th Infantry Division, 103
96th Aero Squadron, 199–200
Non-governmental organization (NGO), 20
Normandy, Battle of, 154–156

Norris, Thomas, 80
North African Campaign, 19, 73, 87, 136, 161, 178
North Atlantic Treaty Organization. *See* NATO
North Korean People's Army, 178–179, 192–197
North Vietnamese Easter Offensive of 1972, 79
Norton, Conrad, 19
Number 12 Prisoner of War Compound. *See* Cowra, Australia
Nuremberg trials, 57, 59, 185

Obama, Barrack, 21, 31
Office of Strategic Services, 152–153
Officer's POW Camp No. 1. *See* Grizedale Hall
Oflag prisoner of war camps
    IV-C, 105
    VI-A, 105
    VIII-C, 105
O'Grady, Scott, **139–142**
Ohio State Penitentiary, 128
One Day in September, 135
154th New York Volunteers, 6
101st Airborne Division, 165, 187–188
174 Squadron (RAF), 156
1 Royal Irish Regiment, 142–144
One That Got Away, 214
Operation Barras, **142–144**
Operation Chavín de Huántar, **144–148**
Operation Dragon Noir, 150
Operation Dragon Rouge, **148–150**
Operation Dustoff, **150–152**
Operation Dynamo. *See* Dunkirk: Operation Dynamo
Operation Eagle Claw. *See* Iran hostage rescue attempt
Operation Finale, 60
Operation Halyard, **152–154**
Operation Iraqi Freedom, 81
Operation Isotope. *See* Flight 571: Tel Aviv Hijack 1972
Operation Ivory Coast. *See* Son Tay Raid: Operation Ivory Coast/Kingpin
Operation Jericho, **154–157**
Operation Jericho, 157
Operation Jonathan, **157–159**
Operation Kingpin. *See* Son Tay Raid: Operation Ivory Coast/Kingpin
Operation Linebacker, 109

Operation Market Garden. *See* Operations Berlin, Market Garden, and Pegasus
Operation Nimrod, **159–164**
Operation Overlord, 155
Operation Pegasus. *See* Operations Berlin, Market Garden, and Pegasus
Operation Rolling Thunder, 36
Operation Thunderbolt. *See* Operation Jonathan
Operation Thunderhead, 49–50
Operations Berlin, Market Garden, and Pegasus, **164–167**
Osan, Battle of, 192–194. *See also* Task Force Smith: Battle of Osan
OSS. *See* Office of Strategic Services
Our Man in Tehran, 10
OV-10 Bronco airplane, 79

P-38 airplane, 154
P-51 airplane, 154
P-61 Black Widow airplane, 27
Pahlavi, Mohammad Reza, 91
Palawan Massacre, 25
Palestine Liberation Organization (PLO), 131–132
Panetta, Leon, 21
Panzer, 51, 165–166
Paris, 1, 3, 7, 10, 17, 18, 71–71, 155, 157
Past Is Alive within Us: The U.S.–Dakota Conflict), 45
Patch, William, 104
Patton, George, 164
Pekerney, Sasha, and Toivi Blatt, 300 others, **169–170**
Penny, Barry, 190–191
Peres, Shimon, 66
Perón, Eva, 138
Perón, Juan, 138
Pha Phim Cu Loc Prison, 49
Philby, Kim, 153. *See also* Cambridge Five
Phillips, Richard, **170–173**
  Captain Phillips, 173
Piegler, Hannelore, 63
Pilcher, Roy, 190–191
Pirates, 20–21, 171–173
Pius VII, 16
PLO. *See* Palestine Liberation Organization
Pluschow, Gunther, **173–176**
Poindexter, John, 30

Pol Pot, 121
Ponchardier, Dominique, 155
Poovey, Junior G., 195–196
Popular Front for the Liberation of Palestine (PFLP), 63, 157
Popular Liberation Army, 148–149
Prisoner exchange systems, 4, 121
Prisoner of war camps
  conditions of, 4
  treatment of prisoners, 5, 7, 18, 25–26, 35, 38, 40, 44, 49, 57, 62, 82–83, 86, 95, 106, 108, 116–117, 121, 177, 194, 203
Puerto Princesa, 25
Puryear, George, 199–201

Queen Elizabeth (Windsor), 38
Queen Elizabeth I (Tudor), 119–120

RAF. *See* British Royal Air Force
Raid on Entebbe, 159
Raiders. *See* Andersonville
Rainbow Six Siege, 164
Rangers. *See* Army Ranger
Rathbone, Charles, 86–87
Reach for the Sky, 19
Reagan, Ronald, 8
Red Cross. *See* American Red Cross
Red Iron, chief, 43
Regulators. *See* Andersonville
Reign, 120
Rescue at Dawn: The Los Baños Raid, 115
Rescue Dawn, 47
Revolutionary United Front (RUF), 142
RH-53D helicopter, 92
Rhode Island Regiments, 39
Ritchie, Steve, 110
Rivera, Maximo, 145
Roberts, Neil C., 188–190
Roberts Ridge, Battle of, 187–190. *See also* Takur Ghar
Romano, Yossef, 133
Roosevelt, Franklin Delano, 73, 153
Roraback, Kenneth, 35
Rose, Thomas, 108
Rowe, James N. (Nick), **177–178**
Royal Australian Air Force, 19
Royal Canadian Air Force, 10
Ruffatto, Barney, **178–180**
Runne, Hermann, 69

Saigon, 24, 35, 150–151
Salim. *See* Mohammed, Oan Ali
SAS. *See* British Special Air Service
Sattler, Friedel, 83–84
Sayeh, Suhaila, 65
Sayeret Matkal Counterterrorist Unit, 67, 157
Scharnhorst prisoner of war camp, 71
Schatz, Henry Lee, 8–9
Schleyer, Hanns Martin, 63
Schreiber, Manfred, 133–134
Schumann, Jurgen, 63–65
Schutzstaffel. *See* SS
Schwandt, Mary, 43
SEAL Team Six, 21–22, 101. *See also* Navy SEALS
SEAL Team Two, 36. *See also* Navy SEALS
2nd Battalion, 9th Marines, 122–123
Second Boer War, 31–35
2nd Infantry Division, 195, 197
2nd New York, 74
2nd Parachute Battalion, 165
Secret Army, 38
Self, Nate, 189
Seoul, Korea, 103, 179–180, 192–193, 1977
Days in Entebbe, 159
7th Air Force, 110
77th Pennsylvania Infantry, 108
Shah of Iran. *See* Pahlavi, Mohammad Reza
Shoah, 204
Shughart, Randy, 15
Siamese Prince, 191
Sibley, Henry, 43–44
Simba. *See* Popular Liberation Army
Simons, Arthur, 181
Simpson, Wallace, 191
Sioux Uprising of 1862. *See* Dakota War of 1862
Sir Percival, 144
6 Days, 164
617 Squadron (RAF), 19
16th Connecticut Infantry Volunteers, 6
16th Illinois Cavalry, 6
6th Ranger Battalion, 26
Skolsky, Tuvia, 132
Skorzeny, Otto, 136, 138
Skyraiders. *See* A-1 Skyraiders airplane
Slabinski, Britt, 188–189
Smith, Charles Bradford, 192
Smith, Jim, 14

Smith, Lloyd G., 99–100
Smith, Victor, 99
Sobibor, 169–170
Sobibor, 170
Son Tay Raid: Operation Ivory Coast/Kingpin, 62, 91, **181–182**
South Korean Army, 192,
SPAD airplane, 45
Spanish-American War, 76
Spitfire airplane, 9–10, 19, 88
SR-71 Blackbird airplane, 49
SS (Schutzstaffel), 57, 68, 83, 89, 136, 169, 170
SS *Anglo Saxon,* 190–191
SS *Columbus,* 68
SS *Mongolia,* 174
St. Helena, 17–18
St. Quentin, Battle of, 72
Stafford, Joe, 8–9
Stafford, Kathy, 8–9
Stalag Luft I, 76, 89
Stalag Luft III: great escape, 10–12, 19, 76–77, **182–186**
Stalag Luft IV, 12
Stalag Luft VII-A, 185
Stalag Luft VIII-B, 76
Stebbins, John, 15
Steinmetz, Francis, 105–106
Streetcar 304. *See* Fields, Kenny Wayne
Stuart, Mary. *See* Mary, Queen of Scots
Student, Karl, 136
Sturmabteilung (SA), 83
Super Six helicopters
  Super Six One, 14–15
  Super Six Two, 15
  Super Six Four, 15
Survived, 191
Svitak, Phillip, 190
Swanwick Camp, 210–211
Sydnor, Elliott, 181

T-39 airplane, 24
Takur Ghar, **187–190**
Taliban, 100–101, 187–188
Taopi, Chief, 43
Tapscott, Robert, and Wilbert Widdicombe, **190–191**
Task Force Smith: Battle of Osan, **192–195**
Tehran, 7, 9–10, 91, 160

Temperelli, John Jr., 150
10th Mountain Division, 15, 187
Terrorism, 1–4, 7–10, 14–16, 20–22, 63–68, 100–101, 131–135, 144–150, 157–164, 187–190
Thatcher, Margaret, 19, 164
3rd Combat Support Battalion, 116
Third Platoon, George Company, **195–197**
Third Reich, 201
35th Tactical Squadron. *See* Black Panthers of the 35th Tactical Squadron
37 Squadron (RAF), 37, 76
Thisted, Poul Hagen, 20–22
Thud airplane. *See* F-105D Thunderchief
Tichener, Caxton, 200
Tinnion, Bradley, 144
Tito, Josip Broz, 152
Toledo, Alejandro, 145
Tom, Dick, and Harry Tunnels, 19, 184
Treaty of Versailles, 176
Trebon, Gregory, 188
Trefftz, Oskar T., 175
Truman, Harry S., 192
Tucker, Rowan, 199–201
Tunnels, Tom, Dick, and Harry, 19, 184
Tupac Amaru Revolutionary Movement (MRTA), 145, 147
Turner, Thomas, 106
25th Infantry Division, 195
21st Infantry Regiment, 192
24th Infantry Division, 178–179, 192, 194
24th Marine Expeditionary Unit (MEU), 139–141
21 Hours at Munich, 135
21 Squadron (RAF), 156
26th New York Cavalry, 75

U-162, 205
U-90 submarine, 94, 96
UH-1B Cobra helicopter, 79
UH-1D helicopter, 151
UH-1H Huey helicopter, 47, 79, 151
Unified Task Force, 15
Unit, The. *See* Sayeret Matkal Counterterrorist Unit
United Nations, 139, 143, 194, 197
U.S. Border Patrol, 68
USS *America,* 61–62
USS *Bainbridge,* 172
USS *Coral Sea,* 122
USS *Florida,* 94

USS *Grayback,* 49
USS *Harold E. Holt,* 122
USS *Henry B. Wilson,* 122
USS *Long Beach,* 24
USS *Kearsarge,* 141–142
USS *Nemitz,* 92
USS *President Lincoln,* 94
USS *Sutherland,* 36

Valley Forge, 40
Van der Stok, Bram, 185
Van Galen, 105
Versace, Rocky, 35
Versailles, Treaty of, 176
Vickers Wellington bombers, 76
Victor Emmanual, King, 136
Vienna, Austria, 13, 17, 66
Vienna, Congress of, 17
Vietcong, 35–36, 112, 177
Vietnam Dustoff Association, 152
Vietnam War, 22–24, 30–31, 35–37, 45–50, 61–62, 79–81, 109–112, 150–152, 177–178, 181–182, 207–208
Vietor, Jurgen, 63–64
Villingen prison, 95, **199–201**
Vincent, Anthony, 145
Vogt, John, 110
Von Werra, 214
Vrba, Rudolf, and Alfred Wetzler, **201–204**
Vugnovich, George, 153

Wabasha, Chief, 43
Waffen SS, 136
Warrenton Jail, 74
Washington, George, 38–40
Wattenberg, Jürgen: Camp Papago Park escape, **205–207**
Webb, Kate, **207–209**
Webster, John, 209
Wegener, Ulrich, 63–65
Weinberg, Moshe, 132
Wellington airplane, 210
Werra, Franz von, **209–214**
  Von Werra, 214
West Side Boys, 143–144
Wetzler, Alfred, 201–204
White, Robert, 36
Who Goes Next?, 87
Widder, 190
Widdicombe, Wilbert, 190–191

Wiesenthal, Simon, 59
Wilkinson, Tim, 15
Willis, Harold, 199
Windsor, Duke and Duchess of, 191
Wirz, Henry, 6
Wolcott, Cliff, 14
World War I, 27–30, 71–73, 84–87, 94–96, 173–176, 199–201
World War II, 10–14, 18–20, 25–27, 37–38, 41–42, 50–54, 56–60, 68–69, 72–73, 76–78, 83–84, 87–90, 97–100, 105–106, 113–116, 124–127, 135–138, 152–157, 164–170, 182–186, 190–191, 201–203, 205–206, 209–214
Wright, Robert "Wilbur," 139–140

Yahia, Abdul Abdullah, 1, 3
Yeager, Chuck, 90

Zoo. *See* Pha Phim Cu Loc Prison
Zouave troops, 72

About the Authors

David W. Mills is an Assistant Professor of Military History at the U.S. Army Command and General Staff College at Fort Leavenworth, Kansas. He thoroughly enjoys teaching field grade officers from the various American military branches, civilians from many federal agencies, and students from numerous allied nations. Prior to this, he was a history instructor at Minnesota West Community and Technical College. He received his PhD in history from North Dakota State University, and he is the author of two previous books on the early Cold War era.

Kayla L. Westra is the Dean of Institutional Effectiveness and Liberal Arts at Minnesota West Community and Technical College. She has an extensive background in teaching and learning, with specializations in online education and faculty development. An English faculty, she has served as an academic dean since 2010. A lifelong advocate for equity in education, she has presented at multiple conferences on topics related to dual enrollment, distance learning, and technology. Additionally, Westra has worked as a professional technical editor and writer for over 25 years. She received her EdD in Educational Leadership from Minnesota State University, Mankato.

www.ingramcontent.com/pod-product-compliance
Lightning Source LLC
Chambersburg PA
CBHW082034300426
44117CB00015B/2474